The Organ in Manitoba

The Organ in Manitoba

*A History of the Instruments,
the Builders, and the Players*

James B. Hartman

THE UNIVERSITY OF MANITOBA PRESS

The University of Manitoba Press
Winnipeg, Manitoba R3T 5V6

Printed in Canada on recycled, acid-free paper ∞

Design: Karen Armstrong
Cover illustration: St. Mary's Academy, Winnipeg, Casavant Frères organ, 1909. All photographs, except as noted, courtesy of the author.

Canadian Cataloguing in Publication Data

Hartman, James B. (James Barclay), 1925

     The organ in Manitoba : a history of the instruments, the builders, and the players

     Includes bibliographical references and index.
     ISBN 0-88755-644-2

     1. Organs - Manitoba - History. 2. Organists - Manitoba - History. 3. Organ builders - History. I. Title

ML563.7.M3H37 1997   786.5'197127   C97-920152-7

The publisher gratefully acknowledges the support for its publishing program provided by the Manitoba Arts Council.

This book has been published with the help of a grant from the Canadian Federation for the Humanities, using funds provided by the Social Sciences and Humanities Research Council of Canada.

Contents

Acknowledgements

THE MAJOR INVESTIGATIONS for this book were largely completed during a six-month research leave from the University of Manitoba in late 1992 and early 1993, and subsequent refinements of the text continued up to the date of publication in 1997.

A number of people assisted my research by making available important information of historical significance. Stanley R. Scheer, vice-president, Casavant Frères, Ltée., provided copies of organ specifications, contracts, correspondence, and several photographs relating to installations of Casavant pipe organs in Manitoba. Richard Greig, chair of the Winnipeg Centre, Royal Canadian College of Organists, allowed access to the records of that association, established in the 1923 as the Canadian College of Organists. My appreciation also extends to those organists, members of the clergy, church secretaries, and parishioners who facilitated access to the organs and to church records. Maureen Dolyniuk, volunteer archivist, St. John's Anglican Cathedral, Winnipeg, was particularly helpful in the latter endeavour. Correspondents in several urban and rural centres supplied useful information in response to survey questionnaires distributed to churches throughout the province. Librarians and archivists everywhere were most cooperative: Alfred Fortier, La Société Historique de Saint-Boniface; staff of the Elizabeth Dafoe Library, The University of Manitoba; and staff of the Provincial Archives of Manitoba and the Manitoba Legislative Library. The interest in and enthusiasm for this project on the part of all these people is gratefully acknowledged.

Introduction

THE HISTORY OF ORGANS IN MANITOBA is a neglected aspect of the musical, cultural, and church history of the province. This book portrays the panorama of the organ—the instruments, the builders, and the players—from the mid-1800s to the present.

The earliest organs in Manitoba were reed organs, or harmoniums, and these relatively inexpensive instruments served church congregations and provided entertainment in family parlours for several generations. With the construction of larger churches, pipe organs became the instruments of choice: the first installation occurred in 1875. Instruments representative of 28 pipe organ builders in Canada, the United States, England, and Europe are to be found in Manitoba; a few of the imports from the United States are now over a century old, and a number of Canadian-made organs are approaching the centennial mark in age. The documentation of the specifications of these instruments reveals changing concepts of tonal design, which in turn can be related to the type of organ music played and heard by early generations. Because theatre organs were part of the popular musical culture, some reports of these instruments and their players have been included. At least a dozen Winnipeg movie theatres, and a few in Manitoba towns, acquired pipe organs in the early decades of the century, but much of the relevant information concerning them has been lost. The few organs in funeral chapels and educational institutions have been documented in the inventory of installations.

The information concerning the instruments, the builders, the players, and their public reception, assembled from survey questionnaires, newspaper reports, church and public archives, and libraries, is presented within the context of five historical periods.

The first period, and perhaps the most important and interesting from the historical point of view, was the "Golden Age" of the organ, a 45-year period up to the end of World War I. During this period well over one-third of all known pipe organ installations in the province occurred. In these early days organ concerts by local and visiting recitalists—some of them internationally acclaimed—played a major role in public musical education and entertainment, and the instruments on which they were played were objects of close attention by the music commentators of the daily and weekly newspapers. Recitals in the larger churches were played before capacity audiences. The parade of visiting recitalists, which began in the 1890s and continued throughout the following years, included such performing luminaries as the prominent American organist William C. Carl; the expatriate English organist and touring superstar, Edwin H. Lemare; the Canadian-born American Lynnwood Farnam; and Ernest MacMillan, later known as Canada's elder musical statesman. In the four decades preceding 1920 slightly more than one-third of all the pieces performed in organ recitals were transcriptions of a wide range of operatic, choral, or instrumental works by major composers. Although this practice, which was widespread throughout Canada, England, and the United States at the time, attracted much criticism, it was defended as broadening access to this realm of musical culture. The vogue gradually diminished in subsequent periods. (The statistical information and generalizations concerning trends in program repertoire provided throughout the book are derived from a computerized database analysis of over 500 known organ recitals by local and visiting players from 1878 to 1959.) In the early 1900s movie theatres began to acquire pipe organs to provide accompaniments to their silent films. Although activities relating to the organ generally were severely restricted during the war years, in terms of organ installations, recitals, and intensity of public interest in the King of Instruments and its players, this period remains unsurpassed in the history of music in Manitoba.

A further period of expansion followed, from 1920 to the beginning of World War II in 1939. These years saw the establishment in 1923 of the Winnipeg Centre of the Canadian College of Organists, a small but enthusiastic group of church musicians who sponsored recitals by local and visiting players and arranged special events for the improvement of church music generally. Most of the officers in the new organization were frequent recitalists, and several of them, such as Hugh Bancroft, Ronald Gibson, Filmer Hubble, and Herbert Sadler, would maintain leading positions in the musical community throughout the following decades. Noted visiting recitalists from other countries included T. Tertius Noble, an expatriate English cathedral organist living in New York; Joseph Bonnet and Marcel Dupré from France, both of whom made repeat appearances; and Alfred Hollins, the globe-trotting blind English organ-ist. Canadian recitalists Healey Willan and Ernest MacMillan, along with Arthur Egerton, the first chairman of the Winnipeg Centre of the Canadian College of Organists, also returned to play in Winnipeg. The early 1920s were also the height of fashion for cinema organs, the culmination of a trend that began around 1915. During this time pipe organs were installed in several of Winnipeg's larger movie theatres, and the activities of theatre organists were frequently reported in daily newspapers.

The period 1940-1949 was one of recession, characterized by the smallest number of organ installations to date and the dissolution of the Winnipeg Centre of the Canadian College of Organists. Both of these trends had war-time causes: a shortage of manufacturing materials that restricted the activi-ties of organ builders, and the entry into military service on the part of musicians. Nevertheless, the French recitalists Joseph Bonnet and Marcel Dupré (now believed to be the greatest organist of his time) returned to play in Winnipeg after absences of many years.

The time for renewal, 1950-1959, was marked by an increase in the number of organ installations that almost matched the first decades of the century, and by the rebirth of the Canadian College of Organists, redesignated as the Royal Canadian College of Organists in the last year of the period. Prominent visit-ing recitalists included the Belgian organist Flor Peeters; Charles Peaker, one of Canada's foremost concert organists who was associated with the Toronto Conservatory of Music for 40 years; and Muriel Gidley Stafford, the first woman national president of the Royal Canadian College of Organists.

The most recent period, from 1960 onward, was one of consolidation and growth. In the 1960s the number of visiting recitalists coming to Winnipeg was greater than in any time before or since; they included such notable play-ers as Peter Hurford from England (he returned in 1995), Canada's Hugh McLean (he returned in 1993); Marilyn Mason, Robert Noehren, E. Power Biggs, and Virgil Fox from the United States; and Anton Heiller from Aus-tria. These players were, and still are, known to the musical listening public on account of their sound recordings. As well, a new generation of local organ players was emerging, several of whom would assume prominent positions in the life of the organ community in later years. The Winnipeg Centre of the Royal Canadian College of Organists continued its yearly round of occasional organ recitals and demonstrations, church music workshops, choir festivals, and other related events. The Centre commenced the publication of a regular newsletter in 1983 to publicize these events and to provide a forum for the discussion of topics of common interest.

A concluding chapter offers some speculation on the future of the organ, considering such factors as the development of electronic organ technology, the respective merits and costs of pipe organs and electronic instruments, the availability of trained organists, changing religious liturgies and the future of organized religion, shifting patterns of church membership and attendance, organ technicians and builders, and public awareness of organs and organ music.

Reports of organ installations and recitals are given verbatim rather than in paraphrased or summarized form. It is only through these direct quotations from original sources that the reader can experience with the greatest immediacy the changing style of music commentary and opinion over the decades, and thus obtain a sense of the relative importance of the organ and its music in the cultural life of the community.

A chronological summary of known pipe organ installations, relocations, and major renovations, arranged according to the various historical periods, is given in Appendix 1: Organ Installations, which also identifies those instruments still in existence at their listed locations. The complete stoplists of all known organ installations in Manitoba are presented in Appendix 2: Specifications of Organs.

The Organ in Manitoba

Manitoba: The Formative Years

Discovery and Exploration

The chief incentive for the exploration of the territories of North America, from the very earliest times, was a sustained interest in trade and commerce on the part of old world companies. In the last of a series of voyages made by the explorer Henry Hudson between 1607 and 1610 under the auspices of English merchants, he entered the bay that now bears his name. The successes of later expeditions were measured in terms of the quantity of furs obtained from the Aboriginal Peoples of the coastal regions. These operations led to the founding in 1670 of the Hudson's Bay Company, which was granted exceedingly wide powers and almost absolute jurisdiction over a vast territory called Rupert's Land. Because the aim of the Company was to secure the North American fur trade and perhaps to find a sea route to the Orient, the tendency was to explore the north rather than the south and west.

The invasion of southern territories was accomplished by French explorers who came from the east by way of the Great Lakes. In 1738 the La Vérendryes, father and sons, paused at the junction of the Red and Assiniboine rivers and established Fort Rouge, now the site of Winnipeg. One of their motives, too, was the hope of finding a sea route to the Orient, and their explorations opened up the great overland fur trade route between Eastern and Western Canada. In 1783 a group of independent traders in Montréal formed the North West Company, whose influence eventually extended to the Pacific coast and to the north and south, posing a serious threat to the Hudson's Bay Company. Both companies built forts where Winnipeg now stands, and the intense rivalry between them erupted into fighting in which the governor of the Red River colony and 21 men were killed in an unfortunate incident in 1816. The conflicting interests were resolved by the merger of the two companies in 1821 under the name of the Hudson's Bay Company.

The first settlers in the Red River district were displaced tenant farmers from the north of Scotland who arrived in three contingents between 1812 and 1814 via York Factory on Hudson Bay. The relocation of the Kildonan Scots was organized by Thomas Douglas, fifth Earl of Selkirk, a prominent Hudson's Bay Company shareholder, after he acquired 187,000 square kilometres of land within the territory of Rupert's Land for the purpose. One of Lord Selkirk's motives was to establish an agricultural settlement in the area to secure the position of the Hudson's Bay Company. A later group of German-speaking Swiss recruited by Lord Selkirk's agent—the Earl had died in 1820—arrived at the colony in 1821. In spite of initial hardships and misfortunes, including severe winters, floods, crop losses, and harassments by the Nor'Westers, the settlement around Fort Garry (Winnipeg) grew steadily. The population increased from approximately 1,500 in 1821 to almost 4,900 in 1847 as the inhabitants engaged in the modestly successful agricultural development of the lands along the banks of the Red and Assiniboine rivers. Following a period of instability in the government of the area, including a rebellion by the Métis majority in 1869, the Hudson's Bay Company surrendered its claim to the area. Problems of authority and jurisdiction were finally resolved by the passing of the Manitoba Act of 1870 that provided for the entry of the province into the Dominion of Canada.

Once the potential of the Red River Valley became known, immigrants began to arrive from the United States, Great Britain, and parts of Europe, thus initiating a period of intense agricultural development of the grass lands and eventual commercial activity in Winnipeg, which was incorporated as a city in 1873.

Music in Winnipeg

In the early days of frontier settlement in Manitoba, the most popular form of music was supplied by the Red River fiddler, whose lively strains caused some young men to wear out several pairs of moccasins during a night of energetic dancing. One of the Métis fiddlers, Pierre Falcon (1793-1876), also known as Pierre the Rhymer, worked for the North West Company for a time. Falcon was one of Manitoba's earliest balladeers; he excelled at putting into song the exploits of adventurers and other local happenings. One of these, which immortalized the Battle of Seven Oaks, became a symbolic legend and a source of identity for the Métis population in their resistance against the English. Falcon eventually settled into farm and family life near St. François Xavier and later served as magistrate in that community.

Pianos

It is believed that there may have been a piano at the Red River Settlement as early as 1833. Documented evidence of the first piano indicates that it was brought from London, England, probably before 1840, by a teacher at the Red River Academy who later married the former chief factor of the Hudson's Bay Company after he retired to the Settlement in 1824. Pianos manufactured in Eastern Canada began to arrive by the mid-1840s. Public demand for pianos was sufficient for the first piano agent to establish a business in Winnipeg in 1872.

Instrumentalists

The musical life of the district accelerated rapidly with the growth of Winnipeg, where the population in 1870 numbered only 500. The first band was formed in 1871 when the instruments of the departing soldiers of the Wolseley Expedition, which had been sent to restore order after the Riel Rebellion, were acquired by some of the residents. Several other bands were organized in the following decade. One of the leaders of musical activities was Captain W. N. Kennedy, a band instructor and the organist of Grace Church, as well as the mayor of Winnipeg in 1875-76, who organized the Philharmonic Society in the early 1880s and invited a conductor from the United States to lead it. Another group of about 35 amateur instrumentalists, the Apollo Club, founded in the 1880s, gave two concerts a year; it was later succeeded by the Winnipeg Orchestral Society. The Winnipeg City Band was organized in the first decade of the present century.

   During the early 1900s several of the larger Winnipeg churches—Grace, St. Stephen's, Westminster, Broadway—organized orchestras that gave periodic concerts. Some of the churches also sponsored secular concerts consisting of instrumental selections, vocal solos or quartets, and literary readings. Newspapers announced and reviewed these entertainments in an attempt to promote quality music in the city. At the same time, the critics disparaged perceived departures from high musical standards; a proposed banjo and bagpipe orchestra was put down as "a fitting accompaniment to noisy and uncultured singing."

Choral Groups

Winnipeg's strong choral tradition began in the later years of the last century, when the amateur singers of the city formed a glee club in 1876. The local Operatic Society, another aggregation of amateurs that produced Gilbert and Sullivan works and other light operas, was established by P. R. Maclagan, one of the city's musical pioneers, who came to the city about 1880 from Montréal to become the organist at Holy Trinity Church. The first choral society in

Winnipeg was organized around 1900. The development of choral activity was stimulated by the participation of local choirs in a Cycle of Musical Festivals conducted by the touring principal of the Royal Academy, London, in 1903. The Winnipeg Choral Society was formed in 1907 by a group of prominent organists and choirmasters, followed by the Winnipeg Oratorio Society in 1908. In 1909 several other church musicians established the Elgar Society; they received a letter from Lady Elgar conveying Sir Edward's best wishes for success. The Winnipeg Male Voice Choir (connected with the Men's Musical Club) was founded in 1916. The Winnipeg Philharmonic Society, a choral group initially specializing in oratorios, was founded in 1922 and renamed the Winnipeg Philharmonic Choir in 1929. A mixed group, the Winnipeg Choral and Orchestral Society, also emerged in the early 1920s, and the Winnipeg Boys' Choir was formed by the Men's Musical Club in 1925. All of these groups were representative of a large number of church choirs and other singing groups, involving all age groups in the community, that raised Winnipeg to a prominent position among the choral capitals of North America up to World War II. The level of choral activity diminished somewhat since that time due to increased activity in instrumental music.

Music Instruction

As soon as trained musicians arrived in Winnipeg, usually from England, they opened music studios in Winnipeg to offer private instruction in voice, piano, organ, and violin. Many of these people were also active in local orchestras or served as church organists and choirmasters. Some took employment in local music stores to supplement their meagre income from professional duties. For example, this advertisement appeared in a daily newspaper:

> Mr. C. J. Newman (Associate London Academy of Music), Organist and Choirmaster, Holy Trinity Church, is now prepared to receive or visit pupils for organ, piano and voice culture. He is also open to accept concert engagements as a pianist, accompanist, or for organ recitals. For terms and appointment, address, for the present, Prince's Music Store. (*Manitoba Free Press*, 25 June 1888.)

Sometimes, such arrivals were treated as newsworthy announcements:

> Mr. C. W. Openshaw, organist and pianist, has arrived in Winnipeg and intends taking pupils for these instruments. Mr. Openshaw has been organist and choirmaster for the past ten years in the Baptist Tabernacle, Southport, England, and the church of the Sacred heart, Accrington, Lancashire, also organist for the famed Accrington Choral Society of over 250 voices. (*Manitoba Free Press*, 23 September 1905.)

In 1894 it was estimated that about 500 people in Winnipeg were engaged in the study of music or related activities. Accordingly, several local musicians perceived that the time was right for the establishment of the Winnipeg Conservatory of Music in that year. In the planning period, the initiator and designated director, Paul Henneberg, travelled to Minneapolis to visit the conservatory there. The prospectus offered a comprehensive program of instruction in piano, organ, mandolin, guitar, clarionet, cornet, violin, violoncello, voice culture, harmony, orchestration, and music history. The intention was to purchase a vocalion specifically for organ instruction.

In 1898 the Winnipeg Piano Teachers' Association met for the first time to discuss curriculum and ways to raise standards of teaching. The development of new musicians was also assisted by the establishment of the Dominion Conservatory in 1903 for instruction in violin. Another larger institution for general music instruction, including organ, was the Winnipeg College of Music, organized by the conductor of Grace Church orchestra in 1903. The Imperial Academy of Music and the Arts, initially affiliated with Die Königliche Hoch Schule, Berlin, Germany, opened in 1908. Along with other musical subjects, the Academy offered instruction in organ; the teachers were two organists from prominent Winnipeg churches.

In 1909 Ralph Horner (1848-1926) arrived in Winnipeg from New York, where he had resided for three years, to assume leadership of the Imperial Academy of Music and the Arts. Born and educated in England, he was a graduate of the Leipzig Conservatory, a former professor at Nottingham University, a choral conductor, composer, and subsequently was a Canadian army bandmaster in 1916-17. In addition to teaching music, Horner became a leading figure in the musical community for many years, and later was referred to as the "grand old man of music" in Winnipeg. Immediately upon his arrival, Horner began contributing a series of informative articles on a variety of musical topics to the weekly newspaper *Winnipeg Town Topics*; their contents ranged from discussions about specific composers and major musical works to discourses on musical aesthetics and practice. These articles contributed to the informal music education of the community and provided helpful background information for current concerts. Later, Horner served as editor of the music page of that publication.

Performing Centres

Although many musical events took place in the larger churches, several other buildings served the needs of Winnipeg's early audiences. The first theatre was the Red River Hall, opened in 1867 above a store; it was also used for church services. The City Hall Theatre opened in 1875, followed by the Winnipeg Theatre and Opera House, originally called Victoria Hall, in 1883. In the same year the inaugural performance in the new Princess Opera House was Gilbert

Advertisement for organ recital,
Manitoba Free Press, 18 June 1888.

and Sullivan's *Iolanthe*; this building was home to the local Operatic Society until it was destroyed by fire in 1899. Recitals were also held in the Y.M.C.A. auditorium.

A longer-lived performing centre was the rebuilt Winnipeg Theatre and Opera House, renamed the Walker Theatre, announced as "Canada's Finest Theatre—Steelcage Construction, Fireproof Throughout" and opened in 1907. Its initial event on the musical culture scene was a triple production of Puccini's *Madame Butterfly* in English, just three years after the opera had opened in La Scala, Italy. In May 1908 the building was the location of what was billed as "Western Canada's First Great Musical Festival," a three-day event including a symphony program, a popular program, and an operatic program.

Music Clubs

The Women's Musical Club, formed in 1894 as a practice and study group, later expanded into concert promotion, sponsoring such international recitalists as Ernestine Schumann-Heink and Ignaz-Jan Paderewski. In 1906 a number of local musical enthusiasts, including the more active church musicians, formed the Clef Club, a social-educational group that sponsored concerts and met regularly for performances and lectures. On one occasion, on 17 April 1909, the group offered a "Made in Winnipeg" program of works entirely by local composers. A later musical promotion group, the Men's Musical Club, was established in 1915 to participate in music making, to encourage the development of young musicians, and to sponsor visiting performers. This club inaugurated the Manitoba Musical Competition Festival in 1918 with 2,500 participants; this annual event continues today with approximately 25,000 performers.

Religious Denominations and Historic Churches

During the 19th century, changes were taking place in the role of music in churches that favoured the introduction of the organ into religious rituals. For example, in the second half of the century Roman Catholic churches in Canada had access to musical publications from France that contained plainsong settings with organ accompaniment, and in 1903 Pius X forbade the use of any other instrument for this purpose. Before the middle of the century, services in Anglican churches were accompanied by any available orchestral instrument, but the importation of pipe organs from England and the immigration of musicians trained in Church of England traditions hastened the acceptance of melodeons in the new settlements. Among the Protestant denominations, at the beginning of the 19th century the Presbyterians allowed neither hymns nor organs, but the laity was more sympathetic to them, and the prohibitions were gradually abandoned after 1872. Congregational and Methodist groups, on the other hand, began to accept organs early in the century, and by its end the larger churches sought to acquire pipe organs, and the smaller ones settled for melodeons. This matter will be revisited in the next chapter in connection with the installation of reed organs in Manitoba churches.

The following brief account traces the establishment of the major Christian denominations in Manitoba during the 19th century. Most of the early organ installations were in churches of these denominations, as their influence spread out from the city of Winnipeg into the rural areas of Manitoba.

Roman Catholic

The Roman Catholic Church was the first to establish missions in Rupert's Land, when two French priests arrived in 1690 to teach the Indians. In 1736 an exploring party under one of La Vérendrye's sons, which included a priest, was massacred by Indians on an island in the Lake of the Woods, east of Winnipeg. The first concentrated missionary efforts in the area of the Red River colony were initiated by the arrival of two priests from Québec in 1818. One of these, the Reverend N. B. Provencher, was later consecrated bishop of the diocese, which became a separate apostolic vicariate in 1844. His authority extended over those portions of the diocese known as Hudson Bay and the

North-West Territories, and his missions reached far into the Mackenzie and Athabasca regions. In 1850 the name of the diocese was changed to St. Boniface.

The first chapel in the district was constructed in 1818, followed in 1819 by a church (later designated a cathedral) to which Lord Selkirk donated a bell. A series of cathedrals followed: the second, begun in 1833, was destroyed by fire in 1860; the third, begun in 1862, was later dismantled; and the fourth, the largest of all, built between 1906 and 1908, was destroyed by fire in 1968. This was the edifice whose prominent twin towers, 46 metres in height, are referred to in John Greenleaf Whittier's poem, *Canadian Voyageur*:

> The bells of the Roman mission,
> That call from their turrets twain
> To the boatman on the river,
> To the hunter on the plain.

The fifth cathedral, a low building of contemporary design placed within the remaining walls of the ruins of the fourth St. Boniface Cathedral, was dedicated in 1972.

In Winnipeg, St. Mary's Parish was formally established in 1824, and the first church edifice was dedicated in 1881, subsequently enlarged in 1895. Elsewhere in the province, the earliest parish churches included St. Pierre Jolys, built around 1878, and Ste. Anne des Chênes in 1895.

St. Boniface College, now the only French-speaking College within The University of Manitoba, traces its beginnings back to 1818 and the earliest days of the Red River settlement.

Anglican

Anglicanism, one of the founding religions of Canada, was brought to this country both by missionaries and by employees of the Hudson's Bay Company. In fact, a Manitoba historian of a century ago asserted that the history of the English Church in the Red River colony, so far as the Protestant element is concerned, is largely the history of the country itself.

The first Church of England missionary to the Red River settlement, the Reverend John West, arrived from England in 1820 by way of York Factory with two Indian boys. At that time the settlement was simply a number of huts widely scattered along the banks of the river. Immediately West organized the first elementary school to teach the children of the local settlers and those of the Native population. In 1822 the Church Mission House was built, and served the dual purpose of church-schoolroom. The church was also attended by Presbyterians, since it was the only non-Catholic church in the settlement at the time. Initially this arrangement was a disappointment to the Scottish

Presbyterians, for West could not speak Gaelic and he used the Book of Common Prayer, but he did make some accommodations later. West's successor replaced this first wooden structure with one of stone in 1883; this was St. John's, or the Upper Church, on the banks of the Red River. The present St. John's Cathedral, the birthplace of the Anglican Church in Canada, is the fourth church on this site and was completed in 1926.

Another mission, known as Middle Church or St. Paul's, had been founded six miles farther down the river in 1824; a church built on this site in 1876-80 still stands, although considerably altered. Yet a third mission station was established in 1827 at the Rapids, otherwise known as St. Andrew's, where a schoolhouse served as the place of worship until a church building was erected in 1832. The present church on this site is the most notable of all: St. Andrew's-on-the-Red, built between 1844 and 1849 on high ground overlooking some shallow rapids in a northern curve of the Red River. The design of this church, like several others in the area, was modelled on those Scottish parish churches familiar to the settlers: a box-like structure of symmetrical proportions, with a pitched roof, side windows, and an attached tower over a central door. This church remains the oldest church in Western Canada west of the Great Lakes.

Another church of historical interest, St. Peter's, Dynevor, was built in 1852-53. It was preceded by another building erected in connection with a mission established in 1836 in an Indian settlement farther down the river from St. Andrew's. St. Clement's Church, Mapleton, just south of the present town of Selkirk, was completed in 1861. For many years the official church of Lower Fort Garry, its bell was brought from England by John West in 1820.

The oldest known wooden (log) church in Western Canada is St. James Anglican Church, completed in 1853. It was built on the north bank of the Assiniboine River on high ground that the local inhabitants had used as a refuge from the devastating flood waters in 1826 and 1852. This church became the focal point of the settlement along the river and gave its name to the surrounding district, now a suburb of Winnipeg. Although it is one of the oldest buildings in Winnipeg, this historically important church is still used in the summer months.

Winnipeg's first church, Holy Trinity, was opened in 1868 following the organization of the parish in 1867 by Archdeacon John McLean of St. John's Cathedral. Finding the walk to St. John's too far, parish members first leased a room in Red River Hall before opening their church, which they expanded two years later. An even larger church building was erected in 1875, followed by the present structure on a new site in 1884. Another major Winnipeg church, All Saints' Anglican, put up its first building in 1884, later replaced by the present larger structure in 1926.

Anglican churches were constructed throughout the rural areas of the province in increasing numbers in the concluding decades of the 19th century, and many of these pioneer churches remain standing today. One of these, St. Mary's Anglican, Portage la Prairie, was built in 1898. By 1891 the Anglicans were the second largest denominational group in Manitoba after the Presbyterians, and their churches contributed significantly to the spiritual, social, and musical life of their communities. The Anglicans also founded St. John's College in 1866 to further the educational work of the church in Rupert's Land; it later became an affiliated college of The University of Manitoba.

Presbyterian

The first Presbyterian missionary to the North-West district, James Sutherland, arrived in 1811, pending the appointment of a regularly ordained minister. One of the stipulations the Scottish pioneers made with Lord Selkirk was that they should have a clergyman of their own persuasion. Following a lengthy delay on this issue, the first Presbyterian organization in Red River was achieved in 1851 with the arrival of the Reverend John Black. In 1851 Kildonan Presbyterian Church was built in the northern part of the settlement; it was modelled after a church of the same name in Scotland known to many of the settlers. This church became the centre of the religious, social, and intellectual life of the community, and is still in use. Besides Kildonan Church, the only other surviving Presbyterian church from the early period is Little Britain (now United), completed in 1874.

In 1868 plans were made for a regular place of Presbyterian worship in a more central location at Fort Garry, and the first Knox Church was completed after the restoration of law and order following the political disturbances of 1869. A second Knox Church was built on the same site in 1879, succeeded by even larger churches at other locations in 1884 and 1917. In 1882 a second congregation, St. Andrew's, was established in the northern part of the city. Augustine Church was erected in 1887 on the south side of the Assiniboine River, followed by the present larger building in 1904. The first Westminster Church building was put up in 1892; the present large edifice was completed in 1912.

Outside of Winnipeg, Knox Presbyterian Church, Neepawa, was built in 1892, Trinity Presbyterian in Portage la Prairie in 1897, and Central Presbyterian in Brandon in 1901.

In 1871 there were only 6 Presbyterian churches in Manitoba, but by 1889 the number had increased to 123. With 7,677 members Presbyterianism now was the strongest religious denomination in the province. The Presbyterians' contribution to education was the founding of Manitoba College in 1871.

Methodist

From 1840 when the Reverend James Evans arrived in Norway House, until 1854 when the English Wesleyan Missionary Society was taken over by Canadian Methodists from Ontario, substantial sums of money were spent in sustaining Hudson Bay missions for employees of Hudson's Bay Company, the Métis, and the Native Indians of the region. Methodism became firmly established in the West when the Reverend George Young founded a mission for the white settlers at Red River in 1868. He travelled extensively in the area, even to the outer reaches of the settlement, to minister to the inhabitants. He also was responsible for the construction of the first Grace Church in Winnipeg, dedicated in 1871, enlarged in 1877, and followed by a new building in 1883. The Wesley Methodist congregation, a spinoff from Grace Methodist in 1881, erected other buildings in succession: one in 1883, then a larger edifice in 1898. Farther away, Neepawa Methodist Church was built in 1892.

The Methodist movement was strengthened by unions of various denominational groups in 1874 and 1884, resulting in an increase in the number of preaching stations from 54 in 1884 to 121 by 1890. The Methodists also erected the Wesleyan Educational Institute near the parsonage of Grace Church in 1873 and established Wesley College in 1877, now the University of Winnipeg. Perhaps because of its activism and acceptance of diverse opinions, Methodism attracted a number of prominent social reformers, businessmen, newspaper writers, and politicians as supporters. At the time of the merger of the Congregational, Methodist, and Presbyterian churches in 1925, the Methodist Church was the fourth largest denomination, following the Roman Catholics, Anglicans, and Presbyterians.

Congregational

The Congregational Church, which derived from the 17th-century English Puritan tradition, entered the missionary field in Western Canada much later than the other denominations. The first Congregational Church was organized in Winnipeg in 1879 upon the arrival of the Reverend William Ewing, who remained for only two years. The first church building was erected in Winnipeg in the early 1880s, followed by a second church in 1890. Central Congregational Church in downtown Winnipeg ranked in size, membership, and importance with the major churches of other denominations, and they were all near neighbours. Other Congregational churches were established in Portage la Prairie in 1888 and in Brandon in 1889. Primarily an urban church, Congregationalism did not perform well in rural settings, and it was not a major component of the United Church in 1925.

———◆•●•◆———

Our church choir singers should remember that the house of
worship is not the place for laughing and giggling. There is too
much levity altogether in the choir galleries of several Winnipeg
churches. (*Manitoba Daily Free Press*, 21 November 1891.)

———◆•●•◆———

Reed Organs

History of the Instrument

The reed organ exists today only as a reminder of a bygone era, but it played an important role in the musical life of the community around the turn of the century. Reed organs were the first organs installed in most churches, and they were also the focus for religious devotions and entertainment in family parlours throughout Canada and the United States.

This type of free-reed instrument is of great antiquity. Early Chinese records dating from 1370 refer to a type of hand-operated reed organ already in use a century before that used a system of slides to select the appropriate reed-equipped pipes and was powered by either a hand bellows or a bagpipe-like skin reservoir. Later developments in keyboard reed instruments included the portable regal, dating from the 15th century, and other experimental free-reed instruments in the 17th and 18th centuries. During the first half of the 19th century at least a dozen variations appeared in Europe, beginning with the French "orgue expressiv" (Bordeaux, 1810), and followed by others with different names: aeoline (Königshofen, c. 1810), euphonion (Stuttgart, 1816), physharmonika (Vienna, 1821), aerophone (Paris, 1828), aeolina (England, 1829), aeolodicon (Thuringia, c. 1830), poïkilorgue (developed by the French organ builder Cavaillé-Coll, 1830), aeolopantalon (1830), seraphine (London, 1833), and harmonium (Paris, 1842). In its day the harmonium achieved a certain dignity by being included in the orchestral instrumentation of Rossini's *Petite messe solennelle* and Dvořák's *Bagatelles for Two Violins, Cello, and Harmonium*. César Franck, Alexandre Guilmant, Sigfrid Karg-Elert, and Louis

Vierne also wrote some pieces for the instrument.

Although the 19th-century reed organ went under different names, all of them used wind-blown metal reeds to produce the sound. The smaller varieties, called melodeons or cottage organs, were compact, table-sized, semiportable instruments. The larger versions were called harmoniums, cabinet organs, parlour organs, or pump organs, and their wind supply was produced by dual foot treadles to power the bellows. These instruments had one or two manuals and from 8 to 10 drawstops. Their fancy cases, decorated with ornate mouldings and carvings, made them desirable pieces of furniture in the Victorian parlours of both city homes and farm dwellings. The larger church models had as many as 20 drawstops and sometimes pedal keyboards; these required an assistant to pump the bellows handle at one side of the case. Often they were mistaken by the public for small pipe organs, for some of them had imitation pipes mounted on the top of the case.

Manufacturers

In the United States one of the first keyboard reed instruments was constructed around 1818, followed in 1836 by a portable "rocking melodeon" or "lap organ" of short compass in 1836. From the mid-1840s onward the more familiar upright keyboard instrument, with keyboards of four or five octaves, prevailed. Improvements in mechanical design of the American organ included an exhaust bellows to power the reeds by suction, in place of the earlier force bellows working on the air compression principle. Reed voicing, developed in the 1850s, provided variations in tone quality to imitate different musical instruments, and the stoplists of these instruments frequently borrowed the names of familiar pipe organ registers. Mechanical ingenuity carried the evolution of the reed organ even further with the development of the vocalion, first patented in 1872 and manufactured from 1886 until about 1910; most were two-manuals with pedals. The heavier reeds of this instrument gave it a smoother, organ-like tone, making it an instrument of choice for some churches—an organist-critic called such instruments "atrocities"—but its relatively high cost was not competitive with that of small pipe organs. The invention of automatic player systems, operated by external "fingers" or internal mechanisms, took place in the late 1890s and the early 1900s.

In the United States and Canada 247 different makers of reed organs have been identified, although some of these companies were quite small and often short-lived. The widespread use of mass-production techniques allowed various distributors, including mail-order houses, to apply their own brand names onto instruments made by large manufacturers. The success of the reed organ business was achieved by aggressive and sometimes gimmicky sales techniques, but often employed "soft-sell" testimonials from prominent musicians of the

THIS

ORGAN

FREE.

THE SUBSCRIBER TO THE

Manitoba Weekly Free Press

who wins the first chance in our GRAND PRIZE SCHEME will secure one
GRAND DOMINION ORGAN—-FREE. No one in Canadian Northwest should
miss this great opportunity. Read our GRAND PRIZE LIST.

100 - SPLENDID PRIZES - 100

Over $1,400.00 Worth of Handsome Premiums to be Given Away !

BALANCE OF 1885 FREE ! -   - ONLY $2.00 TO 1887 !

THE GREATEST OFFER YET MADE.

*In 1885 a reed organ was used to encourage new subscriptions to the
Manitoba Free Press.*

day. Relatively inexpensive, available in a variety of sizes, and requiring little
maintenance, these popular instruments were readily accepted into homes and
small churches, particularly when musical quality was not a predominating factor.

Although many thousands of reed organs were sold throughout North
America during the peak period of their popularity between 1870 and 1910,
the decline of the business as a whole accompanied other innovations in musical entertainment: the player piano, the gramophone, and the radio, all of
which transferred music appreciation in the home from a participatory activity into a passive state. When mass-production techniques were applied to piano
making early in the 20th century, interest in the reed organ began to wane.
Few reed organ manufacturers remained in business after 1930, and apart from
those few instruments still being played in rural churches, the remaining ones
that survive today are collector's items in private homes and museums.

In Canada 57 manufacturers of reed organs have been identified; several
also manufactured pipe organs, such as D. W. Karn Company (c. 1867-1924),
known as the Woodstock Organ Factory in the 1870s. The pipe organ builder
Samuel Russell Warren (fl. 1878-c. 1910) was also a pioneer maker of reed
organs. However, the leading manufacturers were also in the piano business,
as their names proclaimed; they were the major suppliers of reed organs in
Manitoba. One of these, the Bell Organ and Piano Company (or the Bell

Piano and Organ Company, depending on its priorities), claiming to be the largest maker of pianos in Canada, was established in Guelph, Ontario, in 1864. In the late 1890s its peak output amounted to 600 organs and 200 pianos a month. The company manufactured over 170,000 instruments of both kinds before it was sold in 1928.

The Dominion Organ and Piano Company operated in Bowmanville, Ontario, from 1873 to 1936. One of its large reed organs, a 19-stop model with 12 sets of reeds, won an international medal in 1876, and others received prizes in various European exhibitions. The company introduced two-manual instruments for church use in the 1880s and published an instructional manual for reed organ players.

The W. Doherty Piano and Organ Company was founded in 1875 in Clinton, Ontario, and produced about 100 reed organs a month at the outset, increasing to about 400 a month within 10 years. The company established retail outlets in several western cities, including Winnipeg. "Organ" disappeared from the company name in 1913, production was reduced a few years later, and the firm was sold to the Sherlock-Manning Piano and Organ Company of London, Ontario, manufacturers of reed organs since 1902.

The Thomas Organ Company was founded in 1875 in Woodstock, Ontario, by a member of a family that had begun building pipe organs in Montréal in 1832. This prosperous company distributed reed organs around the world and introduced larger "Orchestral" and "Symphony" models alongside its portable instruments. In the early 1900s the company was producing about 150 reed organs a month, along with other pieces of music-related cabinetry. It completed this trend by turning exclusively to furniture making in the 1940s.

The Compensating Pipe Organ Company, in business in Toronto in the early 1900s, offered instruments to Manitoba purchasers through a Winnipeg dealer, the Grundy Music Company. This company installed a two-manual, 14-stop instrument, with full pedalboard, in St. John's Cathedral, Winnipeg, in 1902. It was a hybrid instrument employing both reeds and pipes to approximate true pipe organ sounds in a less-costly instrument. The designation "Pipe Organ" in the company name was misleading, for there is no evidence that the company built actual pipe organs.

Besides these major Candian suppliers of reed organs to Manitoba churches and homes, there was competition from manufacturers in the United States who promoted their instruments through newspaper advertisements. Messrs. Dyer Bros. & Howard, St. Paul, Minnesota, offered Burdett & Woods organs free of duty to Winnipeg residents. Also, the Needham Company, New York, claiming to be the largest organ factory in the world, advertised special designs for churches, schools, lodges, or homes. Several reed organs from the Estey Company, Brattleboro, Vermont, were supplied to Manitoba churches through a Winnipeg agent in the 1880s.

Before railroad connections with Eastern Canada were established in 1886, organs were transported from the east across the northern United States to St. Paul, Minnesota, and then north to Winnipeg by river boat. The *Daily Free Press*, 29 August 1874, reported that "a powerful and well finished organ manufactured by the Dominion Company, Bowmanville, Ont., arrived by the Cheyenne. It is for the Primitive Methodist Church, and will likely be used at the Temperance Hall." In the same year the Manitoba Music Store in Winnipeg offered instruments by both American and Canadian makers, as well as tuning, repairs, and instruction. In 1890 McIntosh's Music House advertised "The Vocalion Organ for Churches, etc; Parlour and Church Organs of every description." The T. Eaton Company sold several models of cabinet reed organs made by the Goderich Organ Company (fl. 1890-1910) through its mail order catalogues in 1900. The basic "Queen" model, with 5 octaves, 10 stops, and 3 sets of reeds, was $29.50; the top-priced "Empress piano-cased" model, with 6 octaves, 12 stops, and 5 sets of reeds, was $75.00 (the lowest priced piano was $150.00). In 1902 J. J. H. McLean's music store invited the public to informal recitals on an automatic self-playing organ, "The Bellolian."

Installations

It is likely that the first reed organ in Manitoba was not imported but was built here. According to the recollections of an early pioneer, the first organ in St. Boniface Roman Catholic Cathedral (the 1833 building that burned down in 1860) was a melodeon made by Dr. Duncan, the medical officer with the regulars, "devoted to music and a very ingenious man." This may have been the same organ (harmonium) acquired by the Grey Nuns sometime after their arrival at the St. Boniface mission in 1844; later they gave it to the parishioners of the Cathedral. One of the nuns, Sister Lagrave, played Dr. Duncan's organ in the Cathedral. The instrument was lost in the fire that destroyed the fourth Cathedral in 1968.

Music in church was not readily accepted by the Presbyterians, for in that denomination throughout the country neither organs nor hymns were allowed; the only singing was metrical psalms. Later a bass viol or flute was used to support congregational singing. This situation continued until 1872, when the Church's General Assembly decided to permit the use of organs, formerly described as "carnal instruments." In Manitoba some members of the Kildonan Presbyterian Church congregation objected to the introduction of a choir and to the idea of having an organ. In a debate on these questions at an annual meeting of the church, an older gentleman announced that if an organ were put in the church he would bring around Old Bob, his horse, "and take the 'kist o' whustles' out of the house of the Lord and dump it by the roadside."

When the organ eventually was put in, another recalcitrant member declared that he would no longer attend services at Kildonan and transferred to St. Andrew's mission church in 1869, perhaps unaware that a small melodeon was used in services there, too. But soon after his daughter was appointed to play the instrument in Kildonan Church he returned there. This repentant parishioner was John "Scotchman" Sutherland, later an elected member of the first Legislative Assembly of Manitoba.

In Winnipeg things went more smoothly, for other religious denominations considered the organ an appropriate aspect of Christian praise. Elsewhere in the country, congregations began to acquire organs early in the 19th century. In Winnipeg a five-stop reed organ was placed in Grace Methodist Church in 1873, and two years later a prominent mill owner presented the Baptist Chapel with a reed organ. Other churches established around this time undoubtedly purchased reed organs, but these acquisitions were no longer reported in the newspapers after pipe organs began to arrive. The first pipe organ in Manitoba was installed in St. Boniface Cathedral in 1875, followed by others in the larger city churches in the remaining decades of the 19th century and well into the 20th century.

Many churches in outlying areas installed reed organs and kept them for many years until they were superseded by electronic instruments. A pioneer recalled an impressive instrument installed in the Deloraine Presbyterian Church when it was built in 1897. The organ had two manuals and pedals, with ornamental pipes, and was powered by the strong arms of older boys or young men who pumped a heavy handle to inflate the two bellows. There was a screen around the pumper's position. She remembered that pumpers earned a reputation of "good pumper" or otherwise. Too much enthusiasm on the part of the pumper made it difficult for the organist to adjust the volume, whereas a "good pumper" had more appreciation for the mood of the music and waited for signals. At one time, during an organ recital, a belt connecting the two bellows broke. The pumper was frantically working the handle, hoping to add more power to the remaining bellows, while the organist was giving signals for more volume, more volume! When the ordeal was over, the pumper was exhausted and drenched with perspiration. That pumper still remembered that occasion vividly at the age of 85.

A two-manual, 16-stop reed organ with "mouse proof" pedals, manufactured by the Bell Organ and Piano Company, was installed in St. Alban's Anglican Church, Oak Lake, Manitoba, around 1890, and it is still in use. The stoplist of this instrument is representative of the instruments supplied to churches in this period.

GREAT	SWELL
Bombardon 16 ft	Cremona 16 ft
Bourdon Treble 16 ft	Euphone 16 ft
Violone 8 ft	Fagotte 8 ft

Melodia 8 ft
Celeste 8 ft
Flute 4 ft
Piccolo 2 ft
Octave Coupler
(one stop name missing)
Great to Pedal

Aeolian 8 ft
Saxhorn 8 ft
Violetta 2 ft
Forte
(one stop name missing)
Swell to Great
Swell to Pedal

PEDAL(?)
Bourdon Bass 16 ft
Pipe Melodia 8 ft
Viola 4 ft

An electric blower was installed in this instrument around 1952 by an inventor whose father had converted many reed organs in England.

A variation on the typical church model harmonium, made by the Compensating Pipe Organ Company, Toronto, was installed in the third St. John's Anglican Cathedral, Winnipeg, in 1902. The names of the stops of this instrument were rather deceptive, since they were identical with those found on pipe organs; the clue is the "Forte" accessory on both manuals, exclusively a reed organ device for maximizing volume. The chief virtues of this instrument were its relatively low cost (perhaps half that of a comparable pipe organ), its smaller space requirements, and its capability of allowing reeds and pipes to be tuned together. Nevertheless, the musical qualities of the organ received a distinctly uncomplimentary judgment by a professional organist: "Compensating organs, of which the less said the better, and which the hearer should be very generously compensated for listening to." ("Few Pipe Organs When Winnipeg was a Hamlet: Diary of the Late James W. Matthews Recalls Early Instruments and Players," *Manitoba Free Press*, 13 December 1924.)

A typical one-manual harmonium, of the kind that graced the parlours of city and farm homes for several decades around the turn of the century, had a divided keyboard that separated its bass and treble registers at middle C. The tonal functions of the drawknobs can therefore be inferred from this array on an instrument made by the W. Doherty & Company in 1895:

Diapason Bass
Principal Bass
Violetta
Bass Coupler
Principal Forte
Sub Bass
Dulciana Bass
Vox Humana
Cello
Piccolo

Diapason Forte
Treble Coupler
Vox Celeste
Principal Treble
Diapason Treble

Doherty harmonium
(1895).

St. Andrew's-on-the-Red Anglican Church is the home of three reed organs. The oldest is a one-manual, 12-stop pump organ built by Trayser & Cie., Stuttgart, Germany. This organ was brought from England through York Factory in the mid-1800s, intended for use in a northern diocese of the Anglican church. In the course of the journey, the York boat containing the cargo overturned on

Trayser harmonium (c.1800),
St. Andrew's-on-the-Red
Anglican Church, near
Lockport, Manitoba.

the Nelson River, but the organ was recovered and brought south to St. Andrew's, where it was left with a local Sunday school teacher who was also the choir leader of the church. The organ was designed to be carried by four men using poles looped through metal rings, two on each side of the case; this allowed the organ to be moved to and from nearby St. Thomas Church. The second harmonium, a one-manual, 19-stop Estey pump organ, now electrified, was provided with a set of ornamental pipes, made of cardboard and painted gold, mounted on the top of the case. The third organ is a two-manual, 20-stop Doherty instrument, built around 1904, originally in St. Alban's Anglican Church, Snowflake, Manitoba. The stop names of these instruments duplicate those of regular pipe organs: bourdon, diapason, dulciana, flute, vox humana, and others, along with pitch level designations: 16, 8, 4, 2. According to the fashion in such instruments, all three organs have ornate carvings on various parts of the casework.

Doherty harmonium (c.1904), St. Andrew's-on-the-Red Anglican Church, near Lockport, Manitoba.

While many foot- or hand-pumped reed organs were converted to electric blowers later in their lifetimes, a final development in the history of reed organs was the electronic amplification of the sounds of the vibrating reeds. The J. C. Hallman Manufacturing Company, which was in business in Kitchener, Ontario, from 1941 to 1977, developed and built 3,000 such instruments, along with 59 pipe organs. Some Manitoba churches purchased the electric tone-generator models through the T. Eaton Company in the 1960s.

Reeds versus Pipes

Writing at the end of the 19th century, a Winnipeg music critic speculated on the future of the reed organ and how it compared with small pipe organs:

> English musical papers now usually contain one or more advertisements of small pipe organs, of moderate price, and although of course limited in power, still powerful enough for small churches, and surely far more preferable to an overgrown harmonium or American organ.
>
> In this western country especially, so many churches want something better than the ordinary little American organ, and yet can scarcely afford the ordinary size pipe organ of at least eight or ten stops; they have at their disposal, say, some four or five hundred dollars; for this sum one of our Canadian firms should be able to supply them with an organ of four or five stops which properly arranged and managed would fill all the wants of a small church. (*Winnipeg Town Topics*, 1 July 1899.)

Prospective Organist: I wish to take lessons on the organ. You teach the organ, do you not?

Professor Lonesomegee: Why, yes! I do; and I shall be pleased to enroll you as a pupil; but, may I ask, what opportunities you have for practice?

Prospective Organist: Oh, we have a fine organ in our house.

Professor Lonesomegee: Delighted to hear it. Two manual and pedal, I suppose?

Prospective Organist: Ah—h'm—I don't quite understand.

P.L.: Two manuals—keyboards, you know—for the hands, and one pedal board for the feet.

P.O.(brightening): Oh, no! Our organ is built quite differently; we have just one keyboard for the hands and two pedals for the feet; one for the right foot and one for the left, don't you know; it is so much easier to pump than those little organs with only one pedal. (*Winnipeg Town Topics*, 30 January 1909.)

[The "Professor's" name is a pun on Melsom Gee, organist at All Saints' Anglican Church at the time.]

Manitoba Pipe Organs and Their Builders

Pipe Organs: A Brief History

The term *organ* is generally defined as an instrument employing a wind-raising mechanism to supply air under pressure through a wind chest or distribution reservoir to one or more graded sets of fixed-pitch pipes activated by a series of valves controlled from one or more keyboards. The invention of the organ is attributed to Ctesibius, an engineer in Alexandria c. 246 BCE, who used air pressure to power various mechanical devices, such as the water clock and catapult. Another of his applications was the use of a pressurized water reservoir to regulate the wind pressure for sounding a row of pipes; hence the term *hydraulis* or hydraulic organ. Originally used outdoors for signalling or ceremonial purposes, this high-pitched, screeching device was also used in athletic competitions in ancient Greece. In Rome the instrument flourished for about three centuries; it was favoured by Nero and other emperors, and was used as an accompaniment to the feasts of wealthy men. Later the use of the organ spread to the Eastern Empire where it assumed ceremonial functions. Organs ornamented with ivory and precious metals became prized as symbols of wealth. The organ is believed to have been introduced into the western Christian Church by a gift to King Pippin III of the Franks from Constantine, the Byzantine Emperor, in 757. Whether the device was a tuneful ceremonial instrument or a military siren-organ is problematical, but it was not a church organ.

The date when organs were first used in the ritual of the Christian Church is uncertain, but they became more accepted by the middle of the 9th

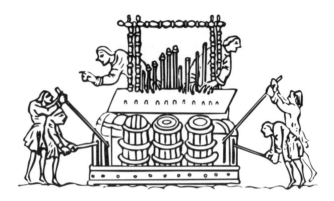

*Hydraulis, illustration from Psalm 150, Utrecht Psalter,
c. 816-830.*

century, following the relaxation of the attitude of the Church against any kind of instrumental music in worship. The use of the organ as a church instrument expanded rapidly, and by the end of the 15th century it had become a fairly uniform instrument whose mechanical and tonal characteristics closely resembled those of today's instruments. The chief factors contributing to its development in this period included the increased number of churches, the establishment of the secular trades, new woodworking and metal technologies, and the development of musical styles. Evolutionary developments included the arrangement of the manuals, pedals, mechanical key action, pipe scaling, wind chests, bellows design, and the use of roller boards that allowed pipes to be mounted above and laterally displaced from their respective keys. By the 17th century organs possessed most of the now familiar varieties of tone related to flue and reed pipe construction, and they were operated by a sophisticated type of mechanical action.

From the 16th and 17th centuries onwards, the organ assumed somewhat different characteristics in various parts of Europe, depending on local religious, political, or economic conditions. In the Netherlands, for example, the organ developed in parallel directions: municipal organs featured solo stops for use in secular concerts and special occasions, while liturgical instruments emphasized the foundation stops required to support congregational singing and reed stops for outlining melodies. It is likely that organ pedals were used in the 14th century, in the same way that Flemish carillons were played by both hands and feet.

The development of the organ in North Germany was most closely identified with the so-called "Baroque organ." The most famous builder was Arp Schnitger (1648-1719), whose unique instruments inspired the young J. S. Bach and other composers of his time on account of their size, scope, and tonal clarity required for contrapuntal music. Although the majority of Schnitger organs contained no wooden pipes, they were characterized by tonally self-sufficient but balanced divisions, including a well-developed pedal; the pipes were mounted in open casework of appropriate functional and visual design, often profusely ornamented. In the southern and central parts of Germany, the most prominent builder was Gottfried Silbermann (1683-1753), whose instruments tended more towards integration. Wooden pipes were used for many of the pipe ranks, and some imitative stops were introduced. Some of these "pre-Romantic" tonal and design characteristics involved less incisive foundation choruses and the weakening of the principle of functional placement of the tonal divisions evident in North German organs. These organs were known to the mature Bach, but they were not well suited to all of his music. The German organ declined after 1720, having lost its identity, and the major composers turned to other media.

In France in the 17th and 18th centuries, most organs exhibited a uniform tonal design distinguished by the fiery reeds demanded by the organ works by Couperin and his contemporaries. In the 19th century the full-bodied tonal innovations in string, flute, and reed sounds in organs by Aristide Cavaillé-

Marienkirche, Lübeck, Germany, before 1475. The open casework and functional visual design are typical of the so-called Baroque organ.

Coll (1811-1899) inspired a school of symphonic composition and playing by such late-Romantic masters as Franck, Saint-Saëns, Widor, Guilmant, Vierne, Gigout, Dubois, and others. The tonal and engineering aspects of Cavaillé-Coll organs influenced organ building in England, and early Casavant organs in Canada followed the contemporary French model, adding improvements in more reliable electric action.

Organs in 16th-century Italy were one-manual instruments, almost uniform in style. Reed stops were rare until some Romantic concessions in reed and string sounds were made in the 19th century. Pedal divisions did not appear until the end of that century. In Spain and Portugal, also, most early organs were one-manual instruments with no independent pedals, but they had more varied registers than Italian organs. Some organs divided the stops into treble and bass halves on the keyboard, allowing a more flexible use of tonal resources. "Toy" stops (birdcalls, drums, bells) were more common than in organs elsewhere. But their distinguishing feature, from the 17th century onward, was the horizontally projecting reed pipes on larger organs, often used in ceremonial occasions.

In England all known early instruments up to the Reformation had only one manual and few stops, although their cases were elaborate and richly decorated. The course of organ building was disrupted by Puritan and political upheavals, particularly the Reformation and in the Commonwealth period, when most organs were destroyed. However, organ building resumed after the Restoration, when some continental traditions were imported. Pedals first appeared in 1720, but were lacking in some important organs even until the mid-1800s; even then, their use was resisted by some players for a long time. English builders in the 17th century developed the "chair" or choir organ at the back of the player, and in the early 18th century the enclosed swell box with adjustable louvred fronts. In the 19th century English organs also increased in size to function as accompaniments to more elaborate musical services. As expressions of civic pride, larger organs were installed in town halls, where they were used in secular solo concerts. The greatest 19th-century British organ builder Henry Willis (1821-1901) excelled in inventive engineering devices for improved control of the organ. He perfected the characteristically English swell organ with its chorus reeds and mixtures, but he still retained other symphonic or orchestral tonal features found in the organs of Cavaillé-Coll. An unfortunate chapter in English organ building was written by Robert Hope-Jones (1859-1914), an inventive telephone engineer who devised the "one-man orchestra" organ. The extreme tone qualities of this bizarre instrument influenced the development of the Wurlitzer theatre organ in the United States in the late 1920s and set back tonal design in both countries for a time. Hope-Jones devised a new type of electric action, connecting the console to the organ mechanism by a flexible cable. W. T. Best, the organist at St. George's Hall,

Liverpool, referred to him as "Hopeless Jones," who "plays his organs at the end of a long rope which ought to be around his neck."

In the southern colonies of America, organs were first imported from Spain in the 17th and 18th centuries; in the northern colonies they were imported from Europe. The first organ building centres began in the northeastern United States early in the 19th century. The first instruments resembled English models, both in construction and acoustical characteristics, followed by others influenced by French and German Romantic traditions. Although the concept of the orchestral imitative organ survived for a while, a reaction occurred in the 1930s that stimulated the production of instruments based on classical models. This organ revival, which had begun with the publication of a critical pamphlet by Albert Schweitzer in 1906 and got under way around the time of the landmark Freiburg Organ Conference in 1926, significantly influenced the course of organ building in Europe as well as in North America. This Organ Reform Movement (*Orgelbewegung*) prompted a number of builders to undertake a contemporary expression of such earlier principles as balanced tonal resources, mechanical action, and free-standing casework. Later developments were influenced by the importation of mechanical-action instruments by European builders; these, in turn, inspired a more sensitive adaption of classical principles by a new generation of American organ builders.

In Canada there was an organ or two in Québec City in the early 1660s. Following a period of importation of organs from Europe, organ building in Canada commenced as early as 1723 and flourished mainly in Québec and Ontario from the mid-19th century onward. Some of the early organ builders learned their trade in the United States, while the Casavant brothers, the Canadian builders, toured Europe and studied organs there. Some members of a later generation of organ builders either emigrated from Europe to Canada or were strongly influenced by the same ideals of organ reform as their counterparts in the United States.

Early Manitoba Organs

The history of organs in Manitoba is largely a chronicle of events in Winnipeg, for the city was the main centre of population and of subsequent growth through immigration from the days of the Red River Settlement, as well as being the focus of commercial activity through the years. The combination of an expanding population, increasing wealth, the growth of the various religious denominations, and the flowering of musical culture resulted in the construction of a number of large churches within a relatively short span of time.

After the founding of the historic churches of the early Red River Settlement, the construction of church buildings throughout Manitoba proceeded in several fairly well-defined phases. Following the arrival of the main line of the Canadian Pacific Railroad in 1886, the exceedingly rapid increase in population was accompanied by the establishment of many new church congregations and the erection of buildings to serve their needs. Winnipeg's population increased from 42,000 in 1901 to 136,000 in 1911 and was accompanied by a boom in all forms of construction, including churches. Many of the business, political, and community leaders, predominantly Anglo-Saxon in origin, were prominent members of larger city congregations, and undoubtedly they exercised considerable influence on decisions regarding the construction, size, and design of church buildings, as well as on the installation of organs.

In St. Boniface three Roman Catholic cathedrals had been erected in succession (1822, 1833, 1862) before other denominations began to construct their houses of worship in Winnipeg. Following the appearance of some of the city's larger churches in the 1880s, the first major boom in church building construction extended to about 1915. Many of Winnipeg's largest and finest churches were built in these early years. The war years 1914-18 and the ensuing short depression slowed but did not halt church construction, and a second wave of church building occurred in the 1920s. After a slowdown during the economic depression of the 1930s and the years following World War II, a third wave of church construction occurred in the 1950s and 1960s. Many of the buildings of the latter period were new ones of contemporary architectural design; they replaced earlier structures that had deteriorated or had become too small for growing and prosperous suburban congregations. The type of organs installed in these churches reflected new concepts in organ design as well as changing architectural requirements. Since the mid-1970s the pace of new construction has slowed once again, due to stability in the population, declining church membership, and economic circumstances generally.

From the outset many of the larger urban church congregations followed the trend established in Eastern Canada of installing adequate pipe organs in their new buildings and of welcoming trained musicians from England to play the new instruments and to direct the churches' musical programs. The pattern of organ installations in Winnipeg reflected but did not exactly parallel the major periods of construction of church buildings. The greatest number of organ installations annually in the city occurred between 1900 and 1930, even through the decade that included World War I. In the following years the number of installations remained fairly constant from one decade to the next, with the exception of the period 1950-59, the second peak of activity; about one-third of the installations in those years were renovations, reconstructions, or relocations of existing instruments. In rural centres most of the early churches did not acquire pipe organs immediately upon the construction of the church buildings, but used reed organs until they could afford pipe organs at a later date. These patterns are evident in the following summary of known organ installations in Manitoba shown in Table 1.

Table 1: Known Organ Installations

	Winnipeg	Rural Manitoba	Total
1875-79	2		2
1880-89	9	1	10
1890-99	6	1	7
1900-09	15	8	23
1910-19	22	3	25
1920-29	19	7	26
1930-39	9	1	10
1940-49	6	3	9
1950-59	18	3	21
1960-69	7		7
1970-79	8	1	9
1980-89	6	3	9
1990-97	4		4
	131	31	162

In the early 1890s Winnipeg's choral tradition was already flourishing, chiefly in the activities of church choirs that presented the works of familiar English composers on special festive occasions and in other concerts through-out the year. Organ recitals become frequent, and newspaper reviews occa-sionally commented on the quality and state of repair of the instruments themselves. Writing in a weekly paper in 1890, a critic remarked that "the organ in Grace church is so meagre in capacity and poor in tone, that it is difficult to take a solo upon it seriously." (*Winnipeg Town Talk*, 23 August 1890.) In another context, it was reported that "Mr. Nelson Barber, the new organist and choirmaster of All Saints' church has arrived from England. . . . It is a pity that he has not a better instrument to play on." (*Winnipeg Town Talk*, 18 October 1890.)

The deteriorating organ at Holy Trinity Anglican Church prompted one critic to assert that even a reed organ would be preferable to the dilapidated structure then in use. Early in 1891 Charles S. Warren of Warren & Son, the Toronto organ builders, was in Winnipeg: "He examined most of the organs in the city, and came to the conclusion that there is room for one or two first-class instruments. He was particularly struck with the unique arrangement of the organ at Holy Trinity, and says Mr. Minchin deserves a chromo for being able to play it at all." (*Manitoba Free Press*, 17 January 1891.)

Then there was the ultimate insult: "The organ at Grace church has arrived at that state of perfection when it is difficult to tell it from a circus calliope." (*Winnipeg Town Talk*, 21 March 1891.)

James W. Matthews was the organist at Central Congregationalist Church in the early 1900s; before coming to Canada from England he was assistant to

Samuel Sebastian Wesley, the foremost English organist of his time, at Glouces-ter Cathedral. He recorded several judgments about the state of organs in some Winnipeg churches in the 1890s:

> Zion church: Very small one manual organ of execrably harsh tone, remind-ing one of Wombwell's Menagerie steam organs. . . . Christ church: Some-what cumbrous two manual organ, maker unknown. Of this organ it should be related that it was the custom of enthusiastic experimenters in organ improvement or construction to try their handiwork on Christ church or-gan, so that eventually the condition of it became appalling. ("Few Pipe Organs When Winnipeg was a Hamlet: Diary of the Late James W. Matthews Recalls Early Instruments and Players," *Manitoba Free Press*, 13 December 1924.)

The quality of organ music at All Saints' Anglican Church improved con-siderably with the installation of a new organ in 1891. The event was duly noted in a daily newspaper that printed the complete stoplist of the organ a week following this announcement:

> Mr. Shaw of Messrs. Warren & Sons, Toronto, is in the city placing the new organ in All Saints' Church, built by his firm, in position. The instrument has been carefully planned and the stops chosen for balance of power and variety of tone. It has two manuals with five stops on each, and provision for two more on the swell and one on the great. Artistically, it will be a great improvement to the church; the front bracketed out into the chancel, pro-jecting about ten feet, and the pipes are tastefully decorated. Mr. Shaw is doubtful whether he will be able to get the organ tuned and ready for use by Sunday, so the special musical service in connection with the dedication of the new instrument will be held on Sunday evening, the 14th inst. (*Mani-toba Free Press*, 7 November 1891.)

The same representative of Warren & Sons was in the city in the following year, working on extensive repairs and alterations to the organ at Holy Trinity Anglican Church. The addition of seven ranks of pipes and renovations of the console—all at a cost of $1,300—yielded a comprehensive three-manual, 39-stop instrument.

In other churches, however, things did not improve much in the following years. W. G. Willmore, an Australian organist who visited Winnipeg in Octo-ber 1894, had the opportunity to try out a number of the city's organs. His judgments were reported in the press:

> Of all the instruments he was most taken with the one in Grace church, which in itself is not much. Knox church organ, he says, is not well put together, the one in Christ church is too cumbersome, Zion church organ is too small, and St. Mary's, while under ordinary circumstances should be the best, is badly kept and needs voicing and repairing. The opinion of Mr. Willmore is valuable; he has been a prominent organist for twenty years, in

two of which he presided over the largest instrument of Philadelphia. In Brisbane he has charge of a $30,000 instrument. (*Manitoba Free Press*, 13 October 1894.)

Even toward the end of the first decade of the 20th century, critics still were delivering verdicts on the state of church organs. St. Matthew's Anglican Church had only a reed organ in 1909, but a reporter hoped for better things to come when the church was able to afford an organ more in keeping with the growth and standing of the church.

The critics offered generous praise for instruments that had been success-fully renovated and for new instruments of high quality. None of the problems that plagued early organs were in instruments manufactured by Casavant Frères, from the time that the company installed its first organ in Manitoba in 1899, and its first in Winnipeg in 1904. Casavant's reputation for high quality was reinforced by the enthusiastic commendations regarding their Winnipeg installations. Following the arrival of a new Casavant organ in St. Andrew's Church in 1904, the chairman of the board of managers reported the opinions of both local musicians and visiting recitalists to the organ builders:

> I have seen a number of local musicians . . . and they told me that the Karn organ simply was not in it with yours. . . . As you know yourselves there are very often traveling salesmen with a good slick tongue which can often turn a committee, but for value give us your instrument every time. (Letter from R. R. Scott to Casavant Frères, 25 February 1905.)

> Mr. Clarence Eddy, the celebrated American Organist recently gave two recitals on our instrument, on which occasion he expressed himself in the most emphatic manner as being delighted with the organ in every respect. (Letter from R. R. Scott to Casavant Frères, 15 March 1905.)

The organist at Zion Methodist Church conveyed the judgment of a visiting recitalist on the recently installed Casavant organ:

> Mr. Arthur Dunham, of Chicago, gave two recitals on my organ lately, and he was most enthusiastic. . . . He told me afterwards that he never played a finer organ of its size before in his life and that it was far ahead of the average organ in the States. (Letter from F. Melsom Gee to Casavant Frères, 3 February 1906.)

The new Casavant organ installed in Grace Methodist Church late in 1907 also received highly favourable comments from the incumbent organist:

> This instrument, which I believe is the largest in Western Canada, was opened on January 1st 1908, and has given the greatest satisfaction to everyone who has either heard or played it. During the past ten months that the organ has been in my charge I have had ample opportunity of testing it and of comparing it with organs of other firms—both English and American. The system

of pneumatic action employed by Casavant Bros. of Quebec is extremely simple and consequently more reliable. The tone of the various stops, both flue and reed, is particularly fine, while the method of control is all that an organist could wish. (Letter from Ernest E. Vinen, FRCO, to *The Edmonton Bulletin*, 24 February 1909.)

After his recital on this organ in 1908, the noted organist Edwin H. Lemare said of the Grace Church organ: "It is an instrument of rare sweetness and capacity, and a delight to handle."

The music columnist P. B. C. Turner monitored the musical aspects of church services by visiting various denominations from time to time and reported on their content and quality under the heading, "Choir News." What he heard at McDougall Methodist Church on Sunday, 28 March 1909, prompted these comments:

I never had much use for mice, and yet after I heard McDougall church organ last Sunday I thought that the immigration department could not do an act of more lasting good to the aesthetic instincts of the younger genera-tion of worshippers who attend McDougall church than might be accom-plished were they to import a colony of mice and give them free homestead entries in the bellows and among the felt and key stickers of McDougall church organ.

For those mice if left long enough would likely do their work well, and confer a lasting benefit to the congregation by stopping that rattling, wheez-ing, groaning combination of tone which passes now under the misnomer of an "organ." And if the mice don't do it well—I suppose that those who were responsible for saddling the church with such an instrument will hate to throw away the hundreds of dollars they sunk into it, and the congregation will have to suffer patiently as they so often do for the blunders of those in charge. Yes! I know all about the history of McDougall church organ. (*Win-nipeg Town Topics*, 3 April 1909.)

The unidentified manufacturer of the offensive instrument, who had sup-plied organs to two other Winnipeg churches before they installed Casavant instruments, probably was a builder in Eastern Canada whose factory Turner had visited some years before in anticipation of establishing a local agency, a prospect he later abandoned after careful investigation. The editorial diatribe against the McDougall organ concluded with this parody of Tennyson's im-mortal ode:

What though the choir knew someone had blundered,
Theirs not to make reply.
Theirs not to reason why,
Theirs but to sing, or die,
While from behind them volleyed and thundered:
Groans and discordant tones,

Sounds as of rattling bones.
How they could sing at all, everyone wondered.
When the noise stopped 'twas rest—rest for three hundred.

A decade later there were still organs in the city that attracted critical comment concerning their decrepit state, in this case the instrument at St.
Matthew's Anglican Church:

> The lady organist, although doing creditable work, did not get an opportu-
> nity to do herself justice for the reason that the organ is a fickle and unsat-
> isfactory affair. The reeds, and, in fact, the entire mechanism of the
> instrument, are in bad order. But when times are better the authorities at St.
> Matthew's will no doubt install an organ commensurate with the size of
> their fine church. ("Music in Churches," *Manitoba Free Press*, 12 January
> 1918.)

In the early years, if organs were referred to specifically in critical reviews
of recitals it was to offer a few words of praise for new installations in the larger
Winnipeg churches. From this time onward organs were not a topic for critical comment for over forty years, when a modern mechanical-action organ was
installed in a Winnipeg church in the early 1960s.

Pipe Organ Builders Represented in Manitoba

Organs manufactured by 28 different Canadian, American, and European
builders have been installed in Manitoba since the first pipe organ arrived in
1875 from Eastern Canada. Some of these manufacturers are represented by
only one instrument, others by a few, and the major Canadian builder,
Casavant, by many.

Winnipeg Builders

In the 1880s Winnipeg had two or perhaps three organ builders, and since it is
likely that some of them were related to one another, they may be counted as
one company. The two partners H. W. Bolton and A. B. Handscomb were listed
as organ builders in the city in 1883. It was this H. W. Bolton, formerly a
Montréal organ builder, who submitted an unsuccessful tender from Winnipeg in 1884 for the installation of a new organ in All Saints' Anglican Church.
There was also Fred W. Bolton, another builder who worked in the city in 1885
and 1886; his name did not appear in the city directory in subsequent years.
Wm. Henry Bolton was listed as an organ builder for 1887 only. In the same
year a one-manual, 5-stop, pipe organ was installed in the Presbyterian Church,
Birtle, Manitoba, by "Messrs. Bolton and Baldwin of Winnipeg." Which of
the three Boltons was involved in this venture is uncertain. As for the col-
league Baldwin, he might have been one of a number of mechanics, fitters,

or carpenters working in the city at that time who may have assisted Bolton in building organs on a part-time basis. No organ builders by the name of Bolton were listed in the city directory in 1888 or in the following years. The Toronto organ manufacturers S. R. Warren & Son described other installations by one of these unnamed Winnipeg builders as "disgraceful failures" in two letters written in 1884 in connection with their proposal for the All Saints' Church organ. The reference probably was to H. W. Bolton, who earlier had installed an organ in Queen's Hall, Montréal, that Warren had been asked to rebuild. A Bolton pipe organ was installed in the Baptist Church, Winnipeg, in 1883, and in Christ Church Anglican, Winnipeg, around 1886. If any of the Bolton organ builders of Winnipeg installed other instruments in Manitoba churches around this time, none of them survive, and there is no remaining evidence of their activities in the area.

Eastern Canada: The Early Years

In 1875 the Montréal builder Louis Mitchell (1823?-1902) accompanied a newly constructed organ across the continent and erected it in St. Boniface Cathedral, on the east bank of the Red River across from Winnipeg, during the week preceding the dedication ceremony on 24 June of that year. Mitchell had been building organs with a partner in his own workshop since 1861, following his apprenticeship with the prominent Montréal builder Samuel Russell Warren, a later competitor. As a young man attending a college in Ste. Thérèse, near Montréal, Mitchell's interest in organ building was stimulated by the music teacher who later would inspire Joseph Casavant in the same direction. Mitchell studied organ building in London, England, but the exact date is unknown. His instruments reflected some aspects of the work of an early 19th-century French organ builder—for a time he imported pipes from France, but never visited there—and their overall high quality led to contracts for installations and restorations both within and outside Québec. Mitchell also supplied a large two-manual organ to the first St. Mary's Church in 1883 soon after the building was constructed. His business ceased operations in 1893.

Samuel Russell Warren (1809-1882), a prominent figure of professional calibre in 19th-century Canadian organ building, was born in Rhode Island, a descendant of one of the passengers on the 1620 voyage of the Mayflower. He acquired his technical skills in Boston before emigrating to Canada in 1836 to build and repair organs in and around Montréal. In 1878 the family firm, now S. R. Warren & Son, relocated in Toronto. The company produced more than 350 pipe organs, along with reed organs, pianofortes, accordions, and flutes. Warren was familiar with the principles of French organ building and had corresponded with Aristide Cavaillé-Coll. Among his innovations were the introduction of harmonic flutes, free reeds, and orchestral stops into his organ specifications. He also patented an octave coupler, and used a hydraulic bellows in a 1861 installation. After his death in 1882, his son Charles Sumner Warren managed the business until 1896, when it was sold to D. W. Karn of Woodstock, Ontario. Winnipeg installations of new Warren organs included a two-manual, 24-stop organ in Holy Trinity Anglican Church in 1878; smaller instruments in Central Congregational, Grace Methodist, and Knox Presbyterian churches in the mid-1880s (specifications unknown in these cases); a two-manual instrument in All Saints' Anglican Church in 1891; a one-manual organ in St. George's Church in 1894; and a two-manual instrument in the College Theatre in 1921. Neepawa Methodist Church acquired a used Warren tracker instrument from an Ontario church in 1921.

Richard S. Williams (1834-1906) was an instrument repairman before establishing a business in Toronto, Ontario, in 1854 to make small stringed instruments, then reed organs and pianos. In 1879 the business was renamed R. S. Williams & Son (later Sons). The factory was moved to Oshawa, Ontario, in 1889, leaving the retail operation in Toronto. A few branch offices were established in other cities, including one in Winnipeg in 1905. In the 1880s the firm specialized in reed organs and pianos, later confining production exclusively to pianos, completing 67,000 of them by 1929; two were placed in Windsor Castle at the request of Queen Victoria. A few pipe organs were made also. The company was sold in 1928, but it continued as a warehouse-type operation until about 1952. Williams's extensive collection of old musical instruments now resides in the Royal Ontario Museum. A large three-manual, 32-stop organ was installed in Grace Methodist Church, Winnipeg, in 1894.

The town of Woodstock, Ontario, became a centre of organ building in the late 1860s, when Dennis W. Karn (1843-1916) joined another local craftsman in building cabinet organs. Besides making pianos in the late 1880s, he began to produce Karn-Warren pipe organs in 1897 following the purchase of the Warren business; however, this alliance was not reflected in the company's letterhead or advertising. Branch warerooms were established in several cities in eastern Canada and in Winnipeg in the early 1900s. After Dennis Karn's retirement in 1909 and the amalgamation of his company with a nearby piano maker, the manufacture of Karn-Morris pipe organs continued under the supervision of Charles Sumner Warren, who remained with Karn for a time. Karn organs were installed in several Winnipeg churches: Westminster Presbyterian in 1899, Augustine Presbyterian in 1905, St. Peter's Anglican in 1910, and Nassau Street Baptist (now Trinity Baptist) in 1911. Other Karn organs were placed in First Baptist, Knox Presbyterian, and St. Mary's Anglican churches, Portage La Prairie, and in St. Matthew's Anglican Cathedral, Brandon, in the early 1900s.

Following the depression of organ building after World War I and the dissolution of the Karn-Morris partnership in 1920, several of the craftsmen living in Woodstock reorganized in 1922 to form the Woodstock Pipe Organ

Builders. Before it ceased operations in 1948, the company had installed organs throughout Canada. In Winnipeg this firm provided two-manual organs for Home Street Presbyterian Church (now Home Street Mennonite) and St. James Anglican Church, both in the 1920s.

Edward Lye (1828?-1919), an English cabinetmaker who settled in Toronto in 1856, founded the longest surviving family business of organ builders in Canada. His company, established in 1864, specialized mainly small, two-manual, tracker-action organs whose tonal design showed an understanding of the principle of balancing strong foundation ranks with appropriate upperwork. Many of these organs, along with several larger instruments, are still in use in Ontario churches. As recently as 1982 a family member was still doing repairs, although The Lye Organ Company officially had ceased operations in the mid-1950s. An Edward Lye tracker organ, Opus 12, was installed in Trinity Lutheran Church, Winnipeg, around 1906. It was taken to Sacré-Coeur Church in 1968 and remained there until it was removed in 1992; it was installed in the Parish Church, St. Norbert, in 1997.

In 1834 Joseph Casavant (1807-1874), a young blacksmith living in St. Hyacinthe, Québec, entered a college in nearby Ste. Thérèse, where he discovered an organ that had been brought from France in an unfinished condition some years earlier. The founder of the college, recognizing his student's mechanical abilities, encouraged him to complete the instrument, which he did, with the help of classic treatises on organ building. Thus began a career that led to the eventual establishment of Canada's illustrious firm, Casavant Frères. By the time he retired from organ building in 1866 after 26 years in the business, Joseph Casavant had supplied organs to 17 churches in Québec and Ontario, but none of them survive.

Joseph Casavant's sons, Joseph-Claver Casavant (1855-1933) and Samuel-Marie Casavant (1850-1929), acquired the essentials of the craft with their father's successor in organ building in St. Hyacinthe. Then they toured Europe for several years, inspecting organs and visiting workshops; Claver had apprenticed briefly with a Versailles artisan before the tour. They returned to St. Hyacinthe in 1879 to open their factory under the now famous name. In the following years production increased steadily as their reputation spread beyond the cities and towns of Québec. While sales were limited to the North American continent until World War II, Casavant organs began to be accepted into churches around the world. From the outset the two brothers were innovators, and they introduced improvements in matters relating to the electric operation of their organs in the 1890s. They ceased building tracker-action instruments entirely after 1905 in favour of pneumatic action (abandoned in 1944) and wholly electric action thereafter.

Following the deaths of the Casavant brothers, the company experienced difficult times in the 1930s due to economic conditions, much standardization of stops, and repetitive tonal design. To maintain profitability, the company diversified its operations into cabinet making and church furnishings for about 40 years. Several imaginative artistic directors (Lawrence Phelps from the U.S. firm of Aeolian-Skinner; and European-trained Gerhard Brunzema, Karl Wilhelm, and Helmuth Wolff), who joined the firm between 1958 and 1965, provided the initiative and fresh insights into the company's operations.

In the early years the Casavant brothers were conservative in tonal matters, seeking to produce in their instruments an ensemble sound of the kind they had heard in old-world models they had examined during their stay in Europe. Now, near the end of the 20th century, most Casavant organs, while mainly French in disposition, exhibit a conventional design that retains both symphonic and modern elements in subtle synthesis. Casavant resumed the construction of mechanical-action instruments in 1961, producing 214 organs with tracker action since that date. By mid-1997 the total output amounted to 3,760 organs of all sizes—almost 1,200 in the past 30 years—and many of these have received enthusiastic testimonials from renowned recitalists. The company had 80 employees in 1997.

The first Casavant organ in Manitoba was a two-manual, 12-stop, mechanical-action instrument installed in the Parish Church, St. Norbert, just south of Winnipeg, in 1899; the most recent installation of a complete organ was in Elim Chapel, Winnipeg, in 1978. Between 1899 and 1988 a total of 78 contracts were completed for the installation of new organs or consoles, and for tonal or mechanical revisions: 65 within the City of Winnipeg and 13 in rural centres. Of the total number of Winnipeg contracts, 37 were complete organs; the remainder were renovations. The 13 organs installed in rural centres were complete instruments. Two Winnipeg churches acquired Casavant organs from other sources in the 1970s.

Some of Casavant's renovations were extensive; others involved the addition of only a few stops, particularly in the majority of contracts completed from 1970 onward. Electro-pneumatic action was first used in a 1917 instrument, a reconstruction of an earlier opus; tubular-pneumatic action was last used in a small organ in 1931. Small unit organs, utilizing from three to seven ranks of pipes, were installed in four Manitoba churches between 1939 and 1947, Casavant's only installations in the province in that interval. This period of relative inactivity was due, at least in part, to the short supply or unavailability of essential raw materials, such as tin for making metal pipes, during World War II and for a year or two following. Thus, Casavant was forced to defer contracts for larger instruments and to limit production to small organs requiring less metal in their construction.

Since the first Casavant organ was installed in Manitoba, 9 of them have been destroyed in church fires, several did not survive the demolition of their church buildings, and others were absorbed into subsequent revisions or rebuilds by other companies. At some time in their life histories, 10 Casavant organs have been moved from one location to another, 8 within Winnipeg. In 1997, 32 Casavant organs remained intact and active in Manitoba: 23 in Winnipeg and 9 in rural locations.

Eusèbe Brodeur, St. Hyacinthe, Québec, assumed control of Joseph Casavant's organ building establishment when the latter retired in 1866. He was the teacher of the Casavant brothers and also the employer of Claver Casavant before the two brothers went to Europe; later he was employed by them. Some of Brodeur's organs still survive in Québec. One of his organs was installed in Immaculate Conception Roman Catholic Church, Winnipeg, in 1896.

St. Hyacinthe, Québec, was the home of another group of organ builders, members of the Casavant staff who established the Compagnie d'orgues canadiennes/Canadian Pipe Organ Company in 1910. This company constructed organs until its equipment was acquired by Casavant in 1931, following closure. Installations in Winnipeg churches included a large four-manual, 44-stop instrument in Holy Trinity Anglican in 1912, a three-manual instrument in First Lutheran Church in 1921, and two-manual instruments in St. Edward's Roman Catholic, St. Giles Presbyterian, St. Jude's Anglican, St. Margaret's Anglican, and First English Evangelical Lutheran, all between 1913 and 1919.

Another prominent 20th-century organ manufacturing business was founded in 1915 by the Toronto organist Charles Franklin Legge (1891-1948), whose brother William F. Legge joined him in 1919 in the C. Franklin Legge Organ Company. It produced over 250 organs, a number of them quite large, including some for customers in North and South America, before ceasing operations in 1947. In the following year, its service contracts were taken over by the T. Eaton Company, the national department store, which also employed William Legge for a while. The company completed the installation of an organ in Neepawa United Church, Manitoba, in 1949. Around that time William Legge resumed private entrepreneurship when he formed the William F. Legge Organ Company in Burford, Ontario; it continued until 1963 when it was purchased by the son of Charles Legge. In Manitoba, Crystal City United Church installed a used C. Franklin Legge organ, Opus 35, in 1927; in Winnipeg, C. Franklin Legge installed an organ in the Province Theatre in 1917; Crestview United Church acquired his Opus 80 (1930) from an Ontario location in 1982; and Our Saviour's Lutheran Church installed a William F. Legge organ in 1954.

Eastern Canada: Recent Years

The French influence in Canadian organ building is evident in the work of Guilbault-Thérien, Inc., formerly Providence Organ Inc., established in 1946 in St. Hyacinthe, Québec. The partners, André Guilbault (b.1937), whose father Maurice Guilbault (1903-1969) had worked for Casavant, and Guy Thérien (b.1947), a voicer for Casavant, joined forces in 1968, when the elder Guilbault retired. The present name was adopted in 1979. When André Guilbault retired in 1992, Alain Guilbault (no relation) acquired an interest in the company. The output of the firm has not been large—38 new installations, mainly in Québec and Ontario, up to 1993—because much of the company's work has involved the restoration and reconstruction of a similar number of Québec organs, some of historical significance. Although their organs exhibit a European orientation in tonal timbres, they are sufficiently versatile for a variety of environments. A two-manual, 12-stop, tracker-action instrument was installed in the Cistercian Abbey, Our Lady of the Prairies, Holland, Manitoba, in 1981.

The continuing influence of the north German organ building ideals of the

Brandon University, School of Music,
Brandon, Gabriel Kney,
1989, 2/9.

17th and 18th centuries is evident in the works of several independent Canadian builders. Gabriel Kney (b. 1929) worked as an apprentice in his home town of Speyer, Germany, and also studied church music before coming to London, Ontario, to join the Keates Organ Company in 1951. In 1955 he was co-founder of the Kney and Bright Organ Company, which specialized in tracker instruments. He established his own company in 1967, still in London. By 1995 he had placed over 128 instruments in Canadian and American locations; the most well-known Canadian example is the large tracker-action instrument in Roy Thomson Hall, Toronto. Gabriel Kney installed the first mechanical teaching organ for the new facilities at the School of Music, Brandon University, Brandon, Manitoba, in 1989.

Karl Wilhelm (b. 1936), who acquired his training in Germany and Switzerland, joined Casavant in 1960, where he initiated the production of mechanical-action instruments. In 1966 he opened his own business, first in St. Hyacinthe, later moving to Mont St. Hilaire, Québec. By

These organs are typical of the case design adopted by several contemporary Canadian builders.
(Left) Messiah Lutheran Church, Winnipeg, Karl Wilhelm, 1974, 1/7.
(Right) Canadian Mennonite Bible College, Winnipeg, Karl Wilhelm, 1977, 2/10.

1995 he had conceived and manufactured 139 mechanical-action organs of all sizes, designed in accordance with the principles of the classical tradition: 73 in various Canadian provinces and 66 in the United States. Two of his small tracker-action organs have been installed in Winnipeg: one in Messiah Lutheran Church in 1974, another in the Canadian Mennonite Bible College in 1977. Both instruments have distinctive sound characteristics as compared with the more conservative acoustical nature of most traditional organs of their size.

Gerhard Brunzema (1927-1992) received extensive technical training in Germany, including a master's degree in organ building, before joining with another prominent European organ builder, Jürgen Ahrend, in the construction and restoration of organs (including several of great historic significance in Holland and Germany) both in Europe and in the United States. He was artistic director for Casavant from 1972 to 1979, before establishing his own business in Fergus, Ontario, where he produced small, transportable, one-manual continuo organs, along with a few larger instruments. The combination of his experience in Europe, then in North America with Casavant, provided him with the opportunity to adapt classical elements to the requirements of contemporary music making. An example of his work is the one-manual instrument installed in the rear gallery of St. James Lutheran Church, Winnipeg, in 1982.

One of Ontario's smaller builders, the Keates Organ Company, began operations in London, Ontario, in 1945, then moved to Lucan, Ontario, and relocated in Acton, Ontario, in 1961. Following the retirement in 1971 of the founder, Bert Keates (b. 1909), Dieter Geissler became president, and the name Keates-Geissler Pipe Organs, Ltd. was adopted in 1990. The company builds about eight organs a year; some have been installed in churches in the United States. The firm also has rebuilt several organs in Canada. A new solid-state console was supplied for the Casavant-hybrid organ in Calvary Temple, Winnipeg, in 1991.

Experience gained in working with Casavant led another of its employees to set up an independent company, Orgues Létourneau Ltée./Létourneau Pipe Organs Ltd. Fernand Létourneau (b. 1944) had been head voicer with Casavant for 14 years, associated with Lawrence Phelps and Gerhard Brunzema, until 1978, when he left the company and embarked on an organ study tour of Europe. Returning to Canada in 1979, he began building organs first in Ste. Rosalie, and later in St. Hyacinthe in 1984. His first organ, a 6-stop instrument, was started in a garage and then displayed in the shop of a cabinet maker; it was later acquired by Hull Conservatoire de Musique, Québec. In its relatively short history to 1993, Létourneau has installed 38 organs in various churches, educational institutions, and music studios in Canada (chiefly the eastern provinces, with a few in the west), the United States, Austria, New Zealand, and several in Australia in the early 1980s. With few exceptions, all

Létourneau organs have mechanical action. The 15 artisans in the Létourneau "family"—a significant number of the employees are related to one another as father-son, brother, cousin, and husband-wife—are also engaged in organ rebuilding and reconstruction: over 40 to date. A new two-manual, 29-stop organ of 35 ranks was installed in Young United Church late in 1993. A few of its ranks are identified as having been inspired by the European builders Dom Bédos, Cavaillé-Coll, and Schnitger.

A European Builder

Only one European builder is represented in Winnipeg: Rudolf von Beckerath, Hamburg, Germany. The first instrument by this maker arrived in Canada in 1959 and was installed in Queen Mary Road United Church, Montréal. This event marked the beginning of the Organ Reform Movement in the country. Beckerath organs are typical of late Organ Reform Movement design, both in terms of their acoustical qualities and the formal box-like casework containing the various divisions of the organ. A "neo-classical," quasi-Baroque, two-manual, 30-stop, tracker-action instrument was installed in First Presbyterian Church, Winnipeg, in 1963. A small Beckerath studio organ, a direct mechanical-action instrument with three ranks of unenclosed pipes, built in 1968, was acquired by the School of Music at The University of Manitoba for use in a teaching studio.

The English Connection

The organ building company William Hill & Son and Norman & Beard Ltd., London, England, was established in 1916 by the amalgamation of the two firms. As part of its overseas operations, the firm built or rebuilt organs in Canada for a number of years following World War II, directing operations from offices in Eastern Canada. The company undertook the major renovation of organs in seven Manitoba churches and retained the services of a Winnipeg technician to maintain them: the Casavant organ in St. Luke's Anglican Church in 1953, the Casavant organ in St. George's Crescentwood Anglican Church in 1954, the Karn-Morris organ in Trinity Baptist Church in 1954, the Casavant organ in First Church of Christ Scientist in 1955, the Casavant organ in First Lutheran Church in 1959, and the Canadian Pipe Organ instrument in Holy Trinity Anglican Church in 1962 (retaining the Casavant console). The firm also rebuilt a Warren tracker organ in St. Mary's Anglican Church, Portage la Prairie, in the 1950s. The results were not wholly satisfactory in every case, for some of Hill, Norman & Beard's reconstructions were not adequately designed to survive the rigors of radical temperature changes in Winnipeg churches, particularly during severe winters.

American Builders

Several organs built in the United States have found their way into Manitoba buildings, three from New England builders and four from companies in the American Midwest. The oldest of these instruments was built in 1850 by George Stevens (1803-1894), who was involved in several partnerships with other craftsmen during his career in the Boston area, beginning in 1822. His instruments were generally conservative in design, for most of his customers were rural churches, and his small-to-medium-size instruments were well suited to support congregational singing. In fact, the small organs of all builders of that time were quite similar in their essential stops. A representative small mechanical-action instrument, obtained through the Organ Clearing House, Harrisville, New Hampshire, was installed in Gloria Dei Lutheran Church, Winnipeg, in 1977.

The Hook factory of organ building was well established in Boston by 1860, although the pace was interrupted briefly during the Civil War. In the year after Frank Hastings became a partner in 1871, the firm's name was changed to E. & G. G. Hook & Hastings, and then to Hook & Hastings when George Hook died in 1880. The factory operated at its peak of activity during that interval, producing an average of 46 instruments a year. Some of them were of record size for the time, up to 81 speaking stops. Although the larger instruments brought desired publicity, the company also produced several models of small, ready-made, moderately priced, stock instruments, available on short notice. The brochures for these organs noted that they were "far superior to any reed organ in every respect, especially in dignity and pervading characteristics of tone, and in durability." One of these tracker instruments, built in 1883 and exhibiting appropriately ornamented metal and wooden pipes, was removed from the Congregational Church in Newton Highlands, Massachusetts, and installed in the First Federated Church of Unitarians and Other Liberal Christians, Winnipeg, in 1924, by Blanchard Bros., official Casavant Frères representatives, after church officials had rejected estimates for a new organ from Casavant Frères and Woodstock Pipe Organ Builders.

Another Massachusetts builder who achieved prominence around the turn of the century was George S. Hutchings (1835-1913). He became involved in organ building when a furniture maker, recognizing young George's talent for constructing fine cabinetry, recommended him to his sons, Elias and George Hook, the celebrated Boston organ builders. George Hutchings entered their factory at the age of 22. After serving in the Union army, he returned to the Hook factory, eventually becoming superintendent, then left in 1869 to form a new business association with several other Hook employees. In 1884 he began building organs under his own name; some of these were of considerable size and featured patented changeable combination pistons. Around 1890 he hired a young man destined to become a major figure in American organ building and design, Ernest M. Skinner, who remained with the company for four years before moving on. Hutchings constructed more than 600 instruments during his lifetime, and many of them still survive. The Hutchings organ in Winnipeg is his Opus 425 (1897), a two-manual, 17-stop, tracker-action instrument obtained through the Organ Clearing House. It had served in two Massachusetts churches before being rebuilt by the Stuart Organ Company, Alderville, Massachusetts, specifically for installation in Christ Lutheran Church in 1980.

There was a tradition of organ building extending back to the middle of the 17th century in the family of George Kilgen, who emigrated from Germany to New York in the 1840s and opened an organ shop there in 1851. The family moved to St. Louis, Missouri, in 1873, and the firm name Geo. Kilgen & Son was adopted in 1886. Following the founder's death in 1902, the firm experienced its most productive years under his son Charles Kilgen (1859-1932). Following a reorganization in 1939, the firm became The Kilgen Organ Company of St. Louis, and it continued to install organs until 1959. An organ by Geo. Kilgen & Son was installed in Grace Methodist Church, Portage la Prairie, Manitoba, in the 1920s and was removed upon the closure of that church to Sparling United Church, Winnipeg, in 1937.

The most successful organ manufacturer in Chicago in the first half of the 20th century was Wallace W. Kimball (1828-1904); he was neither a musician nor an organ builder by training but an enterprising salesman. After settling in Chicago in 1857, his ventures included trading pianos and opening a

Christ Lutheran Church, Winnipeg.
George S. Hutchings, 1897;
Stuart Organ Co., 1979, 2/17.
This organ served in two Massachusetts churches before being reinstalled in Winnipeg.

Sparling United Church, Winnipeg.
Kilgen, c. 1920, 2/13. Installed 1937.

reed organ factory in 1880. Following the suggestion of a young man who joined the staff in that year, the company began building compact, portable, pipe organs to meet the needs of small rural churches. Larger organs—7,386 in all—were built from 1894 until 1942, when the factory closed. A Kimball organ formerly in a movie theatre in Kansas City, Missouri, was installed in a Winnipeg theatre before being acquired by Calvary Temple, Winnipeg, in the 1940s. It was later reinstalled into the chapel of the Temple's new building in 1986.

Another Chicago builder, Frederick W. Smith, installed a unit organ in the Lyceum Theatre in 1920, but nothing is known about his other activities.

The young Danish immigrant Mathias Peter Möller (1854-1937) was first employed as a cabinet maker before building his own organ in 1875 at the age of 21 years. His factory in Hagerstown, Maryland, established in 1881, became one of the largest and most influential in the eastern United States. By the time the business was taken over by his son, the factory had manufactured about 7,000 organs, including the original organ in the U.S. Military Academy at West Point, New York. Most of his instruments were placed in theatres, schools, residences, and auditoriums. One of his modest productions, a two-manual unit organ that developed 20 stops from 5 ranks of pipes, was acquired by the Gardiner Funeral Home in Winnipeg in 1933.

One of the smaller organ factories in the American Midwest is the Wicks Pipe Organ Company, Highland, Illinois. Early in the 1800s John Wick, an organist, constructed his first organ in that city and continued to build organs there with his brothers, Adolph and Louis (1869-1936). The company, incorporated in 1906, continues today with a third generation of the Wick family and many long-term associates. Fully electric action was introduced in 1914, followed by subsequent patented improvements in the 1920s. The firm experienced steady but limited growth, even through the decade of economic depression; today it produces about 80 organs a year. The company installed a "Wicks Giant," a three-manual and pedal instrument of 12 ranks, 150 stops (including bells and percussion accessories), in Winnipeg's Garrick Theatre in 1929, later removed around 1975. J. J. H. McLean and Company, Wicks' agent in Winnipeg, installed a smaller three-manual instrument in a movie theatre in nearby Kenora, Ontario, around 1925. In addition to its larger organs for churches and theatres, the company also made a popular line of compact unit organs for small churches, schools, mortuaries, and homes; many were used as practice instruments in music schools. A self-player attachment was also available, along with music rolls of hymns and other selections suitable for funerals of various religious denominations. Preludes featured some popular pieces by well-known composers, such as Bach, Dvorak, Rheinberger, Schubert, Schumann, Tschaikowsky, and Wagner, that were part of the ordinary repertoire of organists of that time. One of these small instruments, a "Sonatina" model, was installed in Mordue Bros. Mortuary, Winnipeg, in 1940, for a price of $995. The list of 20 stops was derived from three ranks of pipes, and the 16' Subbass pedal stop actually was a rank of 12 harmonium reeds. In 1982 the organ was relocated into the chapel of the University of Winnipeg, but without the self-player attachment.

———•◦•———

The Organ Blower's Epitaph

Under this stone lies Meredith Morgan
Who blew the bellows of our church organ;
Tobacco he hated, to smoke was unwilling,
Yet never so pleased as when pipes he was filling;
No reflection on him for rude speech could be cast,
Tho' he gave our organist many a blast,
No puffer was he
Tho' a capital blower
He could fill double G,
And now lies a note lower.

—*Inscription on a gravestone in a cemetery in Wales*
(Manitoba Free Press, 9 *February* 1918.)

———•◦•———

The Golden Age of the Organ: *1875-1919*

AS THE PERIOD of greatest activity, prosperity, and progress, this 45-year period around the turn of the century was truly the "Golden Age" of the organ in Manitoba. Of the 162 known organ installations in the province, 67 of these, or 41 percent, occurred during this period; they were all new instruments with the exception of three that were relocated from other churches. Both the instruments and the recitals played on them were matters of intense public interest. The opening of a new church organ was a matter of pride and celebration on the part of the congregation, as well as a significant event in the musical life of the city. Winnipeg newspapers described the appearance of the new organs, their mechanical construction, and often included complete stoplists. They also printed both appreciative and critical reviews of recitals by local organists and visiting players (mainly from eastern Canada and the United States), whose programs consisted of a mix of lighter pieces and serious original works for organ by contemporary composers. The many transcriptions of nonorgan compositions that appeared in these programs contributed to the musical education of the general public who attended these events in large numbers. Public entertainment was also provided by the organists of movie theatres, where organs began to be installed after 1915 to provide improvised or arranged accompaniments to silent films. A chronological summary of organ installations during this period is given in Appendix 1: Organ Installations.

St. Boniface Roman Catholic Cathedral, 1875

One of the chief modes of north-south transportation in the early days was the steamboat *International*, which plied the Red River between Winnipeg and Moorhead, North Dakota, in navigable seasons. This boat arrived in the city on 14 June 1875 carrying a pipe organ for St. Boniface Cathedral. Louis Mitchell, the organ builder, accompanied his intrument on the trip overland through the United States from his Montréal factory. The unloading of the cargo on the St. Boniface side of the river was accomplished with the permission of the customs tax collector at the port of Winnipeg; more than 50 men were needed to complete the task.

The organ was the gift of a group of friends of Monseigneur Alexandre Taché in recognition of the 30th anniversary of the date of his departure from Québec for the mission at Red River, and of the 25th anniversary of his appointment as Archbishop of the diocese. At the time of the installation of the organ, about $1,100 had been raised by pupils and associates from the seminary in St. Hyacinthe, Québec. The Archbishop thanked the contributors for the gift of the magnificent organ, which he believed would contribute so much to divine worship, as sign of spiritual harmony and a prelude to the harmonies of heaven:

> Je vous confie . . . l'expression de ma profonde gratitude envers tous ceux qui ont concouru à nous procurer cet orgue magnifique, qui va ajouter tant d'éclat au culte divin, être en même temps le signe de l'harmonie de nos coeurs et comme le prélude des harmonies du ciel. Je vous remercie au nom de la province du Manitoba, puisque ce don généreux lui donne un nouveau trait de ressemblance avec les provinces-soeurs et lui procure une gloire réelle. ("L'Orgue de la Cathédrale de Saint-Boniface," *Les Cloches de Saint-Boniface* 16, 15 June 1917, 184-85.)

Although the specifications of the organ were not given in any accounts of its arrival or installation, the dimensions of the instrument suggest that it may have had about 12 ranks of pipes.

> A large church organ arrived last Monday on the International for the Cathedral of St. Boniface. It was made in Montreal by Mr. Mitchell, the celebrated organ builder. It is the first church organ imported into the North-West, it is 19 ft high, 12 ft 6 in wide, and 11 ft deep. The case, which is already put up, is in the Grecian style, which is well adapted to the architecture of the Cathedral. The Organ weighs 12,000 pounds and costs over $3,200.
>
> We hear that this new organ will be inaugurated on the 24th inst, upon the occasion of the celebration of St Jean Baptist day, and that there will be in the evening a grand concert at the Cathedral, the proceeds of which will go towards the fund for the completion of the church. All the musicians and artists of the Province will be present on the occasion. ("The Church Organ of St. Boniface," *Daily Free Press*, 16 June 1875.)

The promised concert received advance notice through this advertisement:

> The First Church Organ in the North-West
> Twenty-Fourth June
> Grand Concert at the Cathedral of St. Boniface
> Thursday, at 8 o'clock
> Doors open at 7. First class seats, $1; second class seats, 75c.

The account of the celebrations focused closely on the organ:

> The interior of the Cathedral, although not quite finished, is very striking, and the great improvement lately wrought was noticed and admired by those who only visit its sacred precincts on some annual fete day. The altar recess and other portions of the building were decorated by Latin mottoes, and other matters incident to the interior of churches; but the great attraction was THE ORGAN, as it stood in the gallery in all its massiveness and beauty. It is indeed a magnificent instrument, splendidly finished, possessing an admirable tone, and adds in no small degree to the impressiveness of the religious services. . . . HIGH MASS was then performed in a most impressive manner, the thunder of the great organ waking up the sleeping echoes of the Cathedral. . . . The grand feature of the day was the concert in the evening. . . . Father Dugas very effectively wielded the leader's wand, and Brother Hughes presided at the organ. THE PROGRAM was extremely well selected, and admirably adapted to bring out the powers of three first-class artists; it was as follows:
>
> Grande Marche de Gounod
> En Delictus, Grand Choeur (Lambillotte)
> Justus, Duo (Lambillotte)
> Inflammatus (Stabat de Rossini), Choeur et Solo
> Cantique au Sacré Coeur de Jesus (Musique d'Adam)
> Triomphe, Victoire (Smith), Grand Choeur et Solo
> Ave Maria (Musique de Millard)
> Magnificat (Plain Chant Harmonise)
> Chant sur l'air God Save the Queen
> The band of the College added its quota of excellent music.
> ("St. Jean Baptiste—Celebration of the Day at
> St. Boniface," *Daily Free Press*, 25 June 1875.)

The ultimate destiny of the organ was the first instance of organ recycling. In 1921, when the Cathedral purchased a larger instrument from the First Lutheran Church, Winnipeg, the Mitchell organ was removed and divided into two smaller instruments; one went to a school in St. Boniface, and the other to a mission in Lebret, Saskatchewan, both operated by the Oblate Fathers.

Holy Trinity Anglican Church, 1878, 1884, 1892, 1912

Holy Trinity Anglican Church acquired its first pipe organ, a two-manual instrument of 24 stops, installed in the summer of 1878 by Samuel R. Warren & Son. Its formal opening was marked by a concert on 11 July 1878; the newspaper report paid equal attention to the musical content of the event and to the organ:

> The formal opening of the new organ, recently placed in Holy Trinity church, took place yesterday evening, the event being in the shape of an organ recital and sacred concert. There was a very good audience on the occasion, although it would doubtless have been more numerous had not the weather during the early part of the evening been so threatening. And that those present were highly pleased with the concert was evidenced by the applause, with which notwithstanding the sacredness of the edifice, many of the pieces on the programme were received. The programme was capitally rendered, those taking part in it acquitting themselves very creditably. . . . Mrs. Peach presided at the organ, and although having had but a short time to accustom herself to the instrument she fairly astonished her hearers by the excellence of her playing. . . .
>
> The organ is from the establishment of Messrs. S. R. Warren & Son of Montreal and Toronto, and does great credit to that well-known firm. Its price is $3,000, and it is a powerful instrument, containing two rows of keys and full pedale, and twenty-four draw stops. Some of these are of exquisite sweetness, particularly the Claribel Flute, the Viol di gamba, and the Oboe in the swell, and the Dulciana and the Harmonic Flute in the great organ.
>
> The case is of chestnut wood with black walnut facings, and the front pipes are beautifully decorated with *fleur de lis*, and other ecclesiastical designs, in blue, gold and chocolate color. The top is surmounted with carved pinnacles. The body of the organ is contained in a chamber, built specially for the purpose; the front projecting about two feet into the church on the south side of the reading desk, giving a good view to the congregation of the case and ornamented pipes. Mr. Warren having lately visited the principal organ factories in England, France and Germany, now applies to his instruments all the modern improvements, of which we may specially mention the voicing and tuning of the pipes. The present instrument has been carefully constructed in this respect and its builder has succeeded in giving to its notes a softness and sweetness not always heard even in larger and more expensive organs. An important feature in the instrument is the combination pedals both in the great and swell organs, enabling the performer to produce with the greatest ease and rapidity all the changes that may be desired. This, of course necessitates a great deal of nice and complicated mechanism and adds greatly to the cost of an organ, but no instrument is complete without them. ("Holy Trinity Organ Recital and Sacred Concert," *Manitoba Free Press*, 12 July 1878.)

These were the organ selections played by Mrs. Peach:

Overture, Tancredi	Rossini
Traumerei, Romance	Schumann
Offertoire in G	Lefébure-Wély
Marche aux flambeaux	Clarke
Overture, Zampa	Hérold
Silver Trumpets	Viviani

When Holy Trinity Church moved to a new location in 1884, the Warren organ was transferred to the new building, where it was enlarged. The organist at this time was P. R. Maclagan. A native of Scotland, Maclagan showed musical ability early in life and became a church organist at the age of 18. Before coming to Winnipeg around 1880, he was organist at Christ Church, Montréal, for about 11 years. In Winnipeg he served as organist at Holy Trinity Church from 1881 to 1884, and briefly at Central Congregational, St. Mary's, and All Saints' Churches. On one occasion he travelled to New York to play at one of the Episcopal churches there. He was musical conductor of the Musical and Operatic Society, and of the Madrigal Society, before his untimely death of consumption in 1887 at the age of 36. The newspaper report of the new installation remarked both on the capabilities of the instrument and the content of Maclagan's inaugural recital on 17 August 1884:

A good programme was prepared for the inauguration of the grand organ at the above church last evening, when a fair audience gathered to witness the performance. The organ, evidently, was not in a complete state, judging by the manner in which Dr. Maclagan was embarrassed with a few unwelcome sounds. On the whole, however, the organ, with its additional manual, speaks highly of the builder's capabilities. A short interval took place after the selection from Weber's Mass in G, in order to give the organ builders an opportunity to bring to their places some unruly members of the instrument, after which, the organist rendered Rinck's Flute Concerto in good style, although we have heard him to better advantage before, more especially in the execution of the delicate runs which characterize the concerto. Mendelssohn's Andante from Violin Concerto was one of the first pieces rendered. The soft stops of the organ are remarkably sweet, and its clarinette is undoubtedly one of the finest stops which we have had the pleasure of listening to. Of Dr. Maclagan's rendition of the heavy pieces on the programme, we might say that the runs and movements seemed anything but clear, although the sounding capacities of the massive and beautiful edifice are most perfect. . . .

The new organ, which contains many orchestral stops, will aid the able organist materially in the production of Gounod's Redemption, which he proposes to give later on. ("Holy Trinity: Inauguration of the Grand Organ in the New Church," *Manitoba Free Press*, 18 August 1884.)

The advance notice of the inauguration in 1892 of the rebuilt organ at Holy Trinity Anglican Church described the alterations in the tonal design that were part of the remodelled instrument:

> An organ recital will be given next Thursday, the 28th inst, in Holy Trinity church, the occasion being the opening of its grand organ, which has been undergoing extensive repairs and alterations by the firm of Warren & Son, who has been engaged in the work for the past two months. The organ has been thoroughly overhauled and remodelled and several registers have been added, viz: cornopean, traverse flute, piccolo, one rank of mixtures to swell organ, open diapason and 16 foot bell clarinet to great organ, and violoncello to pedal organ, together with those already in use making a very complete three manual instrument of thirty-nine registers. The entire key and register compass is new and of the latest design. The organ being entirely rebuilt with a view to entire freedom of sound to nave and chancel, the power of the instrument augmented by the new stops is fully double its former capacity. Holy Trinity is to be complimented on possessing an instrument which has fine orchestral effects, and is the largest west of Toronto. ("Holy Trinity Organ," *Manitoba Free Press*, 23 July 1892.)

On 28 July 1892, church organists George Dore, Holy Trinity; W. H. Dingle, Knox; and Laurence H. J. Minchin, All Saints' collaborated in a recital program that marked the dedication of the extensively renovated organ:

Coronation March	Rees
Andante, Grand Sonata	Mendelssohn, arr. Warren
George Dore	
Cavatina	Raff
L. H. J. Minchin	
Prelude and Fugue in B-flat	Bach
Adagio Cantabile	Haydn
W. H. Dingle	
Military Movement,	
Symphony No. 12	Haydn
Fugue, Der Tod Jesu	Graun, arr. Warren
George Dore	
Introduction and Bridal Music,	
Lohengrin	Wagner, arr. Eddy
W. H. Dingle	
To Thee Cherubim,	
Dettingen Te Deum	Handel
We Worship God,	
Judas Maccabaeus	Handel
George Dore	

The ensuing review was more preoccupied with the organ itself rather than with the musical event:

Holy Trinity church can now boast undoubtedly the finest organ in the city. There was always the foundation of a fine instrument, but all last winter its condition was lamentable, and the vestry wisely decided to make an effort to have the organ thoroughly repaired and to render it worthy of their fine church. Accordingly repairs and improvements to the tune of $1,300 have been effected with a very gratifying result, as witnessed at the recital last night. The programme was a comprehensive one, so as to exhibit the powers and resources of the organ, but it was too much spun out for many listeners. The church was well filled with an appreciative audience, for whom perhaps the printed request, that there should be no applause, was superfluous. The organist of the church, Professor Dore, and Messrs. Dingle and Minchin, the last named in a minor and less ambitious role, were the performers of the evening, and each in turn showed what the organ could do. ("The Organ Recital," *Manitoba Free Press*, 29 July 1892.)

One of the players, Laurence Minchin, was supervisor of music in Winnipeg schools for a time, before he left the city for Vancouver. Another, "Professor" George Dore, had arrived in the city from Chatham, Ontario, late in 1890, and was a temporary organist at Zion Church, a post which he held for only one Sunday in November. He was the subject of a reminiscence by James W. Matthews, whose diary has been referred to in connection with early organs in Winnipeg:

Professor Dore . . . was an elderly gentleman who played for a time at Holy Trinity and subsequently was organist of the Anglican church in Portage la Prairie. He had the hall marks of a fine musician and claimed, I have no doubt with truth, to have been a fellow chorister with Sir John Stainer and Arthur Sullivan. He was a remarkably clever improviser and a genial soul, and I think of him with kindness as a man with the instincts of an artist and a gentleman. ("Few Pipe Organs When Winnipeg was a Hamlet: Diary of the Late James W. Matthews Recalls Early Instruments and Players," *Manitoba Free Press*, 13 December 1924.)

The installation of a new four-manual organ in 1912 was reported in some detail. The 50-stop instrument, described as "the finest organ in the Canadian West," was manufactured by the Canadian Pipe Organ Company, founded only two years previously in St. Hyacinthe, Québec, by some Casavant staff and headed by Louis B. Madore, also formerly with Casavant:

Mr. Madore is to be warmly congratulated on this example of his artistic workmanship, for it takes an artist to produce a first class organ. Though a little further tuning is necessary to put the instrument into perfect condition it was quite evident last evening that the highest expectations of the congregation are fulfilled—perhaps more than fulfilled. The organ can produce any desired amount of tone from the faintest whisper to a mass of sound that is almost more than the auditorium will properly accommodate. The fifty speaking stops, with their immense variety of combinations, afford an exceedingly satisfactory range of tone-colors. While the tone is excellent, the solo organ stops deserve special mention for their sweetness and purity, some of them being apparently unsurpassable. ("Dedication of Holy Trinity Organ," *Manitoba Free Press*, 28 November 1912.)

The organ recital portion of the opening concert, played by the incumbent organist, Harold St. John Naftel, included these selections:

Carillon in C	Faulkes
Serenade	Goss-Custard
Caprice in B-flat	Botting
Evening Song	Bairstow
Toccata in C minor	Halsey
Arcadian Idyll	Lemare
Allegro symphonique	Brooks-Day

A review of his performance noted that "the organ was hardly completed, and neither was the tuning perfect, but Mr. Naftel showed himself to be the master of his instrument, and the manner in which he handled its complicated mechanism is worthy of all praise." (Herbert Dore, "Holy Trinity's New Organ," *Winnipeg Town Topics*, 30 November 1912.)

Holy Trinity Anglican Church, Winnipeg.
Canadian Pipe Organ, 1912, 4/50;
Casavant console 1950, 4/53.

First Baptist Church, 1883

Early in 1883 the Baptist Church installed a new organ, built by H. W. Bolton & Company, Winnipeg. From the description of the event and the stoplist published in a daily newspapers, it appears that it probably contained two 4-foot registers, one in each manual division:

> The organ is contained in an elegant case, made of black walnut and white pine, and the decorated front pipes present a very handsome appearance. There are sixteen stops in all. There are no reeds at all in the organ. The division of stops is as follows:

SWELL ORGAN	GREAT ORGAN
Stopped Diapason Bass	Open Diapason
Salicional	Stopped Diapason Bass
Violina	Stopped Diapason Treble
Flute D'Amour	Dulciana
Flute Harmonic	Principal
PEDAL	Swell to Pedal
Bourdon 16 feet	Swell to Great
	Great to Pedal
	Tremolo
	Bellows Signal

> The chief characteristic of the organ is its sweetness of tone. The range of effects is necessarily limited on account of the smallness of the organ, but the delightful mellowness of tone is a great relief from the screaming effects of large and more pretentious instruments. ("Baptist Church," *Manitoba Daily Free Press*, 9 March 1883.)

The inaugural recital was played by P. R. Maclagan, one of the city's ablest musicians, on 8 March 1883. The report of his concert at Baptist church paid more attention to the new organ than to the recitalist's program, which consisted of these selections:

Fantasia in C Minor	Hesse
Andante, Symphony in C	Haydn
Overture, Poet and Peasant	von Suppé
Traumerei, Romanza	Schumann
War March of the Priests, Athalie	Mendelssohn

Later in the same year Maclagan gave a recital at Holy Trinity Church on 12 March 1883. Although his program was comprised mainly of transcriptions, the exception was a Bach selection, which was unfamiliar to some members of the audience:

Overture, Egmont	Beethoven
Toccata in F	Bach
Andante, Symphony in C	Haydn
Overture, Poet and Peasant	von Suppé

The effect [the Toccata in F] produced on some of the audience was quite amusing. One gentleman in particular was heard to exclaim: "That's the wildest piece of music I ever heard." Of course those who understood the music thought it anything but wild. ("Holy Trinity Church," *Manitoba Free Press*, 13 March 1883.)

As for the transcriptions, audiences must have responded to them with enthusiasm, for other Winnipeg organists often included Maclagan's choices of Haydn's andantes, Mendelssohn's march, and von Suppé's overture in their own recital programs in subsequent years.

St. Mary's Roman Catholic Church, 1883, 1918

The inauguration of a new organ sometimes was marked not just by the performance of a single recitalist, but by a concert involving the church choir and several soloists. One such concert took place on 20 April 1883, on the occasion of the opening of the new organ at St. Mary's Church. The event was unusual in one respect: Samuel Mitchell of Montréal, the father and associate of Louis Mitchell, who had installed the first organ in St. Boniface Cathedral in 1875, was the featured recitalist. An unusual feature of the two-manual, 18-stop instrument was the assignment of two mixture stops to the great division.

St. Mary's Church was well filled last night upon the occasion of the inauguration of the new organ by Mr. Samuel Mitchell of Montreal, one of the builders. The organ stands in the gallery just over the main entrance, and presents a very handsome appearance. The case is Moresque in design, and is richly decorated, the arrangement of colors ornamenting the front pipes being most effective. The organ has two manuals . . . which are divided as follows:

SWELL ORGAN

Horn diapason 8 ft.	Bass 8 ft.
Melodia 8 ft.	Viol de Gamba 8 ft.
Wald Flute 8 ft.	Violon 4 ft.
Oboe 8 ft.	Tremolo

GREAT ORGAN

Open diapason 8 ft.	Open flute 8 ft.
Dulciana 8 ft.	Flute harmonic 4 ft.
Principal 4 ft.	Trumpet 8 ft.
Fifteenth 2 ft.	Mixture, 2 ranks
Cymbal, 3 ranks	Ventil

PEDAL ORGAN
CCC *to* F

Bourdon 16 feet.	Violoncello 16 feet.

[Couplers]

Pedal to great	Pedal to swell
Great to swell	Octave - Kopel
Pedal check	Bellows signal
Three composition pedals	One expression pedal. . . .

The chief characteristic of the organ is its powerful tone, the reeds are voiced to a high pressure, and perhaps a little too coarse to suit the sensitive ear, but upon the whole it is well suited to the purpose for which it is intended. ("St. Mary's Church: Inauguration of the New Organ—The Recital and Sacred Concert—The Church Crowded," *Manitoba Free Press*, 21 April 1883.

Mitchell's contribution to the concert included these pieces, several of his own devising:

Selection from Carmen	Bizet
Improvisation	Mitchell
Medley of National Airs	Mitchell
Andante	Lefébure-Wély
March à la militaire	Mitchell

The report of his performance commented on Mitchell's sense of humour at the console:

The medley of National airs played by Mr. Mitchell which came after a short intermission, fully demonstrated the capabilities of the instrument. The imitation of the bagpipes greatly amused the audience, and the last expiring croak at the conclusion of "The Campbells are Comin'" elicited the laughter of all. Mr. Mitchell is a very clever manipulator, and the imitation of the fife and drum band was excellent. (*Manitoba Free Press*, 21 April 1883.)

Thirty-five years later, the Mitchell organ was replaced by a new two-manual, 18-stop Casavant instrument. This organ, installed in 1918 at a cost of $3,692, would serve the church for a further 40 years before being rebuilt by the same company.

Victoria Hall, 1884

Winnipeg's Victoria Hall, built in 1883 and later renamed the Winnipeg Theatre and Opera House, was the civic centre for many concerts, musical events, and other entertainments in the early years. Some church congregations held services in the Hall before their own buildings were completed. One of the ventures of the Winnipeg Oratorio Society, which performed there, was to provide an organ for this building. The organ had an unusual stoplist, by church organ standards, but its unique tonal design clearly reflected the intended use of the instrument, as decribed in this newspaper announcement of the forth-coming installation in 1884 (the builder was not identified):

NEW ORGAN FOR VICTORIA HALL

The following description of the organ which is being built by the Oratorio Society for Victoria Hall may prove of interest to our musical readers. The instrument was specifically designed to be used instead of a string band, and as will be seen from the following specification, it contains eleven complete registers, equalling an orchestra of about thirty performers.

LIST OF STOPS

FIRST MANUAL	SECOND MANUAL
1. Viol di Gamba 8 ft	7. Sordino 8 ft
2. Horn 8 ft	8. Prin'pl Violin 8 ft
3. Concert Flute 8 ft	9. Ripieno No. 1 8 ft
4. Clarionet 8 ft	10. Ripieno No. 2 8 ft
5. Harmonic Flute 4 ft	11. Octave Coupler
6. Piccolo 2 ft	12. Tremolo

PEDAL
13. Contra Bass 16 feet

COUPLERS
14. Manual Couplers
15. Pedal Coupler No. 1
16. Pedal Coupler No. 2

ACCESSORIES
17. Composition Pedal No. 1
18. Composition Pedal No. 2
19. Composition Pedal No. 3
20. Signal

In order to leave sufficient stage room, the organ will be very shallow, and will spread across the back of the platform; the dimensions are as follows:—Depth 3ft. 2in., width 18ft., height 21ft. Each manual will have a separate swell, and the whole organ will be voiced to a wind pressure of three inches and a half. The case will be gothic, with carved panels and gilt moldings, and will have an octagonal tower on each side of the centre arch, the whole forming a handsome background to the orchestra. The committee of the Oratorio Society are to be commended for their enterprise. (*Manitoba Free Press*, 12 January 1884.)

Grace Methodist Church, 1885, 1894, 1907, 1917

The first pipe organ in Grace Church was provided by S. R. Warren & Son in 1885, but the details have been lost. A few years later, the Church was considering the purchase of a new instrument, as reported in a daily newspaper:

> The plans and specifications of the proposed new organ for Grace Church have been received from Messrs. Warren & Son, of Toronto. It is understood that nothing definite has yet been decided upon. A number of the most influential members of the church are opposed to putting money into a new organ "until things improve," while there is a feeling on the part of the advocates of the scheme that such an instrument would pay its way and be a good instrument for the church. That such an organ as the Messrs. Warren propose to build would be a boon alike to the church and to the city at large, there can be no doubt. Let the order be given at once, by all means. (*Manitoba Free Press*, 14 March 1890.)

The financial situation apparently did not improve immediately, for the project was deferred for several years, when an order for a large organ was placed with R. S. Williams & Son, Toronto and Oshawa. When it was installed in Grace Church in December 1894, the existing instrument was transferred to Westminster Presbyterian Church. The new organ attracted considerable attention in the press and was the subject of several advance notices. One newspaper report of the event featured a drawing of the organ and consisted entirely of a lengthy technical discourse on the innovative features of the instrument,

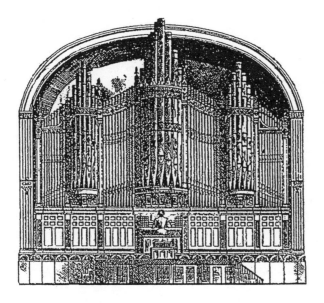

Grace Methodist Church, Winnipeg.
R.S. Williams & Son, 1894, 3/34. The installation of this instrument attracted much attention in the press of the day.

including its tubular-pneumatic action, key action, bellows, draw-stop action, combination pedals, and voicing. Specifically it noted that the tubular-pneumatic mechanism, entirely new in the Northwest, would not be affected by climatic changes. The complete specifications of the three-manual, 34-stop instrument were also included.

GREAT		SWELL	
Double Open Diapason	16	Bourdon Treble	16
Open Diapason	8	Bourdon Bass	16
Gamba	8	Open Diapason	8
Doppel Flute	8	Viol di Gamba	8
Wald Flute	4	Concert Flute	8
Principal	4	Aeoline	8
Twelfth	2 2/3	Stopped Diapason	8
Fifteenth	2	Traverse Flute	4
Mixture	III	Violina	4
Trumpet	8	Flautino	2
		Mixture II	
		Vox Humana	8
		Oboe	8

CHOIR		PEDAL	
Geigen Principal	8	Double Open	16
Dulciana	8	Violone	16
Bourdon	16	Melodia	8
Harmonic Flute	4	Violoncello	8
Harmonic Piccolo	2	Trombone	16
Clarinette	8		

MECHANICAL REGISTERS

Swell to Great	3 Combination Pedals to Great
Swell to Choir	3 Combination Pedals to Swell
Choir to Great	Tremolo Pedal to Swell
Great to Pedal	Great to Pedal double acting
Swell to Pedal	
Choir to Pedal	
Bellows Signal	(*Manitoba Daily Free Press*, 17 November 1894.)

J. Warren Andrews, organist at Plymouth Church, Minneapolis, played the opening recital on the new Grace Church organ on 8 December 1894:

Organ Concerto No. 5	Handel
Gavotte in F	Martini
Communion in G	Batiste
Toccata and Fugue in D Minor	Bach
Ave Maria	Arcadelt

Largo	Handel
Fantasie pastorale	Lefébure-Wély
Reverie of Home	Andrews
Variations on Air, America	Flagler

More than half of the review consisted of a series of observations on the theme that the organ needed "a good shaking down," for an intermittently sounding pedal-note marred the opening selection and some of the valves were sticking. Also, the instrument tended to go out of tune before the end of the program, perhaps due to a drop in the temperature of the church on the cold winter evening. Nevertheless, the voicing was rated as excellent, as were the English-style diapasons and the reeds, some of them imported from France. The reviewer was disappointed that only two hundred people attended, and that the majority of them were heading for the door before the concluding piece was finished. ("The New Organ: Inaugural Recital by Mr. Andrews of Minneapolis," *Manitoba Free Press,* 10 December 1894.)

Casavant Frères installed their largest organ to date, a four-manual, 46-stop instrument, in Grace Methodist Church in November 1907; the price was $7,150. The event was celebrated by a concert that included the choir, soloists, and a recital by the organist, George Bowles. Several years before, a music critic had remarked that "Bowles would have been a great organist if he hadn't decided to become a bank manager." His skill in accompanying both the solos and choruses of *Messiah* in a public presentation by the Grace Church choir of 100 members in 1906 had also been praised in print as contributing to the success of the performance. Bowles's program at the opening of the new Grace Church organ on 1 January 1908 included:

Laudate Dominum	Lemmens
Mater amabilis	Salomé
Melodie in E	Rachmaninoff
Sonata in E-flat	Rheinberger
In paradisum, fiat lux	Dubois
On the Coast	Dudley Buck
Idyll in E-flat	Lemare
March in E-flat	Dubois

The ensuing review was unique insofar as it combined general descriptions of the organ and the performer's recital, all coloured by poetic editorializing:

> Organ recitals as a rule are never enticing to the average concert goer, unless there is some special interest attached to the occasion. On the night of New Year's day, however, there was really something happening, for a splendid new organ was to be opened in Grace church. The largest instrument in the city was to undergo a rigid test as to its reliability in all departments, to ascertain the equilibrium of contrasts, and to unfold a rich palette of tones

from the heavy foundation stops upwards to the varied harmonic flutes, to the whole reed family, not forgetting the intervening mutation and compound stops, which give what is called "body" to the perfect organ of modern construction.

It will take Mr. George Bowles, the organist, some time to get thoroughly acquainted with his new "chest of whistles," but as far as could be judged from the exhibition of its qualities this week, the congregation have every reason to be satisfied with their magnificent auxiliary to the musical services of the church.

Mr. Bowles developed the solo stops to the intense delight of the seven or eight hundred people present in the church. They admired the pianissimos and were duly awed by the thundering acclaim of the full organ, for he had wisely chosen for performance pieces of varied nuances, illustrated from the works of Dubois, Lemare, Salome, and Lemmens, but the piece de resistance was that noble sonata in E flat by that man among men—Rheinberger.

Behold, the movement is calm, large, and like a Bach composition it grows, it is building up strength, rises to a majestic height, and the finale.

Bah! What are the pretty nothingness of a soft reed solo compared with the full toned instrument about which Adelaide Porter beautifully unburdened her poetic soul: "Only the organ's voice with peal on peal / Can mount to where those far-off angels kneel."

That the new organ is a noble toned instrument is certain, and reflects the highest credit upon the firm who built it, Casavant Bros., of Ste. Hyacinthe, near Quebec; but it may be doubted whether the reeds will remain in tune for any length of time owing to the variations in temperature of a church heated by hot air. Even the reed instruments in orchestral work, notably the oboes, are affected by climatic changes. Is there no remedy for this? (*Manitoba Free Press*, 4 January 1908.)

The American organist Edwin H. Lemare came to Winnipeg to perform on the new Casavant organ on 17 and 18 April 1908. On the afternoon before his first recital, he sent a telegram to the company: "Toronto and this organ really beautiful. Sincere compliments from E.H. Lemare." Later he offered a more detailed judgment on the instrument to the music committee, which in turn was reported to the manufacturers:

Respecting our previous correspondence and your letter of the 15th inst., we had Mr. Edwin H. Lemare go over the organ carefully and pronounce his opinion upon it which Mr. Madore will advise you was very favorable indeed. . . .

Mr. Lemare suggested the removal of the Doppel Flute and the substitution of a No. 2 Scale Diapason on the Great, also to take out the Geigen Principal and substitute an eight foot Clarabella on the Great. I may say that Mr. Lemare's views harmonize with your own on the Cathedral Roll, the adjustment not being necessary to the organ but the building itself.

Mr. Lemare further suggested that when the organ would be transferred to a larger building that a 32 foot Open Large Scale would be very benefi-cial, and he further added that if the money was plentiful, a heavy pressure 15 inch Tuba outside the swell box could be added with great effect.

While we are not likely to consider the two latter suggestions at the present time, it might not be amiss for you to favor us with your criticism of Mr. Lemare's suggestion.

I may say that we were greatly delighted with Mr. Lemare's playing upon our new organ. He was very greatly pleased with it. We may possibly ask you to change the flat [pedal] key board to the concave, but shall wait until our new organist from England arrives, which will be early in June. (Letter to Casavant Bros. from J. W. W. Stewart, 28 April 1908.)

The 1907 organ was severely damaged in a fire on 17 February 1917, and was promptly restored, with improvements, approximately to the original speci-fications, at a cost of $6,500.

The eventual fate of the Grace Church organ provides a unique story in the history of organs in Manitoba. Around 1942 Stuart Kolbinson, then a young man 24 years old, was working with C. Franklin Legge, the Toronto organ manufacturer, servicing a small Winnipeg organ built by a local company, prob-ably Bolton. Legge introduced his assistant to the Grace Church organ, say-ing, "This will be for sale someday." Legge's prediction proved correct. Although Grace Church was regarded as the mother church of Methodism in the west, the wealthy congregation of the downtown church drifted away into the new city suburbs over the years, and the church building was demolished in 1955 to make way for a parking lot. Kolbinson bought the Casavant instrument for $2,000, dismantled it, and transported it to his prairie farm in the Kindersley district in Saskatchewan, where it was stored for several years. By 1963 Kolbinson had constructed a special building to house the organ, and it was ready to play. As stories of the heritage instrument spread, organists from as far away as Oregon came to try it out. Kolbinson left the farm in 1971 to enter the hotel business in Vancouver, then moved to Victoria, leaving his organ behind at the farm. After selling the farm in 1976, he returned there in 1979 to pack up his organ for the trip to Victoria. Although the organ had remained in an unheated building for several years, it played well except for being a lit-tle out of tune. Kolbinson, now retired, built a large extension to his Victoria home, including a tower, to accommodate the large instrument. In earlier years, Kolbinson had visited France to examine and play instruments by classical French builders, so the knowledge he acquired there, together with his expe-rience in organ construction, voicing, and tuning, provided a necessary back-ground for his restoration of the Grace Church organ, which he accomplished with various parts from Casavant Frères. In these letters, Kolbinson reminisced on how he became interested in organs at an early age, his acquisition of the organ, and its present state:

I have collected many books on the organ that interested me, the first being "How to Build a Chamber Organ" by Milne, in 1936. I had seen the article with a picture of a decent looking organ built by boys in a Technical school in England. This was in a music magazine "The Etude" which my father subscribed to even in the depression. (We were farmers then.) I was 16, just finished Grade Twelve, and of course didn't have the resources or expertise to even attempt such a project.

Nevertheless, that book gave me the idea of owning my own organ some day, and in less than ten years I had a 2 manual professionally built organ installed by myself in my parents' home. In the meantime I had managed to get my B.A. as well as working with professional organ builders which made the project within my means. I only had the organ a few months, however, as I had to sell it in order to get the cash to get a home and property of my own, which also would be the home of Grace Church organ ten years (1955) later. This also was in Saskatchewan, Kindersley district. . . .

Of course, the type of programmes played by Lemare and Bowles would never be offered today by serious musicians. Consequently the organ had to be changed to a certain extent to be able to give a good account of itself for modern players. Still, there is a good solid base remaining of the older style which many of the post-war organs lack, a richness due to many 8' ranks, modified somewhat though some of them may be. . . . Meanwhile old opus #301 goes on, singing every day! (Letter to the author from Stuart Kolbinson, 30 June 1992.)

I have had many difficulties, but it is worth it, and I am sure that after I am gone the organ will still be the pleasure of those who will in the future have care of it. There is no reason why it won't be singing a century from today.

I was not able to install the case, since it required a height of 28 feet. Unfortunately the lovely oak casework was also stolen probably by the same criminals who took the pipes. However, I bought the casework of another Casavant and hope to work it in to its present position.

Occasionally I have a visit from someone who knew old Grace Church in its glory days, but as time passes these get fewer as the passing years take their toll. All the clever hands that built it so well have long since laid down their tools for the last time. All honor to them, who took leather, wood, lead, tin and zinc and fashioned an instrument whose voice shall always sing their praise. ("Some notes regarding Opus 301," for the author, to Casavant Frères, 1992.)

Presbyterian Church, Birtle, 1887

The earliest known installation of a pipe organ in rural Manitoba was in a small town in the western part of the province; it was made by Bolton and an associate, a Winnipeg builder who was active in the 1880s. This event was chronicled in a report on the state of music in the town at the time:

On his arrival here in 1882 your correspondent found only one miserable little melodeon and two pianos in the whole place. . . . Early in the spring of 1887 the Presbyterians, who had been holding their services in the Town Hall, decided to build a church of their own and succeeded in erecting and opening a very comfortable building by the 19th of June, but not satisfied with this they went a step further and substituted a small but good "pipe organ" for the reed organ they had hitherto used. They now claim [incorrectly] to have the only pipe organ in the country west of Winnipeg. It was built by Messrs. Bolton and Baldwin of Winnipeg and is valued at $1000. At present it has only one manual with four stops, viz:—open diapason, stopped diapason, dulciana and principal and a Burdon [sic] set of pedal pipes, it also has a tremolo and swell box. This is just a start, I have no hesitation in saying that in another year or two there will be an addition to it in the way of a "swell organ" which will give them an A 1 instrument for a small church. On the evening of October 29th we opened the organ with a concert and organ recital. . . .

In conclusion I think you will agree with me that this is quite a go-ahead little town. This last year we have built two churches worth $5000, placed a $1000 pipe organ in one of them and subscribed over $200 to a band, all this is a town of less than 3000 inhabitants. ("Birtle, Man.," *The Musical Journal*, 15 April 1888.)

All Saints' Anglican Church, 1891, 1917

In 1883 a site was selected for All Saints' Anglican Church at the intersection of Broadway Avenue and Osborne Street, where the present edifice now stands. Within a year services were conducted in the unfinished building. One of the ideals of the founders of this parish was that worship services should place more emphasis on the musical and ritualistic aspects of worship than was customary in Anglican churches in Winnipeg at the time. Accordingly, the nucleus of a substantial organ fund was established by the Ladies' Aid Society in 1884; even the Girls' Guild obtained some money from their activities that they wished to save for the organ. For a time a small pipe organ was rented from a Winnipeg dealer, then a reed organ was purchased from Mason & Hamlin Organ and Piano Company, Chicago, pending the outcome of inquiries regarding the purchase of a pipe organ. Not all of the fund-raising activities of the Ladies' Aid Society were exempt from criticism, however, as this anonymous letter complained:

> Ch. of All Sts. has just been formally opened by the Bishop of Ruperts Land. 2 things in connection with the church and its opening are public property, and neither is creditable to those concerned. . . . [One] matter is the illegal, immoral lottery which the church is sanctioning for the benefit of the organ fund. A bed quilt or something of the sort is to be gambled for, the proceeds

of the swindle to go to the church. All Saints Church is improperly named, it should be called All Sinners. To expect true Christianity in a fashionable church seems as absurd as to expect to find decency in a monkey house. (*Winnipeg Siftings*, 23 February 1884.)

Three builders are known to have submitted specifications and cost estimates for the proposed organ. In 1884 H. W. Bolton, Montréal and Winnipeg, offered to build a two-manual, 18-stop instrument for $2,500. Nevertheless, a friend of the Church Warden, residing in Ottawa, who was knowledgeable about pipe organs, offered some frank opinions in this letter:

Don't have Bolton. Have you never heard of a Wily Winnipegger of the Queen's Hall organ of Montreal! Warren is rather dear but there is a man in Toronto Edward Lye who puts up a great many two manual organs. He is cheap and I believe good. I have a small 2 manual of his in my house but as it has only 1 stop for each manual and has passed 18 months alongside of a hot stove pipe it has not had a fair chance. I am however well enough pleased with it to think it worth your while to get someone to call on him in Toronto and see some of his organs of which he has built several. In Montreal there is a new man called Casavant, the cleverest tuner I ever met with and if one can believe Davies he is one of the best in the country for small organs. Davies is not always quite disinterested as we know but I think you should make inquiries about him in Montreal. He tunes nearly all the organs here and has put up one or two, and Davies who is now fixed here at St. Albans raves about him—Casavant Frères Organ Builders, Montreal, will find him. (Letter to All Saints' Church Warden from J. M. F. Harrison, 31 March 1884.)

About the same time the Toronto firm S. R. Warren & Son entered their bids for the construction of a new organ: a two-manual instrument for $4,400, and a three-manual instrument for $5,300. Their letter concluded with these pronouncements:

The fact of there being other tenders for the work, would make no difference in our figures.

We are tendering for first class work, and we find that it cannot be done for less money than we ask for it and allow a living profit.

While we think you will find our prices compare favorably with those of first class builders, we cannot come down to the level of men who have made such disgraceful failures as the Queen's Hall organ in Montreal, which by the way we have just been asked to rebuild. (Letter to Fred W. Laffery, Winnipeg, from S. R. Warren & Son, 28 March 1884.)

Warren was unrelenting in his criticism of Bolton; in a covering letter accompanying the preceding correspondence, he reiterated his low opinion of his competitor:

We are aware that there is a builder in Winnipeg but we should think that your congregation would hardly care to take the risk of entrusting the work to a man who has made so many disgraceful failures as the Queen's Hall organ in Montreal and in fact everything he has attempted. (Letter to C. J. Brydges, Ottawa [Land Commissioner of the Hudson's Bay Company and Honorary treasurer of the Synod of Rupert's Land], from S. R. Warren & Son, 28 March 1884.)

Casavant Frères declined to submit specifications and a cost estimate until the church furnished further details about the environment in which the organ would be installed. Specifically, the company inquired about the size and dimensions of the building, the placement of the organ, and whether it was desired to have a complete organ initially or a basic instrument that could be enlarged later, "otherwise we should be exposed to make specification of an organ that would not suit the church at all."

All of the church's inquiries were premature, as it turned out, for in 1888 the Ladies' Aid Society decided to concentrate on paying off the debt on the church building and to defer any outlays for a new pipe organ until that goal was met. At last, in 1891, the society was in a position to apply its available funds to the long-cherished purpose of providing an organ for the church, which was installed later in the year. The successful applicant for the work was S. R. Warren & Son, Toronto; the installation of the instrument was completed late in November 1891. The total cost was $1,837.40, of which $1,000 was payable immediately, and the balance in two equal installments payable in November 1893 and 1894. The specifications were as follows:

GREAT		SWELL	
Open Diapason	8	Horn Diapason (Grooved Bass)	8
Dulciana	8	Aeoline	8
Melodia	8	Stopped Diapason (Treble)	8
Stopped Diapason (Bass)	8	Stopped Diapason (Bass)	8
Principal	4	Traverse Flute	4
Fifteenth	2	Mixture	III
Trumpet	8	Oboe and Bassoon	8
		Cornopean	8

PEDAL		MECHANICAL REGISTERS
Bourdon	16	Great to Pedal
		Swell to Great
		Swell to Pedal
		Bellows Signal
		Tremolo
		Great to Pedal Reversible
		Two Combination Pedals
		to Great Organ

A week before the opening concert, this announcement appeared in a daily
newspaper (with some inaccuracies regarding the stoplist):

> Mr. Shaw of Messrs. Warren & Son, Toronto, is in the city placing the new
> organ in All Saints' Church, built by his firm, in position. The instrument
> has been carefully planned and the stops chosen for balance of power and
> variety of tone. It has two manuals with five stops on each, and provision for
> two more on the swell and one on the great. Artistically, it will be a great
> improvement to the church, the front bracketed out into the chancel, pro-
> jecting about two feet, and the pipes are tastefully decorated. Mr. Shaw is
> doubtful whether he will be able to get the organ tuned and ready for use by
> Sunday, so the special musical service in connection with the dedication of
> the new instrument will be held on Sunday evening, the 14th inst., when
> the choir will sing Tours "Magnificat" in F, and Trimmel's anthem "The
> Lord is King." The choir is very strong at present, numbering about twelve
> men and eighteen boys. (*Manitoba Free Press*, 7 November 1891.)

With the expansion of the parish that accompanied the increase in Winnipeg's population around the turn of the century, the need for a new church
building became apparent as early as 1905, although the question was not resolved for over 20 years. While the war was going on, it was decided that a
new pipe organ would provide a fitting memorial to members of the congrega-

All Saints' Anglican Church, Winnipeg.
Casavant, 1917, 3/37; console 1959, 3/48.

tion who had lost their lives in the conflict. A committee was formed to make inquiries about various makes, designs, and prices.

> The result of this committee's work was the placing of an order with Messrs. Casavant Frères of Québec, the well-known manufacturers, for a new pipe organ at a price of $8,344 to be delivered in July 1917 . . . and it is pleasant to relate that the Ladies' Aid Society again came to the front and very generously offered to meet each installment of $500 with interest as the same matured. The organ was duly installed as a memorial to the men of All Saints' who fell in the war and was dedicated on Sunday the 16th September 1917, the Church being crowded. The old organ was at the desire of the Ladies' Aid Society presented to the Congregation of St. Alban's Church in the City of Winnipeg. (*History of All Saints' Church*, n.d.)

The three-manual, 37-stop instrument, later enlarged and refitted in 1959, is the present organ in All Saints' Church.

Westminster Presbyterian Church, 1894, 1899, 1912

Westminster Church had a reed organ until 1894, when it acquired a Warren pipe organ from Grace Church after the latter congregation had installed its large three-manual instrument. Then, five years later, D. W. Karn, Woodstock, Ontario, completed the installation of a two-manual, 24-stop instrument early in the year, but none of the published reports of the event printed the complete stoplist. Even so, the tonal result was praised by two critics; one of them offered a brief comparison with other city organs, while another highlighted the visual appearance of the instrument:

> The indications are that the new Westminster church organ will wear well, and that its diapasons and bourdon bass will mellow and ripen with age.
>
> To compare these tones with those in Holy Trinity is as much to say that they are very good indeed, for there are some instruments in the city with such harsh pedal voices that time will never soften, therefore in this respect Westminster is to be congratulated. (*Winnipeg Tribune*, 22 April 1899.)

> The opening recital on the new organ at Westminster church will undoubtedly be one of the most interesting musical events of the season. The congregation of the church have not spared money or trouble in the matter of the new and handsome instrument. Its appearance conforms to the style of the church. The woodwork is of antique oak, rich in color but simple and unaffected in design. The coloring of the pipes is subdued, the ground being green shaded and softened to a light cream and adorned in crimson and gold. The large pipes in front have a fine effect, being boldly placed on a circular bracket. The whole appearance is pleasing and unostentatious. The quality of the instrument must be judged by its use but the writer has had the privilege of hearing its voice and predicts a most satisfactory and

pleasing quality of tone. The right thing appeals to most people. The tutored and the untutored alike know when they are satisfied. (*Manitoba Free Press*, 15 April 1899.)

The opening concert on 21 April 1899 was a collaborative event involving four organists and the church choir; the players were Mrs. Billington, the resident church organist; George Bowles, Grace Church; James Matthews, Congregational Church; and Laurence Minchin, All Saints' Anglican Church. The organ selections were few in number and light in character:

Marche cortège	Dubois
Russe Varied	Cramer
Barcarole	Bennett
Largo	Handel
Overture, Occasional Oratorio	Handel

The concert itself was ignored by one newspaper, and the critic of another confessed to leaving early for another engagement, a performance of the very

Westminster United (formerly Presbyterian Church), Winnipeg. Casavant, 1912, 4/49; console 1951; revisions, 4/54.

popular light opera, *Princess Bonnie*, at the Winnipeg Theatre, which received extensive coverage. Accordingly, the organ recital received only a very brief comment, more in the nature of a complaint about the program:

> It would have been advisable, perhaps, if more room had been made in the programme for organ pieces and less attention paid to the vocal selections . . . the audience seemed to feel that they would like to have heard more from the instrument itself, which is a very superior one. . . .
>
> The tone of the organ, both as to value and quality is excellent, soft and mellow, without any harshness, and exactly suited to the size of the church. (*Manitoba Free Press*, 21 April 1899.)

In 1912 the church installed a large four-manual, 49-stop Casavant organ in its new building, at a cost of $10,500. This organ, modified with a new console and several additional ranks in 1951, as well as a tonal revision in 1985, is the grandest organ in Winnipeg in the Romantic tonal tradition. For this reason it has served as the location for many concerts and recitals by local players and world-renowned organ virtuosos over the years.

St. John's Anglican Cathedral, 1902

The story of the Parish of St. John's began in the summer of 1817, when Lord Selkirk met his settlers on the banks of the Red River and gave them the property where he stood for a mission church and manse, erected a few years later. In 1833 the decaying buildings were replaced by a new Upper Church on the grounds of the present Cathedral. The Red River Academy, a boarding school for the children of the officers of the Hudson's Bay Company and for the training of native missionaries, was also constructed. In 1862 a new Cathedral was completed that served the congregation until 1920, when it was declared unsafe. It was demolished in 1926 to make way for the present Cathedral, begun in the same year.

It can be assumed that music in the 1862 Cathedral was provided by reed organs until an organ committee was appointed in 1900. In the following year the purchase of an up-to-date model Compensating Pipe Organ (Improved Style "O") was approved, and in 1902 the order was placed for the instrument, costing about $407. The arrival of the new organ, a two-manual hybrid instrument combining both reeds and pipes, received detailed and enthusiastic coverage in a weekly newspaper:

> The St. John's Cathedral is to be congratulated on the installation of its new organ, not only on account of the quality of the instrument, but also on its having been built for the Cathedral in time for the ordination of the new dean. The organ is a large Compensating pipe organ, supplied by the Grundy Music Co., Ltd., and judging from its preliminary trial last Sunday, both the Cathedral and the Grundy Music Co., Ltd., should be well pleased with it.

The reeds are beautifully sweet in tune and very powerful in volume, while the pipes either in solo or in combination with reeds are grand and the two together make a combination that is simply superb.

The predecessor was a similar style of the same make and earned golden opinions from all who heard or played on it, and the new one is a much more powerful and expensive instrument; indeed it almost seemed too powerful for the Cathedral's capacity when played at its full limit last Sunday. . . .

Up to a short time back, lovers of music despaired of being able to obtain a pipe organ worth the name under a price running into thousands of dollars, but now they may take heart for the Grundy Music Co., Ltd., are doing quite a business in these organs at prices ranging from $360 to $1600. . . .

It is to be conceded that it is a very good thing indeed for churches, large or small, Sunday Schools, concert halls, etc., that it is now brought within their means to obtain a high grade organ, producing genuine pipe organ music, one that takes up less than half the space of any other instrument producing a similar musical result, (thus saving expensive alterations), and one that, as has before been said, can produce such beautiful effects with reeds and pipes, played together,(they can be tuned to each other at any temperament) and one, which can be bought for half the price that has hitherto prevailed for instruments of similar volume. Similar musical results have never been produced before. (*Winnipeg Town Topics*, 9 August 1902.)

The published specifications of this unusual instrument were as follows:

TWO MANUALS AND PEDAL
Compass of Manuals CC to C 61 notes
Compass of Pedal CCC to F 30 notes

GREAT ORGAN
1. Principal 4 ft
2. Melodia 8 ft
3. Aeoline 8 ft
4. Open Diapason 8 ft
5. Bourdon 16 ft

SWELL ORGAN
6. Piccolo 2 ft
7. Flute d'Amour 4 ft
8. Violin Diapason 4 ft
9. Salicional 8 ft
10. Harp Aeolian 8 ft
11. Stopped Diapason 8 ft
12. Clarionet 16 ft

PEDAL ORGAN
13. Bourdon 16 ft
14. Violone 16 ft

COUPLERS & MECHANICAL STOPS
15. Octaves to Great
16. Swell to Great
17. Great to Pedal
18. Swell to Pedal
19. Tremulant
20. Blowers Signal

ACCESSORIES
21. Balanced Swell
22. Forte to Great Organ
23. Forte to Swell Organ
24. Wind Indicators
25. Compensating Lever in Great
26. Compensating Lever in Swell

St. Stephen's Presbyterian Church, 1903, 1906

When St. Stephen's Church was erected in 1903, it acquired a new organ through a rather unusual sequence of events. In the same year the Winnipeg College of Music opened, with a staff of 15 teachers who offered courses in piano, organ, voice, violin, harmony, and theory. The College had ordered a two-manual $2,000 organ from an unidentified Toronto builder, probably either Warren or Williams, for installation in their building. How St. Stephen's acquired their organ was reported in a weekly newspaper:

> When it came to making alterations in the new college building it was found that it would be impossible to erect the organ there without inconvenience and a large expenditure of space—and the college business is growing so fast that space is a very valuable consideration. So, in this dilemma a convenient arrangement was made with the authorities of St. Stephen's church by which the organ will be placed in that church, used at the services and be available for college purposes during the week. The fine instrument is now being put up and will be used for the first time on Sunday, Mr. Guy V. Dingle, the organist of St. Stephen's, presiding. (*Winnipeg Town Topics*, 31 October 1903.)

The organ was only in use for about three years, however, when it was replaced by a three-manual, 26-stop instrument, installed by Casavant Frères in 1906 at a cost of $5,050.

St. Andrew's Presbyterian Church, 1904

A new three-manual Casavant organ, purchased by the church at a cost of $5,060, was formally opened on 24 March 1904. One report of this event served the educational purpose of informing the general public about the characteristics and construction of organs generally. It included paragraphs touching on the place of the organ in church worship, and such recent mechanical improvements as tubular-pneumatic action and the balanced crescendo pedal. Turning to the organ itself, the critic (a local organist) commended the quality of the many stops and the promptness of the speech of the pedal pipes, but questioned the lack of brightness in the tone of the full swell and the lack of heaviness in the pedal organ. Overall, however, he concluded that "the instrument in its entirety must be regarded as an excellent specimen of a modern organ and possessing so very many obvious points of superiority, that any modifications that might be suggested could only be regarded as points of individual taste." (J. W. Matthews, "Opening of the New St. Andrew's Church Organ," *Winnipeg Town Topics*, 26 March 1904).

The recitalist was Robert D. Fletcher, whom Matthews, in his diaries, recollected as "a medical student and an enthusiastic amateur" (he received his medical degree in 1903). He was awarded a Master of Arts degree from The

University of Manitoba in 1902 for his treatise, "The Church Organ—Its Evolution—Some Famous Instruments." The opening paragraph of his 21-page dissertation accurately reflected prevalent attitudes towards the organ as a rival of the orchestra:

> There is probably no instrument which has so engrossed the public attention, as well as Musicians generally, as the organ, embodying in its completeness almost all the principal effects obtained from band or orchestra in solo as well as ensemble playing, even surpassing these in some respects, and as capable of the most delicate pianissimo as the thundering forte.

His program, shared with vocalists and the church choir, included pieces in the "modern" style that were intended to demonstrate the capabilities of the instrument:

Festival Fantasia	Tschirch
Meditation	Lemaigre
Toccata	Dubois
Largo	Chopin
Funeral March	Chopin
Chant sans paroles	Holmes
Prelude to Le Déluge	Saint-Saëns
Andantino in D-flat	Lemare
War March of the Priests	Mendelssohn

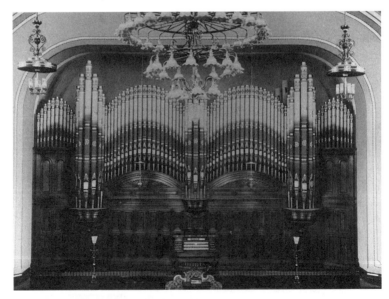

St. Andrew's Presbyterian Church, Winnipeg.
Casavant, 1904, 3/28. Photo from Casavant archives.

Augustine Presbyterian Church, 1905

The D. W. Karn organ in Augustine Church, a three-manual, 28-stop instrument, is the first organ installed in Winnipeg that remained relatively unaltered until 1994, although it underwent refitting and renovation several times in the intervening years. Although Casavant submitted a proposal whose stoplist was almost the same as Karn's, the company was not awarded the contract. The tonal design of the $4,000 Karn organ seems to have been inspired by the Romantic tradition of French and English organ building in vogue at the time. During the construction of the church building in 1904, some alterations were required to accommodate the large pedal pipes:

> We have made a new design of [the] case as it would be impossible to place the design of case that was submitted to you previously inside of the arch, as there was not sufficient height for the pipes. As it is, we have made this design to suit the proposed alterations in your organ chamber, and you will see that we have found it necessary to bring the large pipes on either side of the keyboard part of the way down to the floor in order to get them in the arch, but we think that the design which we have sent to the architect should be quite satisfactory, as it will look well and is the only way in which we can treat the organ in connection with these large double open pipes. (Letter to J. P. Robertson from D. W. Karn, 30 May 1904.)

The American organist Clarence Eddy, the most widely known player in the country, had opened more organs than any organist of his day and performed at many world fairs, including the Paris Exposition in 1899. He played two recitals for the opening of the Augustine organ, one on 21 February 1905 and another on the following day. This was his first program:

Chromatic Fantasie	Louis Thiele
Chant du soir	Bossi
Scherzo	Bossi
Sonata No. 5, Op. 80	Guilmant, dedicated to Clarence Eddy
Legende (New)	F. Seymour Hastings
Fanfare d'orgue (New)	Harry Rowe Shelley
The Swan	Saint-Saëns
Pilgrim's Chorus, Tannhaüser	Wagner, arr. Eddy
Sursum corda (Elevation)	Elgar, arr. Lemare
Fugue in D Major	Bach
March of the Magi Kings	Dubois
Berceuse	Wheeldon
Concert Overture in E-flat	Faulkes

The account of this event combined a description of the organ with a running commentary on Eddy's program:

Augustine Presbyterian Church, Winnipeg.
Karn, 1905, 3/28.

Light and color were transformed into waves of melody at Augustine church
last evening before a delighted audience of between seven and eight hundred music lovers, assembled at the first of the two inaugural recitals on the
new organ by Mr. Clarence Eddy, a pastmaster on the great church instrument. The church is as new as the organ so there were no grim ghosts of bygone Covenanters to protest against the introduction of a musical instrument
in the kirk, but even had there been they would have been soothed by the
carnival of sound which the magnificent instrument produced under the
master touch of the world-wide famous American organist.

The organ is set in an alcove on a level with the gallery and above the
choir. It was manufactured by the Karn Organ and Piano company, of

Woodstock, Ontario, of which Mr. Wright is the local manager. It is a splendid instrument, the largest and best in western Canada, with over 2,000 speaking tubes; and, thanks to its large open diapasons, it has a wide volume of sound which is unequalled by many even larger instruments. Mr. Eddy himself is delighted with it. "It is brilliant," he said, "and it was a pleasure to me to play on it."

The programme was a delightful one so wide was its scope as to display the organ's every capacity, but demanding by its great variety of technique a great deal from the organist. The numbers were arranged in an admirable sequence presenting fine contrasts. It was arranged also on an ascending scale of merit. Each number led to something better—a perfect crescendo of execution. It occupied nearly two hours and a half, but the audience remained enrapt to the close. (*Manitoba Free Press*, 22 February 1905.)

Eddy was an indefatigable recitalist during his stay in Winnipeg, for he also played two programs on the recently installed organ in St. Andrew's Presbyterian Church on 23 and 24 February 1905; the concert on the second day was made possible by the cancellation of an engagement to play a recital in Brandon, Manitoba.

Zion Methodist Church, 1905

The second Zion Church was one of the city's most imposing churches, whose architectural design reflected the Greek revival style used in a number of banks and other public buildings constructed in the early years of the century. In the same year that the new church was completed, a three-manual Casavant organ with 37 speaking stops was installed at a cost of $6,200. In the opening services on 22 October 1905, the new organist Fred M. Gee (1882-1947) was at the console. Gee had emigrated from Wales to Winnipeg in 1902 and opened a studio to teach piano and organ. In the following year he joined the staff of the Winnipeg College of Music and became organist-choirmaster of Westminster Presbyterian Church. For several years after his arrival in Winnipeg, until around 1907, he was referred to as F. Melsom Gee, perhaps to preserve a family identification with his father, Melsom D. A. Gee (1852-1921), who followed his son to Canada in 1906 and served as organist at All Saints' Anglican Church, 1907-21, and was also one of the founders of the Winnipeg Oratorio Society. At the inaugural services for the new organ Fred Gee presented a brief but dramatically structured program that moved from meditative introductory selections by recent composers to a march by Guilmant, followed by an arrangement of Handel's ever-popular, rousing *Hallelujah Chorus*, and ending with a sonorous and virtuosic *offertoire* by the fashionable French organist-composer Louis James Alfred Lefébure-Wély that represented a transition from the sacred to the secular world.

Another "opening recital" was given on the new organ on 18 January 1906 by Arthur Dunham, organist at Mt. Sinai Temple, Chicago. The delay of several months may have been due to the difficulty of securing a suitable visiting player on relatively short notice. In the course of correspondence in connection with arrangements regarding the organ installation, an official of Zion Church had asked for some suggestions from Casavant Frères, mentioning that he was thinking of securing a recitalist from Minneapolis. Presumably he was unsuccessful in the wider search, for Dunham eventually was chosen. Dunhams's program on 18 January 1906 consisted of several transcriptions of works by Dvorak, Boccherini, Gounod, and Wagner, but also included one of Mendelssohn's organ sonatas and a fragment of a Widor organ symphony; the player also presented one of his own compositions.

Fort Rouge Methodist Church, 1906, 1911

In November 1906 Casavant Frères installed a new two-manual organ in Fort Rouge Methodist Church Sunday School; the price was $2,750. This was their fourth contract to be completed during 1906, and three other Casavant instruments would be installed in larger city churches in 1907. An observant music reporter commented: "That our churches are beginning to realize the importance of pleasing musical services is evident from the fact that so many are installing beautiful new Casavant organs." (*Winnipeg Town Topics*, 1 December 1906.) F. Melsom Gee (Fred M. Gee), organist at Zion Methodist Church, played the inaugural recital on the new organ on 16 November 1906. He opened his program with an arrangement of Franz von Suppé's lively and durable *Poet and Peasant Overture*, and concluded with a postlude by Louis James Alfred Lefébure-Wély and an *offertoire* by Edouard Batiste, one of the most popular French recitalists of his time and a contemporary of Lefébure-Wély; in between he played several pieces of a more relaxed nature by composers of the day.

A larger three-manual, 33-stop Casavant organ was installed in the main church building in 1911 at a cost of $6,560; it is the second oldest instrument by this company still active in Manitoba.

Broadway Methodist Church, 1907

An advance announcement of the installation of the new three-manual Casavant organ at Broadway Methodist Church described the mechanical features of the instrument in some detail, noting that it was the first divided organ in the city, with the decorative pipes distributed among six arches on both sides of the chancel. The tubular-pneumatic action, the adjustable combination action, and the rotary-fan wind supply all were regarded as wonderful achievements of mechanical genius. As for the tonal design:

Fort Rouge Methodist Church, Winnipeg.
Casavant, 1911, 3/33.

The general scheme of the organ is so comprehensive so all-embracing in
tonal quality that while it is a wonderfully complete and brilliant church
organ, lending itself to the support of the choir and congregational singing,
it is no less by the exceeding richness of its solo stops, a perfect solo organ,
and splendidly suited for the performance of modern organ compositions.
(*Winnipeg Town Topics*, 23 March 1906.)

The arrival of this new organ, which cost $6,375, was not only a matter of
pride for the congregation and an event of interest to general public, but it
also provided an opportunity for local organists to inspect and play the instrument. Five city organists performed at a private trial of the instrument on 23
April 1907: Maud Cross, St. Andrew's; James W. Matthews, Central Congregational; J. C. Murray, St. Stephen's; F. Melsom Gee, Zion; and F. G. Tollitt.
Leading members of the congregation and several city clergymen also attended
the performance.

Most of the organists present played on the instrument and all expressed
their admiration of its beautiful tone, also the mechanical accessories. The

new organ has 36 speaking stops and 13 couplers, being one of the largest and finest instruments in the west. Dr. Fletcher, the recently engaged organist, is to be congratulated on his appointment. . . . Mr. J. C. Casavant, head of the firm of Casavant Frères, was also present. (*Winnipeg Town Topics*, 27 April 1907.)

Broadway Methodist Church, Winnipeg.
Casavant, 1907, 3/36.
Photo from Casavant archives.

Young Methodist Church, 1907

The installation of a smaller organ in a less prestigious church was accorded much less attention by musical journalists. The opening of the two-manual, 16-stop Casavant organ—the contract price was $2,750—in Young Church received only a few lines:

> The instrument is not large, having only two manuals, but it nevertheless admirably adapted to the requirements of the church in every respect. The registration is evenly balanced and the voicing excellent, while in appearance it is most artistic and an ornament to the church. . . . Miss Mayhew, organist of Knox church, performed several numbers in an artistic manner, revealing the beauties of the various solo stops to the evident satisfaction of a large audience which filled the auditorium of the church. (*Manitoba Free Press*, 3 May 1907.)

Wesley Methodist Church, 1908

Wesley Church was established in a small building in the northern part of Winnipeg 1881 as a spin-off from Grace Methodist, the central downtown church of that denomination. A period of expansion followed, involving two new buildings in rapid succession, one in 1883 and another in 1898. As one critic put it, Wesley Church "staggered under a load of discords" produced by two unsatisfactory organs by unidentified makers before it became financially able to install a two-manual, 17-stop Casavant instrument in the latest edifice in 1908 at a cost of $3,255. Even so, both the installation, the inaugural concert, and a subsequent recital were largely ignored by the press, perhaps because Wesley Church was somewhat beyond the fringe of the circle of prestigious downtown churches. The report of the event was brief:

> The Casavant Bros., of Quebec have just installed one of their beautiful two-manual organs at Wesley Church, which will be opened by Miss Maud Cross, the new organist of the Church, on Good Friday evening at 8:15. Solos will be rendered by Mrs. Pingle and Mr. Davidson Thomson, and by other good local talent; the choir, under the leadership of Mr. J. E. Williams will render selections from Haydn's "Creation," and Stainer's "Crucifixion."
> (*Winnipeg Town Topics*, 18 April 1908.)

On 19 July 1908 Minor C. Baldwin, a touring organist from New York, offered a recital at the church, but neither his program nor an account of the performance was reported.

About a decade later the Wesley congregation disbanded, following the transition of the area surrounding the church to a warehouse district and the accompanying deterioration of the middle-class housing area. When members of the congregation began to move to new residential districts elsewhere in the city, in 1919 the Winnipeg North District of the Methodist Church gave permission to sell the Wesley Church property. Around this time the organ was acquired by First Church of Christ, Scientist, which had just completed the superstructure of a large new edifice on the south side of the Assiniboine River in the central part of the city. In 1955 the organ was reconstructed, several stops were added, and a new console was supplied by Hill, Norman & Beard, the British firm active in organ rebuilding in Winnipeg in the mid-1950s. The future of the organ is uncertain, for the church, including the pipe organ, was listed for sale for the first time in 1993.

St. Luke's Anglican Church, 1910

The Parish of St. Luke's, Winnipeg, had its beginning in a small store in the Fort Rouge district; it was within easy walking distance to Holy Trinity Anglican Church for adults, but too far for children. The establishment of the mission and Sunday School in the vacant store was so successful that the

St. Luke's Anglican Church,
Winnipeg.
Casavant, 1910, 3/30.
Echo organ 1912, 3/36.
Hill, Norman & Beard,
1953, 4/61.
The location of the echo
organ at the rear of the
church is unique in
Winnipeg.

congregation took on the ambitious project of erecting a stone church, completed in 1905. Four years later, in the course of discussions about the improvement of the building, the matter of a suitable organ was raised. Accordingly, the St. Luke's Organ Guild was formed in 1909 by the women of the church for the purpose of raising funds for the purchase of a pipe organ. Immediately the members set about canvassing for membership subscriptions, holding sewing meetings and sales of work, publishing one thousand copies of St. Luke's Cook Book containing paid advertisements, and holding various entertainments and social gatherings. Within one year their enthusiastic endeavours had yielded over $2,000, the first payment on the organ, leaving a balance of about $3,500 to be paid.

The installation of the Casavant organ, a three-manual, 30-stop instrument, was completed late in 1910 and was pronounced satisfactory by a committee of the vestry.

> The organ was delivered on November 4th, and was first played by the organist Mr. James Bending on December 10th; and the first strains heard from the completed instrument were "Praise God from whom all blessings flow," as expressive of our thanksgiving for this beautiful instrument, and as indicative of the purpose for which it had been installed. (*St. Luke's Church Year Book*, 1911.)

In November 1912 a new 6-stop echo organ was presented to the church by a wealthy parishioner; the $1,500 mechanism was installed in the church tower and connected electrically to the main organ.

St. Giles Presbyterian Church, 1913

Late in 1913 St. Giles installed a three-manual, 30-stop organ made by the Canadian Pipe Organ Company. The newspaper announcement of this event published the complete specifications and informed the readers:

> The cost of this magnificent instrument was upwards of $6,000, and St. Giles church is to be congratulated on having an organ worthy of its surroundings, and which will undoubtedly be a great help to the services of the church. Fred M. Gee, organist of Augustine church, Fort Rouge, will preside at the console at the opening services, Sunday, Dec. 14, both morning and evening, and has also been engaged to give the opening recital at 8:30 p.m., Monday, Dec. 15. Mr. Gee's services are in great demand for the opening of new organs, and in every instance his masterly work at the console has been very highly commended by the most exacting critics. He is "admitted to be one of the best organists in the Dominion," and it is safe to predict that in his hands the magnificent new organ at St. Giles will be shown to its best advantage. (Manitoba *Free Press*, 6 December 1913.)

The inaugural recital by Fred M. Gee on 15 December 1913 contained these selections:

Commemoration March	John E. West
Cantilène	Dubois
Gavotte, Mignon	Thomas
Marche funèbre et chant séraphique	Guilmant
The Swan	Saint-Saëns
Scherzo	J. R. Rogers
Evening, The Cuckoo, The Bee	Lemare
The Evening Star, Tannhaüser	Wagner
The Pilgrim's Chorus, Tannhaüser	Wagner

Every available seat in St. Giles' Church was taken last evening when the inaugural organ recital was given by Fred M. Gee. The very fine and comprehensive programme served the double purpose of showing to advantage the extensive resources of the new organ and of proving Mr. Gee's exceptional ability as an organist. An instrument of three manuals, 30 speaking stops and up-to-date improvements affords a player very good opportunities, and Mr. Gee made admirable use of them. His playing was notable for clearness and accuracy, and especially for variety and appropriateness of expression. ("St. Giles Organ Recital," *Manitoba Free Press*, 16 December 1913.)

The organ is still in use (the church building is now designated Burrows Bethel Mennonite Church), although five ranks have been removed from the swell division since it was first installed.

Local Players

In the early days organ recitals in the larger churches were played before capacity audiences, and they were much more frequent than they are today. Sometimes they were shared performances involving church choirs, vocalists, or other instrumentalists. Occasionally the music columnists who reported on these events were also organists or musicians; in such cases the quality of musical commentary often was high. For the most part, however, most of these reviews were purely laudatory descriptions, exhibiting little sensitivity to the refinements of musical interpretation.

An early organ recital to be reported in detail was given by J. C. Dunster, organist at Holy Trinity Anglican Church briefly in the mid-1880s, at Central Congregational Church on 11 May 1885:

Festival March	J. C. Dunster
Andante	Lefébure-Wély
Chorus, For Unto Us	
a Child is Born	Handel
Andante	Batiste
Grand offertoire	Batiste
Grand Fugue in A Minor	Handel
Cavatina	Raff
O Gloriosa Virginium	J. C. Dunster
Chorale Fugue, Cum Sanctu	Mozart
Adagio cantabile	Haydn
Overture, Zampa	Hérold

The review was extremely general, with some attention given to the social aspects of the event:

The organ recital in the Congregational Church last evening by Mr. J. C. Dunster, in aid of the choir fund, was well attended despite the threatening character of the weather. The assemblage included nearly all the leading musical people of the city, and therefore the applause which was so freely given could not be characterized as fulsome, as a competent as well as a critical audience meted out the praise. It was the first opportunity that has been afforded the citizens of Winnipeg of hearing Mr. Dunster, as his sojourn here has only been of a few weeks' length, and from the flattering encomiums which preceded him a great deal was naturally expected, and there is no question that the most exacting were more than satisfied. Mr. Dunster's rendering of the difficult program proved him to be an organist of the highest order. Where every number was given with such effect and artistic accuracy it could be but a matter of taste to particularize.

The combination of the various stops were so carefully arranged that the listeners forgot for the time that the organ used was a comparatively small one. ("Pedals and Pipes: Mr. Dunster's Organ Recital a Brilliant Success," *Manitoba Free Press*, 12 May 1885.)

P. R. Maclagan, the organist at Holy Trinity for several years beginning in 1881, was in demand as a recitalist at various other churches. His program at St. Mary's Church on 10 November 1885 consisted of these selections:

Prelude, Lohengrin	Wagner
Toccata and Fugue in D Minor	Bach
Sonata in F Minor	Mendelssohn
Reverie, Algerian Suite, Gavotte	Saint-Saëns
Grand Sonata in D Minor	Guilmant

The review referred to the educational intention of his program:

The recital of organ music given by Dr. Maclagan in St. Mary's Church on Tuesday evening was attended by a large and fashionable audience, including most every professional and amateur organist in the city. The programme was an unusually heavy one, and contained representative compositions of nearly all the Great Masters, classical and modern.

The programme contained an analysis of the various compositions lending an additional interest to the performance, which, it was announced, was intended to be instructive as well as entertaining. The audience was led to expect a great deal, from the fact that Dr. Maclagan has been practising steadily of late, and judging from the expression of satisfaction heard on all sides, they were not in any way disappointed. The technical difficulties of some of the pieces, notably the Guilmant sonata, are enormous; yet they were all performed, not only with apparent ease, but with a degree of artistic finish seldom or never heard in the country. The pedal playing was remarkably clear and wonderfully "legato," the most rapid passages being executed as smoothly as if on the pianoforte. Those who had heard previous recitals by the Dr. on Holy Trinity church organ regretted that he had not as good an instrument under his fingers, the weakness of the swell being particularly apparent; nevertheless the performance was probably superior to anything hitherto executed by that talented artist, and his many friends who were present expressed their delight at again enjoying his masterly interpretations. ("Dr. Maclagan's Recital," *Manitoba Free Press*, 11 November 1885.)

Holy Trinity Anglican Church was the site of many organ recitals in the early years; it had a fine instrument and competent musicians to perform on it, and the church was centrally located. One such concert was this duo performance there by J. C. and F. Dunster on 17 June 1886:

Grand Organ Concerto in B-flat	Handel
Andante, Symphony in B-flat	Haydn
Allegretto, Barcarole,	
Concerto No. 4 in E	Sterndale Bennett
Grand Organ Sonata No. 4 in B-flat	Mendelssohn
Overture, Occasional Oratorio	Handel
Allegretto	Guilmant
Grand Pedal Fugue in E Minor	Bach
Minuetto, O Glorioso Virginium	J. C. Dunster
Grand Chorus, For Unto Us	Handel

Although the newspaper account of this event did not deal in depth with either the music or the performance, it was typical of the level of reviews of organ recitals in the early days:

> Holy Trinity Church was filled with a select audience last evening on the occasion of an organ recital by Messrs. J. C. and F. Dunster. It was the debut of the latter gentleman in Winnipeg and his skillful performance upon the organ last evening established his reputation at once. He gave selections from the leading composers of the day in a perfect manner, and charmed his many listeners. And no less pleasing and effective was the performance of Mr. J. C. Dunster, whose abilities as an organist are acknowledged by competent judges. (*Manitoba Free Press*, 18 June 1886.)

Other local organists also contributed to the development of musical culture by offering solo recitals. Kate Holmes (whose first name was never revealed in newspaper references or reviews,it was always "Miss Holmes"), organist at Grace Methodist Church, played a recital at Christ Church Anglican on 18 May 1892:

Marche religieuse	Guilmant
Adagio, Sonata in B-flat	Beethoven
Minuet	Boccherini
Larghetto	Mozart
Offertoire in D	Batiste
Flute Concerto	Rinck
Allegretto in B Minor	Guilmant
Overture, Poet and Peasant	von Suppé

While the review was highly appreciative, especially of two of the transcriptions, the inadvertent reference to "her exceptional ability, for a woman," would not pass late 20th-century feminist criteria unchallenged:

> Christ church was well filled last evening by a music loving audience, who had gathered together to hear and appreciate what is not too often heard in this city, high-class music, well played on the organ. To very few women is given such power over the master instrument as to Miss Holmes, who is the

organist of Grace church. Without apparent effort, she handles the keys in a manner that proves her exceptional ability, for a woman, on the organ.

The programme which was selected was a very comprehensive one, and was well calculated to exhibit the resources of the fine instrument that Christ church now boasts. If it lacks the full rolling tones of the grand old organs, which modern makers, beyond adding a few novel stops and scientifically improved apparatus, do not seem to be able to improve upon, the Christ church organ is still an instrument of which the congregation should feel proud and they should endeavor to clear its debt with alacrity. Miss Holmes was particularly successful in the graceful and melodious sonata in B flat by Beethoven, and in Rinck's Flute concerto, in which the flute stop passages were admirably brought out. . . . Before the recital commenced the Rev. Canon Pentreath in a few introductory remarks said that education for the appreciation of music of high class was equally necessary as training in other sciences. He announced that there would be a recital of high class sacred music every month in Christ church. The proceeds of the collection would go to the organ fund. ("Organ Recital," *Manitoba Free Press*, 19 May 1892.)

The gap between the public appearances of teachers and their students was particularly short in the case of Kate Holmes and her "best pupil," Florence Morgan, who was appointed organist at Christ Church Anglican in the following year.

Robert D. Fletcher played his first reported recital at Holy Trinity Anglican Church on 27 September 1898; eventually he was appointed organist at the church, probably due to his demonstrated competence at a number of recitals he played there and at other locations. His program consisted of a mix of familiar transcriptions and original pieces by several minor composers of the day:

Triumphal March, Naaman	Costa
Berceuse	G. Delbruck
Largo	Handel
Offertoire	Edw. M. Read
Serenade	Gounod
March	John S. Camp
Meditation	Lemaigre
War March of the Priests, Athalie	Mendelssohn

The reviewer remarked that the large attendance at his recital was evidence of popular interest in organ music,

Music—a branch of the art that, speaking locally, does not hold its proper place in public esteem. There is usually an absence of vulgar clap-trap at organ recitals, and in a beautiful church like Holy Trinity the refined and restful surroundings add much to the impressiveness of such occasions. Tuesday's programme was by no means a formidable one, in fact there was not a "big" number on it; but its performance was characterized by care and skill as to execution, and intelligence as to registration. (*Winnipeg Town Topics*, 1 October 1898.)

Another reviewer remarked on the size of the crowd, but also dwelt on the youth of the performing artist and some faults of organ recitals generally:

> The organ recital at Holy Trinity church last night was attended by a very large number of people. The splendid gathering was a tribute to the worth of the talented young organist, Mr. R. D. Fletcher—a tribute well deserved.
>
> Mr. Fletcher's musicianly good taste was not displayed more in his playing than in the arrangement of his programme. The twelve [sic] numbers were well chosen, and the entertainment was concluded by half past nine o'clock—scarcely an hour an a half in length—in striking contrast with other organ recitals, which have been stretched out to a point of tediousness. The programme was performed precisely as printed; there being no substitutions "by request," and the misguided enthusiasts addicted to the encore mania were for once effectually silenced. That is the advantage of a recital in an Episcopalian church.
>
> Mr. Fletcher watches over the Trinity organ as tenderly as a mother watches over her young, and the instrument was in perfect condition for the recital. Eight numbers were played by the young instrumentalist—the term young may well be applied, for he has not yet reached manhood's state— and all were of a pleasing character. By the word pleasing is not meant trashy, for every selection was of a high standard. (*Manitoba Free Press*, 28 September 1898.)

Another in his series of recitals was given in Holy Trinity Church on 11 September 1900. The advance announcement of his concert program was reassuring with regard to the readiness of both the recitalist and the organ:

> All the numbers are of the highest class and are well calculated to show off Mr. Fletcher's ability as an executant. The organ during the past week has been looked over and pronounced in first class condition by a St. Paul expert. (*Manitoba Free Press*, 8 September 1900.)

Grand Chorus	Dubois
Allegro grazioso	Tours
Scherzo	Rheinberger
Toccata	Dubois
Andante No. 1	Stainer
Festival Fantasia	Tschirch
The Broken Melody	Van Biene
Intermezzo sinfonica	Mascagni
Chant due Rei Rene	Guilmant

In addition to a descriptive commentary of the pieces that Fletcher performed, the report also included some thoughtful reflections on organ playing in general and of musical interpretation in particular:

The large crowd which gathered at Holy Trinity church last evening to hear
Mr. R. D. Fletcher's organ recital crowded the building throughout, but all
were satisfied at the close of the programme that the merits of the music
fully made up for the inconvenience and slight discomfort of the crowd.
Organ recitals are more uncommon than they should be and fine organ playing is still more uncommon, the consequence being that last evening's audience fully appreciated what was presented for their enjoyment. . . . There is
a danger in organ music of relying too entirely on the mechanical effects for
the interpretation of the work and while these effects are very necessary, in
fact indispensable, nothing can take the place of a sympathetic, artistic de-
livery on the part of the performer himself. There are very few organists in
the west who can entertain an audience as did Mr. Fletcher last evening.
(*Manitoba Free Press*, 12 September 1900.)

Fletcher's apparent fondness for transcriptions was not exhibited consist-
ently throughout his performing career, however. In his recital program on 24
September 1901 at Holy Trinity Church, he abandonded them entirely, pre-
ferring to stay with tuneful pieces by composers of original works for organ:

Entré dans le style classique	Pierné
Berceuse	Edmundstoune Duncan
Fanfare	Lemmens
Gavotte moderne en ut	Tours
A Sunset Melody	Vincent
Prelude and Fugue in F	Bach
Christmas Offertory	Jules Grison
The Question and The Answer	Wolstenholme
Andantino in D-flat	Lemare
Grand choeur	Guilmant

Fletcher's great popularity can be gauged by the large attendance at his recitals. He had a dedicated following in other social circles, for he also played
ragtime piano pieces at "smoking concerts," where groups of men spent eve-
nings playing cards amid the fragrant odour of superb Havana cigars and being
entertained by singers, small orchestras, and instrumentalists. Although ragtime generally was denounced as musical rot that makes money (*Winnipeg Town
Topics*, 1 June 1901), a critic deplored the meagre collection received at
Fletcher's September organ recital: "His talents will some day be more substan-
tially appreciated than in a community in which an audience of one thousand
'music lovers' contribute the magnificent collection of forty dollars and fifteen
cents." (*Winnipeg Town Topics*, 5 October 1901.)

Immigrant organists from England were given an early opportunity to dis-
play their musical capabilities. Frank G. Wrigley, formerly a pupil of Dr. Joseph
Cox Bridge, organist at Chester Cathedral, England, offered this program at
Westminster Presbyterian Church on 9 June 1903:

Prelude in C	Rachmaninoff
Allegretto	Wolstenholme
Postlude in D	Smart
Andantino in D-flat,	
Chant sans paroles	Lemare
Conzour	King Hall
Marche religieuse	Guilmant

One review of his recital was bland and uninformative: "He proved himself to be a very capable organist and made an impression that was distinctly favorable. His technique is admirable and his interpretations are characterized by good taste." (*Winnipeg Town Topics*, 13 June 1903.) Another commentator, however, had very little of significance to say about his musical interpretations. Rather, the critic seized the opportunity to deplore the disturbing theatrical displays of other organists, as well as the slovenly practices of some music critics:

A recital at Westminster church last night was the medium adopted for the introduction of Mr. Frank G. Wrigley, a young English organist, who recently crossed the herring pond to make his home in this land of illimitable opportunities.

Mr. Wrigley was welcomed to Winnipeg by an audience which included many of our leaders in affairs musical and won a verdict which was altogether favorable.

He played a programme well calculated to illustrate the high standard of his technique and to evidence, if not brilliantly, at least talent beyond mediocrity, as well as good taste, as an interpreter of organ music.

Mr. Wrigley is to be praised for the smoothness of his playing and to be commended for conducting himself on the organ stool as a rational human being instead of imitating the Jumping Jack contortion antics which mar the work of many organists.

He played intricate and difficult passages without any agonizing squirming or tortuous writhings and changed combinations without any of those gymnastics which are irritating as well as distracting.

The substitution of selections for those on the printed card was a mistake. It always is sometimes a fatal one for learned critics who have been known to fall into the snare of glibly describing the rendering of compositions which were not rendered at all.

Mr. Wrigley comes to Winnipeg at an opportune time, a time of prosperity and of musical expansion.

We have now only a few good organists—shortly, come to think of it, we are to lose one of this few, and the newcomer should have no difficulty in securing the recognition he is entitled to.

Without detailing his numbers, it may be said that had he played nothing else but the magnificent March Religeuse of that brilliant Frenchman,

Alex. Guilmant, his talent and fine technique would have been abundantly manifested. (*Manitoba Free Press*, 10 June 1903.)

A new generation of organists was emerging in Winnipeg in this period. One of these, Eva Ruttan, received keyboard training in the city before leaving in 1905 to study with Henry S. Woodruff, organist and musical director of Westminster Presbyterian Church, Minneapolis. On her return to Winnipeg two years later, she opened a studio to accept students in piano and organ and also assumed the position of organist at the new Fort Rouge Methodist Church, where she remained until 1909. Her first public recital on 15 October 1907 included the following pieces:

Prelude and Fugue in B-flat	Bach
Suite gothique	Boëllmann
Andantino	Lemare
Overture, Stradella	Flotow, arr. Buck
Fanfare	Lemmens
Cradle Song and Prayer	Guilmant
Introduction to Act 3, Lohengrin	Wagner

The critical review favoured the lighter works:

The lady shows distinct improvement in her manipulation of the difficult instrument, and plays with fine expression. Her best numbers were "Fanfare" by Lemmens and Lemare's "Andantino." Good organists are not so many in the city but that a new recruit to the ranks will be warmly welcome. (*Winnipeg Town Topics*, 19 October 1907.)

J. C. Murray, organist at St. Stephen's Church, was the subject of favourable commentaries by Winnipeg music critics. One wrote at length:

In most of these churches the work of the organist calls for no special comment. For they are all fairly good, much better, in my opinion, than the average choir with which they are associated. But the organ playing in St. Stephen's church does call for special comment, because it makes its special appeal to every highly artistic instinct of one's being.

The ordinary organist draws a few stops and plays through a simple hymn tune with very little change of registration, as though its interpretation mattered little. Not so, Mr. J. C. Murray of St. Stephen's church. With him the most delightful changes of registration are constantly introduced in keeping with the sentiment of the work, and yet not foreign to the spirit of the music; and the general effect is most inspiring. . . . I write these things for no other purpose than art's sake—purer art. . . . So, for this purpose, I call special attention to Mr. Murray's playing of the organ and suggest that connoisseurs who seek inspiration in the tones of the king of instruments when masterfully handled, may find it by visiting Ralph Connor's church. (*Winnipeg Town Topics*, 20 February 1909.)

Murray apparently was not a frequent recitalist, but clearly he was well known and appreciated in the musical community. In 1908 a London publisher issued an album of his arrangements of selected Elizabethan lyrics. He played this program at St. Stephen's Church on 6 May 1909:

Symphony, Sonata in D Minor	Guilmant
Song, It is Enough	Mendelssohn
Fantasie in E Minor, The Storm	Lemmens
Improvisation on a given theme	
Triplet of Bagatelles	Grieg
Intermezzo	Chipp
Andante, Surprise Symphony	Haydn
Finale, Casse noisette Suite	Tschaikowsky

In an exceedingly complimentary review of his recital, the writer returned to an earlier theme of the musicianship of local organists as compared with visiting recitalists. The favourable comparison was perhaps not wholly justified, considering the relatively light character of Murray's program:

> There are few organists or musicians in this country of the artistic calibre of Mr. Murray. . . . [It] is an achievement of record to hold the interest of a mixed audience in an organ recital given by one who does not come heralded with world-wide fame. . . . Mr. Murray's manipulation of the resources of the organ suffers little in comparison with such world famous organists as Edwin H. Lemare and Clarence Eddy. His playing has the same clearness of execution, the same breadth and dignity, the same easy command of resources, and mastery of the art of rapid construction in improvisation. (*Winnipeg Town Topics*, 8 May 1909.)

Later in the year Murray announced a recital composed entirely of transcribed works by Richard Wagner. Although this concert on 6 November 1909 at St. Stephen's Church was not well attended, the reviewer praised the player for this unusual venture but chastised the musical public for its indifference, returning to a comparison with international touring organists:

> I cannot help but say that our dozens of church organists show more curiosity than love for their art when they turn out en masse to hear Edwin H. Lemare, of London (good as he is) and W. H. Hewlett of Toronto, in recital, while they do not avail themselves of the opportunity of hearing Mr. Murray, who, to my mind, is much in advance of the latter player as a concert organist. . . . While the resources of St. Stephen's organ are inadequate to convey the manifold orchestral color tints of Wagner's music, an approximate reading can be given when a player of Mr. Murray's resourcefulness essays the task. (*Winnipeg Town Topics*, 13 November 1909.)

Murray later received a warm tribute from an organist-diarist:

> Mr. Murray had been an occasional pupil of Guilmant, i.e., I think he had benefited on several occasions on courses of lessons designed for pupils, who could have the time to run over to Paris from Great Britain and sit at the feet of the great master. Mr. Murray was a superb player and maintained the highest traditions of organ playing. He was a man of delicate constitution, in fact, his later days were a constant fight, waged with courage and high spirits, against ill health. But his playing had a charm and finish that will not be easily forgotten, and he was a most generous fellow-artist, as I have good reason to testify, having received much kindness and hospitality from him in the matter of permission to indulge in practise on the instrument at which he presided—a very excellent specimen of Casavant's build. His sudden and untimely decease was a great loss to musical Winnipeg. ("Recalling Early Organists: From the Diary of the Late Jas. W. Matthews," *Manitoba Free Press*, 3 January 1925.)

Late in 1911 nine local organists launched a series of half-hour organ recitals before Sunday evening services at Broadway Methodist Church. The performers all were prominent organists at the larger city churches: Robert D. Fletcher, George Bowles, Ernest E. Vinen, James Bending, Fred M. Gee, James W. Matthews, Melsom Gee, Lillian Mayhew, and Mrs. J. V. Dillabough; but the programs for these performances were not published.

The content of recital programs by local organists still exhibited a balance between serious musical compositions and lighter pieces, often transcriptions, for the entertainment of those members of the audience with less discriminating tastes in organ music. During the months of November and December 1913, there were four recitals by city organists. Robert D. Fletcher, at Broadway Methodist Church, gave two recitals in November. The first, on 1 November 1913, was devoted exclusively to transcriptions of works by modern French composers such as Saint-Saëns, Massenet, and Debussy. His second recital on 8 November, however, had a more balanced content:

Adagio, Sonata No. 2	Mendelssohn
March in G	Smart
He Shall Feed His Flock, Messiah	Handel
Romance in D-flat	Lemare
Largo in G	Handel
Berceuse	Spinney

On the following day, his assistant Frederic Watson duplicated the program, with the exception of the Handel transcription. On this occasion the program was shared with a soloist.

Although transcriptions had a strong appeal for the audiences, and organists themselves showed no indication of abandoning them, the practice was not entirely approved by leaders in the music community. Ralph Horner, the Music Director of the Imperial Academy and Music Editor of a weekly newspaper, commented on this issue within the context of an article that advocated an expanded program of more frequent organ recitals in city churches as a means of increasing public familiarity with good music:

> The organ is a most noble instrument, capable of expressing the noblest and highest human emotions, but also the deepest religious feelings; and because of its facility of execution and its power of producing so many kinds of color, the modern organ is an instrument eminently adapted for solo use. There are so many splendid solos written for the organ which we seldom have the opportunity of hearing. We occasionally hear one in the offertory and sometimes another as a postlude to play people out of the church—and that is all! . . .
>
> I am not an advocate for playing arrangements of orchestral music on the organ, for the attempt to illustrate or imitate the orchestra only results in disparaging the "King of Instruments," but in the absence of a Symphony Orchestra these organ recitals can be the means of making people acquainted with orchestral compositions which otherwise they would never hear. . . . (Dr. Ralph Horner, "Music," *Winnipeg Town Topics*, 17 February 1912.)

The War Years

During World War I, 1914-18, only three large city churches were completed in Winnipeg. The number of organ installations was also severely restricted. New organs were placed in two rural Manitoba churches and about seven in Winnipeg churches. The large Grace Methodist Church instrument was extensively renovated by Casavant. Two theatre organs were also installed in Winnipeg in this period. Nevertheless, organ recitals continued to be offered by local organists every month, sometimes even more frequently. Although these recitals were announced in advance, only a few were reviewed in the newspapers, generally in a perfunctory fashion. Perhaps the performances of local organists were coming to be regarded as less worthy of comment than those of prominent visiting recitalists, or the frequency of the recitals by local organists was beyond the capabilities of music columnists to report. Since the size of the audiences remains unknown, it is therefore impossible to judge the extent of the popularity of organ recitals at this time.

Organ recitals in the war years occasionally were the vehicles for raising funds for patriotic charities. One of a number of Red Cross Fund benefit recitals was given by Ernest E. Vinen, organist at Grace Methodist Church, where he had served since arriving in Winnipeg in 1908. Previously Vinen was organist at St. Augustine's Church, London, England for 20 years. As conductor of the Elgar Society in Winnipeg, Vinen's ability in developing choral activity in the city was recognized by both the press and the public. Vinen and Fred M.

Gee both played separate programs for the benefit of the Red Cross Fund at two of Winnipeg's largest churches during 1915.

In addition to his post as organist at St. Stephen's church, Fred Gee offered private instruction in organ. One of his successful students was Rodolphe Pépin, who had been organist at Sacred Heart Roman Catholic Church for three years before Gee presented him in a public recital. Pépin's program at Stephen's Church on 1 May 1916, in aid of the Patriotic Fund, included these selections:

Larghetto, Allegro Vivace,	
Sonata No. 2	Guilmant
Adagio, Sonata No. 2	Mendelssohn
Romance in D-flat	Lemare
Gavotte, Mignon	Thomas
Vorspiel, Lohengrin	Wagner
Intermezzo in D-flat	Hollins
Marche pontificale	Lemmens
Cantilene pastorale	Guilmant
Toccata	Dubois

The ensuing review of Pépin's recital was complimentary with regard to his performance and accurately prophetic of his future achievements:

> An organ recital of unusual merit was given in St. Stephen's church last evening by Rodolphe Pépin, a gifted pupil of Fred. M. Gee. Mr. Pépin's programme was of a highly interesting character throughout. . . . The rendering of Guilmant's "Cantilene Pastorale" and the Dubois' "Toccata" convinced one of Mr. Pépin's ability as an organist who should in time command a good deal of critical respect in more serious programmes. The young player's success last night was assuredly due to the meritorious character of his work. ("Organ Recital at St. Stephen's Church," *Manitoba Free Press*, 2 May 1916.)

Pépin, still a pupil of Fred. M. Gee, played another recital at St. Stephen's Church on 29 May 1917; it was praised for its "keen musical insight and marked technical proficiency" and "intelligent elucidation of an altogether exacting programme." (*Manitoba Free Press*, 30 May 1917.) By now Pépin was the organist at St. Boniface Cathedral, a position he held until June 1919, when he left Winnipeg for the United States to join the New England Conservatory of Music in Boston.

Arnold Dann was one Winnipeg organist who achieved prominence in the field of music education. Shortly after arriving in the city to become organist at Grace Church, he opened a studio and secured an academic appointment at Wesley College:

> With the assistance of several talented teachers . . . [Dann] will conduct classes in all grades for the study of pianoforte, harmony, musical aesthetics, and interpretations. . . . Mr. Dann is planning to give a series of organ and

piano recitals personally. In addition he will deliver his popular lectures on "Music and War," "The Complete Organist," and "The Rise and Development of the Tune." (*Manitoba Free Press*, 31 August 1918.)

Dr. Riddell, principal of [Wesley] College, recognizes the importance of music as a communal asset and the necessity of placing it in Winnipeg on the same footing as other arts and sciences. The services of Arnold Dann, the well known piano virtuoso, and successful director of music at Grace church, have been engaged. He has been given a professorship and a place on the faculty of the college. ("Wesley College to Inaugurate Music Department," *Manitoba Free Press*, 14 September 1918.)

Dann was an active recitalist during his time at Grace Church, and he also encouraged his pupils to perform in public. A newspaper article in 1919 reported that his recital series had been drawing great crowds. The frequency of his concerts clearly reflected the enthusiastic reception they received on the part of the musical listening public, even though transcriptions rarely were included. Dann served as organist at Grace Church and held his teaching appointment at Wesley College until he left Winnipeg in 1923 for the United States, where he later became organist and choirmaster at a new one million dollar church in Pasadena, California, in 1924.

Most of the church organ recitals in the concluding years of this period were not free-standing events, but were short performances after the regular Sunday evening church services, usually with other musical selections by the choir or soloists. Even weekday organ concerts by local players were often shared with other performing musicians.

Visiting Recitalists

One of the earliest concerts by a visiting organist to be reported at some length took place at the Central Congregational Church on 30 September 1890. It was given by the touring recitalist Frederic Archer, who had moved to the United States from England in 1880. While in England he had played over 2,000 recitals on the new organ at the Alexandria Palace without repeating a program. The advance notice of his Winnipeg appearance contained extravagant praise for the recitalist:

> The coming of Frederic Archer, who may be said to be the finest organist in the world, is being looked forward to with a great deal of interest by lovers of all classes of music. As organist, he produces such effects as few have ever heard from that instrument, and which those who have heard say can never be forgotten. Effects unlike and beyond those commonly associated with organ music, which are said to charm all who hear them. (*Manitoba Free Press*, 27 September 1890.)

For an admission fee of 50 cents, the audience heard a program comprised chiefly of transcriptions of orchestral or operatic works by familiar composers:

Fantasia in F Minor	Mozart
Clock Movement	Haydn
Gavotte, Mignon	Thomas
Marche nuptiale	Guilmant
Borree	Handel
Overture, Die Freischütz	Weber
Prelude and Fugue	Bach
Larghetto, Concerto in C	Beethoven
Allegretto, March in C	Lefébure-Wély
Shadow Air, Dinorah	Meyerbeer
Overture, William Tell	Rossini

In a retrospective account of this event, one critic chose to emphasize the orchestral capabilities of the organ:

> The organ in the Congregational church is one of only ordinary size, and the wonderful use to which it was put by Mr. Archer shews how a persistent study of the capabilities of the instrument will do in the hands of a thoroughly well educated musician. Where every piece was played in so masterly a style, it is almost impossible to select any one for special comment. The most generally popular, because the best known, of his selections were undoubtedly the overtures. That to "William Tell" was a fine conclusion to the concert. Throughout the instrumental colouring was as far as possible maintained and transferred from the orchestra to the organ. . . . In the overture to "Der Freischutz" the reproduction of Weber's weird and sonorous orchestration was marvellous, and this was probably (I write with hesitation) the best of an excellent recital. (*Winnipeg Town Talk*, 4 October 1890.)

Another critic agreed, but acknowledged the fine performance of original organ masterpieces and the general enthusiasm of the audience for the whole program:

> Mr. Archer's reputation is so firmly established in the musical world that all were quite prepared to find the numbers by Bach, Handel, Haydn, Mozart, Beethoven, Weber, Rossini, Guilmant, Meyerbeer and Wely equally well interpreted. If some were better rendered than others they were certainly the two overtures, although the Bach fugue was splendidly done and at a much more rapid tempo than most organists would dare attempt.
>
> The great master's programme was most delightfully varied; the dainty Wely Allegretto, the "Dinorah" song and the Thomas [and] Guilmant number[s] contrasting sharply with the great Bach and Mozart pieces and the overtures. The opening Fantasia is a wonderful composition, a masterpiece for the organ, and has never before been played in Winnipeg.
>
> Mr. Archer is probably the greatest musician who has ever visited our

city. Perhaps it is not generally known that he is an exquisite pianist.

It should be mentioned that judging from the applause that followed each selection he seemed to be thoroughly appreciated, and after the wonderful performance of the Freischutz overture, the delighted audience begged for more, and Mr. Archer very kindly played a beautiful march with a marvelous pedal passage. (*Manitoba Free Press*, 1 October 1890.)

Less than a year later Archer returned for another recital at Congregational Church. This time he was on a tour to Pacific coast cities, including an recital engagement at the Mormon Tabernacle in Salt Lake City, Utah. On 4 May 1891 he played these selections:

Toccata in D	Grison
Andante from E-flat Symphony	Romberg
Offertoire in D	Batiste
Larghetto - Clarionet solo	Mozart
Fugue in G	Krebs
March in E-flat	Lefébure-Wély
Allegro con moto, Quintette in A	Mendelssohn
Canzone	Guilmant
Scherzo Pastorale	Grieg
Gavotte	Handel
Overture to Semiramide	Rossini

One critic commented:

Mr. F. Archer's Organ Recital in the Congregational Church was the great musical event of this week. The first point which struck one was the admirable variety of the programme. Many and varied were the styles represented, though of organ music proper only the modern French school was represented. . . . The organ did not seem in such good condition as it was when Mr. Archer was here before. I suppose that must be ascribed to our trying climate. (*Winnipeg Town Talk*, 9 May 1891.)

The literary style of another review was reminiscent of the report of Archer's recital in the preceding year; therefore it was probably prepared by the same writer:

As a solo organist Mr. Archer is universally admitted to be one of the greatest of the present time. With rare intelligence he unites much tenderness and a fire which is all his own. Consequently he invariably carries his audience with him, as he did last night. His exquisite playing can be appreciated by those of his audience who are deficient in musical knowledge as well as by those who may be said to belong to the class of educated musicians. If his playing happens to be the first really great organ playing they have heard they do not need a professor to tell them where to applaud. If, on the contrary, they belong to the class mentioned, they applaud all the more, for well they know how rare this kind of work is. He has qualities as an interpreter of organ music possessed by but two or three artists in the world. . . . Those who had the pleasure of listening to the artist will not soon forget his delightful performance. The only regret is that Winnipeg had not an instrument more worthy of the gifted performer. (*Manitoba Free Press*, 5 May 1891.)

On 18 July 1898 the Canadian organist Frederick H. Torrington, then principal of the Toronto College of Music, organist at Metropolitan Methodist Church, Toronto, and an influential figure on the Toronto music scene, gave an organ recital at Grace Church; admission 25 cents. While more than half of his lengthy program of 18 pieces consisted of transcriptions, the remainder included mostly lightweight pieces for organ; the exception was Bach's *Toccata in F.*

The tradition of inviting internationally known organists to perform in Winnipeg churches began early in the 20th century. The New York organist William C. Carl was on his way to give an inaugural recital on an organ at Dawson City, Yukon, when he consented on short notice to give a performance at Grace Church on 17 July 1903. His program, shared with a female vocalist, included works by some contemporary and modern composers:

Symphony in D, 2 movements	Guilmant
Prelude and Fugue in D Major	Bach
Allegro, Organ Concerto No. 10	Handel
Carillons de Dunkerque	Calaerts
La vendredi	Tombelle

The event received a lengthy review that exhibited both wisdom and wit. Referring to Spitta's analysis of the Bach work, the writer commented that "to many musicians this number was one of the most satisfying that Mr. Carl rendered, his playing being clear and dignified throughout and affording the hearer the exquisite pleasure of intelligently grasping the texture of this marvellous piece of musical tapestry." As for the work by the French amateur composer, de la Tombelle, a programmatic piece that portrayed various natural cataclysms,

Probably very few present had the slightest idea of what an earthquake would be like, but the taste for music of this kind is ever present. . . . From an organist's standpoint these pieces are very useful as giving an opportunity to work up the less used portions of the organ, and to let air through various bunches of harsh sounding pipes, whose interiors are stagnant for want of use. Impressive as the effect doubtless was, probably no person in the audience was so profoundly moved at these imitations of nature's darker moods, as was the man at the bellows. ("Mr. W. C. Carl's Organ Recital," *Winnipeg Town Topics*, 18 June 1903.)

On one occasion Winnipeg was host to a visiting musician who was both a singer and an organist. Rosa d'Erina, described in an advance notice as "the distinguished Irish prima donna and organist," gave an organ and sacred song recital at St. Boniface Cathedral on 8 October 1905. She played these organ selections:

Overture to Masaniello	Auber
Elévation	Batiste
Fantasie pastorale	Lefébure-Wély
Overture, Zampa	Hérold
Organ Fantasie on Irish Airs and the old March of Brian Boru, composed A.D. 1014, on the eve of the battle of Ciotarf	
Grand March, Queen of Sheba	Gounod

The review on the following day only noted that "the organ in the Cathedral was somewhat out of tune in the reeds, but this defect was scarcely perceptible under the artist's masterly manipulation of the instrument." Two weeks later this organist gave a similar recital at Immaculate Conception Church, except for the substitution of the Overture to Alceste by Gluck for the opening selection, the elimination of the Hérold Overture, and the replacement of the Gounod March by Sousa's Imperial Edward March at the end.

Late in 1905 F. Melsom Gee (Fred M. Gee) declared that he intended to negotiate with some prominent American organists to come to Winnipeg for recitals. This initiative was the first of a series of successful ventures on his part in bringing musical artists to Winnipeg. Gee later became a full-time music impresario; in 1927 he established the highly successful Celebrity Concert Series that brought hundreds of internationally acclaimed performers to Winnipeg until it was discontinued in the late 1960s, some 20 years after Gee's death.

Gee brought the American organist Arthur Dunham to Winnipeg on 18 October 1906, the performer's second visit to the city in the year (he had played a belated opening recital at Zion Methodist Church in January). The advance notice of Dunham's appearance mentioned a testimonial from Charles-Marie Widor: "I am able to conscientiously say of this young organist that he is an artist with a very promising future. He is very intelligent and very musicianly. He has superb technique on the organ and a profound respect for the best in art." Dunham's portion of a concert given at Knox Presbyterian Church consisted of:

Allegro and Vivace, Organ Symphony No. 6	Widor
Pastorale in G	Dunham
Prelude and Fugue in D Major	Bach
Evening Song	Bossi
Elegy	Coleridge-Taylor
Fantasy on Old English Airs	Best

Melodie in F	Rachmaninoff
Marche nuptiale	Guilmant
Funeral March and	
Seraphic Song	Guilmant
Grand Chorus in G Minor	Hollins

The review of his recital on the new three-manual Casavant organ was enthusiastic:

> Organ recitals are usually regarded as rather tedious and probably because of that [others] were called upon to participate. . . . Mr. Dunham did such wonderful things with the unlimited source of melody at his command that his large audience was lost in rapture. . . . His manipulation of the stops, pedals, and keyboard proved him to be a technician of rare training and ability, while his readings of the various scores were those of an artist of lofty mind and aspirations. (*Winnipeg Town Topics*, 20 October 1906.)

Another reviewer's report of the same recital was equally euphoric, describing Dunham's performance as "a revelation in the art with which this very skillful executant is endowed to the fingertips. It was a great performance, and one that must have waked to ecstasy every dormant craving of musical expiration." The reaction of the audience was such that Dunham offered two "encores" in the midst of the scheduled program: a *Minuet* by Boccherini and the *Pomp and Circumstance March* by Elgar. Moreover, the reviewer concluded, "although the concert was prolonged until a late hour, he had to doff his overcoat when on the point of leaving, and repeat the Minuet to a goodly company who insisted on remaining behind." (*Manitoba Free Press*, 19 October 1906.)

The most famous of touring recitalists to visit Winnipeg in the early years was the expatriate English organist Edwin H. Lemare (1865-1934). He was born in the Isle of Wight and was awarded a scholarship to the Royal Academy of Music in 1878. While there, his talent attracted the attention of the noted English organist William T. Best. At the age of 19 his exciting organ recitals at the International Inventions Exhibition made front-page news in London newspapers. The termination of his appointment at fashionable St. Margaret's Westminster Church following altercations with the church authorities marked the beginning of his touring career. Lemare left England late in December 1899 and played his first North American recital in New York on New Year's Day 1901 to the enthusiastic acclaim of critics who compared him favourably with the organist Guilmant and the pianist Paderewski. He was often thought of as an American, because of his appointment in 1902 as organist at the Carnegie Institute, Pittsburgh, and posts as city organist in San Francisco and several other cities, following extensive tours in the United States, in Canada, and in Australia after 1900. At the height of his popularity, this showman and superstar of the organ played to capacity audiences throughout the world. Lemare was particularly skillful in transcribing orchestral compositions for the organ and in improvising, and his technical facility in playing legitimate organ compositions was also highly praised. Some of his performances on a player organ illustrate his mastery of the instrument. Although he was highly regarded as a master of the orchestral style of organ playing in his day, when it fell from fashion, so did Lemare's reputation. Recent reassessments, however, have recognized his musical accomplishments. Some of his own works required a high level of technical virtuosity to perform. Of all his compositions, the *Andantino in D-flat* (later popularized in the song *Moonlight and Roses)* appeared frequently in his programs and in those of other organists. Lemare came to Winnipeg to give two recitals on the new Grace Methodist Church organ on 17 and 18 April 1908, and his appearance was the focus of great interest on the part of the general public, city organists, and music critics. As an advance announcement of his visit stated,

> The mere mention of this great artist's name requires no supplementary remarks for those who have heard of his wonderful ability as an organist. As to the brilliancy of execution and command of orchestral effects, all who have heard him seem to agree. (*Manitoba Free Press*, 11 April 1908.)

Lemare's first program consisted of:

Pomp and Circumstance March	Elgar
From the South	Lemare
Prelude and Fugue in G Minor	Bach
O Star of Eve, Tannhäuser	Wagner
The Ride of the Valkyries	Wagner
Carillon	Wheeldon
Marche funèbre et chant séraphique	Guilmant
Trumpet Overture	Mendelssohn

On the following evening he performed:

Prelude and Fugue in D Major	Bach
Curfew	Hersman
Arcadian Idylle	Lemare
Andantino in D-flat	Lemare
Sonata No. 6	Mendelssohn
Vorspiel, Parsifal	Wagner
Scherzo in F	Hoffmann
Improvisation on a given theme	
Concert Fantasia on the tune Hanover	Lemare

One critic wallowed in uninhibited hyperbole regarding the first recital:

> This magnificent organ recital . . . surely marked a red letter day in the city's musical history. It is beyond the capacity of any ordinary critic to do justice

to the gorgeous display of his marvellous technique and his wonderful command of the magnificent instrument at his disposal. Certainly no one who followed him in any single number of his carefully compiled analytical programme will have the temerity to suggest that it has been surpassed by anything of the kind on this continent at all events. (*Manitoba Free Press*, 18 April 1908.)

However, another columnist offered a more thoughtful analysis of Lemare's playing and compositions:

And I have this to say—that in our own city and among our own organists—there are men of talent and musical ability who, with the same opportunities and environments, would command as much applause as some of our visiting artists. But, of course, being local musicians they are supposed to possess only very ordinary ability. . . .

To revert to Lemare, I wish to say that barring the unfairness of the kind of eulogism used, I can endorse most of what the critics have said as to his superb mastery of the king of instruments, and yet after Good Friday's performance, I was just a little bit disappointed. . . . I compare him with concert organists of his own class. . . .

Not that I was disappointed in Mr. Lemare's playing—far from it. His technique is brilliant and his complete mastery of the organ self-evident—just a little too self evident, I thought—and whether it was my own fault or not I seemed to be unable to forget the performer in the higher contemplation of the performer's beautiful music.

I make one exception. In Mr. Lemare's own works I was able for a brief period to forget the player in mental enjoyment of his delightful compositions. (P. B. C. Turner, "Lemare Among the Organists," *Winnipeg Town Topics*, 25 April 1908.)

The point of the critic's disappointment apparently was Lemare's extroverted stage personality, a trait he was seen to share with his great American contemporary Clarence Eddy, who had performed in the city several years earlier. This characteristic was absent in the English concert organist Frederic Archer, another visitor to Winnipeg, who exhibited "complete abandonment of conscious personality while the spell of the music was on him." In the writer's opinion, Archer's performance was characterized by more constructive originality and greater interpretive depth, qualities of performance that he thought lacking in both Eddy and Lemare.

Another critic, "The Strolling Musician," thought that the strongest item on Lemare's program was Mendelssohn's *Sonata*, but with respect to Lemare's improvisations and compositions there were certain misgivings:

Lemare, in his extemporization, gave us a good many bars of commonplace chordal pizzicatos, which on the pianoforte might be termed vamping; this however, was followed by some artistic variations and modulations including a fugal movement in the pedals.

When playing his "Andantino in D Flat" Lemare did not give the stac-
cato movement as marked, but played it in a somewhat legato style. This is
a sweet little piece and very useful. In fact all Lemare's compositions are
more or less idealistic dreams with fancy coloring. But his transcriptions of
other composers' works never fail to make them better than they really are.
In short, Lemare has a wonderful faculty for interpreting music. ("Lemare at
Grace Church," *Winnipeg Town Topics*, 25 April 1908.)

Lynnwood Farnam (1885-1930) was a Canadian organist who became a
legend in his own time. Born and trained in Montréal, he held several church
positions there and taught at the McGill Conservatorium until accepting a post
at a Boston church in 1913. The story is that he impressed the audition committee by presenting the members with a list of 200 pieces he had committed
to memory, stating that he was willing to perform any of them. He was hired
immediately. After the war he was organist-choirmaster at a prominent New
York church. By 1920 he had given 500 organ recitals. At the time of his death
at the age of 45, he was Head of the organ department at the Curtis Institute
of Music, Philadelphia. His pupils included a number of prominent Canadian
and American organists. Although he did no improvising and composed only
one piece for organ, he was one of the great interpreters of his time, introducing audiences on the North American continent and in Europe to contemporary organ music, particularly that of French and American composers.

In the spring of 1905, during a visit to some friends in Winnipeg, he played
on the organs at Grace, St. Andrew's, and Augustine churches, but these were
not public recitals. The report of Farnam's visit remarked that although he was
only 20 years old at the time, if he fulfilled his present promise he would some
day be one of the world's foremost organists. Farnam returned to Winnipeg again
in 1908 and 1909 to play recitals on the Karn organ at Augustine Presbyterian
Church. On the last of these, on 13 September 1909, he presented these selections:

Toccata in A-flat	Hesse
Romance in D-flat	Lemare
March No. 4, Pomp	
and Circumstance	Elgar
Cantabile in B Minor	Loret
Toccata and Fugue in E Major	Bach
Finale, Symphony No. 2	Widor
Andante cantabile, Symphony No. 4	Widor
Scherzo, Symphony No. 4	Widor
Allegro, Symphony No. 6	Widor

The ensuing review was warmly appreciative in a general way:

The audience, comprising practically all the professional organists of the
city, and the higher musical element, gave the brilliant performer a hearty

welcome, and the enthusiasm over the wonderful technique and musicianship were manifested again and again. . . .

The whole recital was from memory and executed without apparent effort, a feat seldom, if ever, attempted by the great organ geniuses of any
country. (*Manitoba Free Press*, 14 September 1909.)

The performances of all visiting recitalists did not receive uncritical praise.
The energetic and influential Canadian organist William H. Hewlett (1873-
1940), heralded as "one of the most brilliant players of Western Canada,"
came to Winnipeg from Hamilton, Ontario, on a visit in his capacity as an
adjudicator and examiner. A thoroughly experienced organist and one of the
co-directors of the Royal Hamilton Conservatory of Music in 1907, he was a
respected organ recitalist and an expert on church-organ installation. Nevertheless, his recital at Broadway Methodist Church on 21 June 1909, according to the reviewer, was technically flawed, and his choice of music was thought
to be condescending. Perhaps the critic was beginning to tire of noisy transcriptions of orchestral works:

[The Tempest in the Alps (Breitenbach), the Battle of Waterloo, and the
Battle March of Delphi] appeal to the popular imagination but they are, I
fancy, hardly the kind which a thoughtful educationalist would place before
his students as worthy of serious study, and their value upon a programme of
this nature is to be questioned. . . . The organ arrangement of the hackneyed
"Tannhauser March" and "William Tell" overture gave rather an imperfect
conception of their true orchestral tone color, and some of the lighter numbers were such as may be heard any Sunday in a dozen churches of this city.
. . . We expected a programme of scholarly works of which there is such a
vast amount of good material at the concert organist's disposal; and we expected clean, authoritative readings of them. (*Winnipeg Town Topics*, 26 June
1909.)

Gatty Sellars, the solo organist at Queen's Hall, London, who had also given
concerts at the Crystal Palace Music Festival, visited Winnipeg in 1911, accompanied by William Short, the King's Trumpeter. Sellars was condemned
in print for promoting his own compositions too vigorously. His recital at Grace
Methodist Church on 15 November 1911 consisted of these pieces:

Concert Toccata in C	Purcell J. Mansfield
Repose	Sellars
Cradle Song	Sellars
Allegro appassionata, Sonata No. 5	Guilmant
Aubade	Ernest Halvez
A Sunset Melody	Charles Vincent
Tone Poem: The Church Triumphant	Sellars
Toccata in F Minor	Bach
Introduction to Act 3, Lohengrin	Wagner

At *Twilight*	Sellars
Cantilène rustique	Sellars
Carnival Overture	Sellars
Descriptive Pieces:	
La Garde, Storm at Sea	Sellars

Local critics had some reservations about with the program and Sellars' interpretative style:

> There is one thing in the playing of Mr. Sellars that is frequently disconcerting to those who like to hear a pronounced rhythm: he is inclined to take capricious liberties with the time. This was particularly apparent in the "Lohengrin" selection, where many phrases were so condensed as almost to give the impression that some notes were dropped out. Not that his feeling for rhythm is at fault, for many pieces were played in a simple, straightforward, rhythmical manner, showing no trace of capriciousness, hence the charge must be brought against his interpretation. In other respects, there was little to criticize adversely.
>
> In praise of Mr. Sellars it may be said that he understands most thoroughly the resources of his instrument and shows great skill in using them. His playing of his "Storm at Sea" must have been a revelation to everybody in the audience. It was absolutely sensational. The organist seemed transformed into a magician, producing rolling thunder, dashing water, roaring and shrieking winds—all the features of a terrible storm—with appalling realism. Of course such things lie outside the sphere of pure music, but they are exceedingly effective. ("Gatty Recital," *Manitoba Free Press*, 16 November 1911.)

Another critic was less forgiving with regard to the frequency of Sellars' own compositions on the program: "Mr. Sellars cannot be called a great organist, and his compositions—of which he played no less than ten out of the sixteen numbers given—are not what one would stamp as standard." (*Winnipeg Town Topics*, 18 November 1911.)

Sellars made another appearance in Winnipeg about a year later, when he played several recitals at St. Andrew's Presbyterian Church. The first, on 2 October 1912, was poorly attended, probably due to insufficient advertising. In a review of this concert two selections of a programmatic nature, one of them composed by the performer, were singled out for special mention:

> After the rendering of such numbers as Rubenstein's "Russian Patrol," there remains no doubt about Mr. Sellars' exceptional mastery of the resources of his instrument. Quite wonderful are his imitations of the marching and music of a regiment of soldiers, approaching, passing and receding. Even more realistic was his imitation of the sounds of a violent thunderstorm. Mr. Sellars has a special aptitude for such things and they appeal forcibly to the many people who are fond of the sensational in music. . . . His own compositions,

of which he played several, reveal a gift of melody and a knowledge of effective registration. ("Gatty Sellars' Recital," *Manitoba Free Press*, 3 October 1912.)

A few days later he played two recitals, one in the afternoon and the other in the evening, on 7 October 1912. Now another critic abhorred the intrusion of the highly programmatic piece, "Storm at Sea," which Sellars played again on this occasion: "The imitation of a storm, however clever, was too realistic and sensational to be classed with good music. If Mr. Sellars intended to play down to the people, he succeeded admirably." (*Winnipeg Town Topics*, 12 October 1912.)

The only visiting recitalist of the following year was Henry Woodruff of Minneapolis, who played at Knox Presbyterian Church on 1 January 1913. His program consisted of these selections:

Suite gothique	Boëllmann
Andante cantabile	Widor
Daybreak, Peer Gynt Suite	Grieg
Concert Overture in F	Faulkes
Processional, Lohengrin	Wagner
Berceuse	Delbruck
Prelude in F	Guilmant
Thème religieuse	Thome, arr. Guilmant
Fanfare	Lemmens
Marche brilliante	Lefébure-Wély

The critic's reaction was a qualified one, describing the Lemmens piece "too trite to have had a place in a serious organ recital," and "as there was no organ composition by Bach, Mendelssohn, Rheinberger, or even Smart, we had little opportunity of judging his ability in pedal work." (*Winnipeg Town Topics*, 7 January 1913.)

The opening recital of the following year was by Arthur Dunham, organist of Sinai Temple, Chicago, who returned to Winnipeg after an interval of seven years. He played this program at Knox Presbyterian Church on New Year's Night, 1 January 1914:

Suite gothique	Boëllmann
Romanza in D	Dunham
Prelude and Fugue in G Major	Bach
Elévation in E-flat	Rousseau
Scherzo in D	Rousseau
Fanfare, Concert Etude	Shelley
Prayer and Cradle Song	Guilmant
Rhapsody on Catalan Airs	Gigout
Finale, Symphony No. 5	Widor

The event was not only musically successful, but also socially fashionable:

> Arthur Dunham, an organist of Chicago, gave a recital in Knox church last evening under the distinguished patronage of Sir Daniel and Lady McMillan, Sir William and Lady Whyte, and Sir Hugh John and Lady MacDonald. A good-sized audience was present and was richly rewarded; for Mr. Dunham is a soul-satisfying organist and he had a delightful programme. He has a remarkably clear technique, a fine sense of rhythm, and a thorough appreciation of extensively varied styles of music. His interpretation of every number was marked by admirable taste. One of them was a beautiful composition of his own, a "Romanza in D," which so pleased the audience that he had to add Boccherini's Minuet as an encore. There were continual demands for encores, and his responses were very generous. (*Manitoba Free Press*, 2 January 1914.)

The next performance by a visiting recitalist was given by Albert D. Jordan, London, Ontario, who had served as organist at the Panama-Pacific Exposition in San Francisco. The advance notice informed the public that "Mr. Jordan scorns the dry-as-dust organ literature and as a programme-builder has few equals." His recital at Westminster Presbyterian Church on 29 June 1915, under the auspices of the Ladies' Aid for their Red Cross work, consisted of these pieces:

Concert Overture in D Minor	Hollins
Melodie in E	Rachmaninoff
Ungarische tanz	Brahms
Fantasie in F Minor	Mozart
La cygne	Saint-Saëns
Badinage	Victor Herbert
Andante cantabile	Widor
Toccata in F Major	Widor
Elégie	Massenet
Aragonaise, Le Cid	Massenet
Overture, Carnaval	Dvorak

The mix of tuneful organ compositions and popular transcriptions was well received by the audience, as the reviewer noted:

> His programme as played last night, constituted a brilliant achievement not only from a technical standpoint, but also from the viewpoint of skill in registration.
>
> Few organists are able to present an entire programme so as to hold the interest of an audience till the end. This Mr. Jordan succeeded in doing, and it was surely a tribute not only to his ability as a player of high rank, but as a recitalist who knows what to give the public. His other encore numbers were Nevin's "Love Song" and Schubert's "Serenade." (*Manitoba Press Press*, 30 June 1915.)

A few years later the Men's Musical Club of Winnipeg brought Herbert A. Fricker (1868-1943) to the city to play at Westminster Church. Fricker acquired his early musical training while a chorister, and later assistant organist, at Canterbury Cathedral, England. In London he studied with Frederick Bridge and Edwin H. Lemare, followed by a career as city organist, symphony orchestra conductor, and choirmaster in Leeds. Fricker came to Canada in 1917 to become conductor of the Toronto Mendelssohn Choir, a position he held until 1942. His frequent cross-border musical acitivities began immediately with his choir's program with the Philadelphia Symphony Orchestra under Leopold Stokowski. He was also an active organ recitalist—he composed several pieces for the instrument, along with choral works—and served as president of the Canadian College of Organists in 1925-26. His program on 28 May 1919 consisted of these selections:

Concert Overture in C Minor	Fricker
The Question and The Answer	Wolstenholme
Prelude and Fugue in D Major	Bach
Fantasia on the Hymn	
Tune Hanover	Lemare
Ave Maria	Schubert
Entr'acte in G Major	Schubert
Military March in D	Schubert
Largo and Allegro in F Major	Handel
Gavotte, Mignon	Thomas
Tone Poem, Finlandia	Sibelius

The recital was reviewed by Ralph Horner, a prominent Winnipeg musician and educator. He was more forgiving about the inclusion of transcriptions on this program than of the practice of orchestral transcriptions generally, which he had condemned in print several years earlier:

> The programme last evening was so varied in character that it served to show the famous artist at his best. It was literally a feast of good things, which not only gave keen pleasure to the audience. but which was also a valuable lesson to all who try to play the "king of instruments."
>
> The Concert Overture in C Minor, composed by the organist himself, is a good example of his talent for composition, and it was evidently written to show his powers as a performer. It is orthodox in form and charming in style, and the general effect is enhanced by the clever treatment of the subjects. The pedal work was excellent and the registration showed great taste. . . . His last number was his own arrangement of "Finlandia," a tone poem by Sibelius. Thanks to him, it is one of the few orchestral pieces which has been effectively transferred to the organ. The applause was so great at the end of this that he came back and delighted everyone with Mendelssohn's "Cornelius" march. ("Noted Organist at Westminster," *Manitoba Free Press*, 29 May 1918.)

A year later one Canadian and one international performer came to Winnipeg in the same week in May 1919. The Canadian was the man who eventually would become recognized as the country's elder musical statesman, Ernest MacMillan (1893-1973). Apart from periods of time spent in England completing work for his FRCO diploma and a music degree at Oxford, in France studying piano, and in Germany as a prisoner of war for four years, he remained in Toronto from 1919 onward, teaching organ and piano. His lecture-recital appearances often consisted of an organ recital and recollections of his activities during the period of his detention in Germany, when he conducted camp musicals and worked on various compositions. MacMillan played a full program at Westminster Presbyterian Church on 13 May 1919:

Triumphal March	Hollins
Barcarolle, Piano Concerto No. 4	Sterndale Bennett
Fantasia and Fugue	Bach
The Question and The Answer	Wolstenholme
A Song of Sunshine	Hollins
Largo, New World Symphony	Dvorak
Allegro cantabile	Widor
Toccata, Symphony No. 5	Widor

A few days later the English organist T. Tertius Noble (1867-1953), formerly organist of Ely Cathedral and York Minster, and now in charge of music at St. Thomas's Episcopal Church, New York, visited Winnipeg. He played this program at Grace Methodist Church on 16 May 1919, supported by the choir and a soloist:

Overture, Athalia	Handel
Two Preludes	Stanford
Chant solennel; Pastorale	Vodorinski
Andante in G Minor	Boëly
Elizabethan Idyll	Noble
Solemn Prelude, Gloria Domini	Noble
Finale	Noble

Trends in Repertoire

The content of organ recital programs over the years can be attributed to a variety of factors: the performers' backgrounds, training, musical interests, and technical abilities; reverence for musical tradition and the attraction of the new; the perceived musical preferences of audiences; and the tonal resources of the organs. In Winnipeg in the early 1900s there were only a few orchestras or instrumental groups that could provide public performances of musical masterpieces of the past or of contemporary works. Nevertheless, access to this realm of musical culture was broadened by the inclusion in organ recitals of many transcriptions of operatic, choral, or instrumental works by major composers. This practice, which was also evident in England and the United States, eventually attracted much criticism, but at the time it served the valuable function of providing the public with opportunities to hear works that otherwise would remain relatively unknown.

In the four decades preceding 1920, there were 111 known organ recitals, consisting of 733 selections in all. Slightly more than one-third of all the pieces performed were transcriptions of a wide range of works by the major composers of the 18th and 19th centuries. The most frequently performed pieces were derived from Wagner's operas and Handel's choral works, including the latter's ever-popular *Hallelujah Chorus* and *Largo*. Haydn was represented by arrangements of his symphonic and chamber works. Audiences also heard organ interpretations of marches by Gounod (*Marche militaire*), Mendelssohn (*War March of the Priests* from *Athalie*), and Chopin (*Funeral March*), along with arrangements of Grieg's *Peer Gynt Suite* and Dvorak's *New World Symphony*. Transcriptions of von Suppé's *Poet and Peasant Overture*, as well as of Beethoven's overtures and some of his piano pieces, were also presented. The frequency of performance of organ transcriptions of works by these and other composers during this period is given in Table 2.

Table 2

	Number	Percent
Wagner	27	11
Handel	24	10
Haydn	13	5
Gounod	11	4
Mendelssohn	10	4
Chopin	9	4
Grieg	9	4
Dvorak	8	3
Von Suppé	8	3
Beethoven	7	3

As for original works, Alexandre Guilmant's organ compositions were the most frequently played, led by his *Marche funèbre et chant séraphique*; the earliest recorded performance of his *Sonata in D Minor*, written in 1874, occurred in 1885. About the same time Bach's toccatas, preludes, and fugues began to be played often, but almost none of his chorale preludes; more than half of their performances were by several visiting recitalists. The first known performance of his *Toccata and Fugue in D Minor* was in 1883. Mendelssohn was first represented in 1885 by his *Sonata No. 1 in F Minor*, composed about forty years earlier. Pieces by Louis Lefébure-Wély, the fashionable Parisian organist who demonstrated instruments of the leading builder Cavaillé-Coll in the mid-1800s, rapidly became recital favourites; one of his works was played in the first known organ recital in Winnipeg in 1878, about ten years after its publication. However, the works of Charles-Marie Widor were not included in the programs of touring organists until 1905. Interest in the compositions of Edwin H. Lemare escalated following his recitals in Winnipeg in 1908, and local organists included many of his lighter works, such as the later-popularized *Andantino*, in their programs for many years. The compositions of Alfred Hollins, however, began to appear in the programs of both visiting and local players at least a decade before his visit to Winnipeg in 1926. The frequency of performance of original works for organ by these and other composers during this period is given in Table 3.

Table 3

	Number	Percent
Guilmant	52	11
Bach	35	7
Lemare	34	7
Widor	18	4
Batiste	16	3
Lemmens	16	3
Hollins	14	3
Lefébure-Wély	14	3
Mendessohn	14	3
Wolstenholme	14	3
Dubois	11	2
Boëllmann	10	2

Theatre Organs and Organists

Moving picture theatres were the chief form of popular entertainment in the cities and towns of Manitoba and elsewhere in the early years of the 20th century. For several decades the weekend editions of Winnipeg newspapers devoted several pages to reports on current films and previews of coming attractions, theatre by theatre. The larger movie houses also had resident vocal soloists, instrumentalists, and orchestras that gave brief concerts before screenings of motions pictures or during intermissions. Vaudeville acts and sometimes local military bands were featured in these events, too.

Theatre organs first were used to provide musical backgrounds to the dramatic scenes in silent movies. Sometimes these sonic backdrops were improvised spontaneously by the organist, sometimes they were adaptations of composed music. In some respects the theatre organ was a competitor of the orchestra, for the pipe ranks and stop lists of these organs mimicked orchestral instruments. They were also equipped with a variety of percussion devices, such as drums, traps, xylophones, bells, and chimes. Organ consoles were elaborately decorated structures, often of coloured glass backlighted to silhouette the player. Sometimes they were mounted on hydraulically operated platforms that allowed the organist, seated at the console, to rise dramatically into the audience's view from beneath floor level, playing all the while.

A bizarre instrument called the "Fotoplayer" was installed in Winnipeg's Bijou Theatre in 1915. This automated music machine was probably a direct descendant of the "Orchestrion," which employed a barrel organ mechanism arranged to play flue-type organ pipes, ranks of reeds, and percussion devices with the aim of imitating the various instruments of the orchestra. Although the first Orchestrion-type instrument was conceived by Thomas Dallam and presented to the Sultan of Turkey in 1599, more recent varieties were demonstrated at Buckingham Palace and in London, England, in the summer of 1851. Successors to this device in the late 19th century were the Organette, sets of free reeds activated by an exhaust bellows and controlled by paper rolls or other means, and the "Pianola," a trade-name for one make of player-piano.

As for the "Fotoplayer," several models of these relatively inexpensive music machines were manufactured by The American Photo Player Company, New York, and installed in theatres throughout the United States and elsewhere, where they added to the public's enjoyment of silent films. This mechanical wonder included a pressurized reed organ section and perhaps several ranks of organ pipes, along with various sound effects, all of which could be played manually or by means of paper rolls. Some models had a device for shifting quickly from one roll to another to follow the mood changes of the film. The single keyboard was centred between two sound cabinets that housed the electric blower, wind chests, and special effects devices. It was billed as "The Ninth Wonder of the World, The Musical Masterpiece that Expresses the Griefs, Joys, and Triumphs of the Artists; that Supplies the Unspoken Words in the Pictures—Magnificent Orchestral and Organ Tones." The arrival of this sound machine in Winnipeg, said to be the only one of its kind in the country, was described in a daily newspaper:

> The instrument has many novel features, the chief of which is the inclusion in its capabilities of the reproduction of all "picture effects" such as the rushing of water, the screech of the wind, the firing of pistoles, the chiming of bells, the beating of drums, etc. The operator just sits at the keyboard and presses the buttons directing these effects as he thinks best. . . . A Fotoplayer takes the ordinary piano-player 88 note rolls, and there is a large selection to choose from. It also includes all the instruments in a full orchestra. (*Manitoba Free Press*, 20 November 1915.)

The Dominion Theatre in Winnipeg introduced an innovation intended to provide its patrons with advance details of the music they would hear accompanying the motion picture: printed programs. Perhaps this move was inspired by the usual practice of providing advance programs of church organ recitals. These were the selections the organist, W. Fish, played during the screening of *Temptation*, starring Geraldine Farrar (a cellist also was featured on the program):

La Traviata, Fantasia	Verdi
Entr'acte	Helmasbor
Adieu - Mélodie	Karganoff
Meditation	G. Drumm
Largo, New World Symphony	Dvorak
Romance	Tschaikowsky
Musical Gems	Tschaikowsky
Danse mélodique - Intermezzo	L. L. Loth
Cupid's Dart - Novelette	L. Donneberg

("Innovation at the Dominion," *Manitoba Free Press*, 12 May 1917.)

Organ recitals of current popular music and transcriptions of familiar light classics took on an independent life of their own with the advent of talking pictures. These performances, like those of theatre orchestras, were additional attractions to the current motion picture being shown, and often featured special music for the Christmas season, for example. It is interesting to note that theatre organists endeavoured to maintain high standards in their selections of music, whether to accompany the motion picture or for short recitals during intermissions:

> Modern theatres have for some time been equipped with splendid pipe organs. Good orchestras have been introduced, and are now a recognized feature. The music is one of the chief attractions.
>
> One organist who plays at a large picture house said recently, "besides recital programmes and special organ solos, I gave request numbers to get the musical pulse of our audiences. Only once have I received a request for ragtime or any real cheap piece. On one occasion I had a request for a Bach Fugue." ("Music," *Manitoba Free Press*, 23 March 1918.)

Some theatre organists earned a living out of this activity, while others occupied posts as church organists at the same time. Their careers, involving moves from one theatre to another, or presiding at the opening of a new instrument, were usually reported in the entertainment sections of the newspapers, perhaps in the belief that their fans would want to follow them from theatre to theatre.

The installation of a new organ in the Province Theatre in Winnipeg in September 1917 created a high level of interest. The three-manual, electric-action instrument (claimed to be the only organ in Winnipeg so equipped), containing 2,000 pipes, was supplied by the Toronto organ builder C. Franklin Legge. The $20,000 instrument also had a self-playing mechanism that allowed the instrument to perform on its own in the absence of a trained organist. The organ was formally opened on 10 September by George E. Metcalfe, "The Organist Supreme" from the Pacific Coast, who amused the theatre customers with a steady stream of improvisations on the "Wonder Organ" throughout the afternoon and evening. At the time, the theatre was featuring a hand-coloured film, *Mayblossom*, made in France by Astra-Pathé. Eventually the theatre appointed a regular organist, and its newspaper advertisements highlighted "Dolman at the Organ."

The theatre organist Walter Dolman had a career as a church organist before and after his experience in Winnipeg cinemas. Born in England in 1875, he became a church organist in Burton-on-Trent around the age of 14. After coming to Canada in 1903, he lived in Toronto and worked for a while with F. H. Torrington, principal of the Conservatory of Music, then moved to Chatham, Ontario. For a short time he was a church and theatre organist in Detroit, Michigan, before coming to Winnipeg around 1918 to play at the Province Theatre, then at the College, Dominion, National, and Starland theatres. At the Starland in 1923, he inaugurated a regular program of community singing on Friday nights. In 1925 he moved to Brandon, Manitoba, to play at the Strand Theatre. The appointment was short-lived; by the year's end Dolman was back in Winnipeg. This time he was at the Capitol Theatre, where he offered a daily series of "twilight recitals" in the late afternoon and early evening: the program included a mix of music by modern masters, older composers, and popular numbers in vogue with the younger set. Occasionally he served as substitute organist at St. Matthew's Anglican Church. In 1928 he moved to Kenora, Ontario, to become organist at Knox Church in that town, where he remained until his death in 1947.

The performances by theatre organists ordinarily were not within the scope of music critics, with some exceptions:

> The beautiful Christmas music rendered on the Province organ this week by Prof. Walter Dolman is one of the most enjoyable features of the season at this theatre. It adds greatly to the success of the programme. Prof. Dolman plays these selections with deepest sympathy. (*Manitoba Free Press*, 27 December 1919.)

A year after the installation of the Province Theatre organ, the question of the influence of the theatre organ generally on the development of an appreciation for mainstream organ music was the subject of a borrowed newspaper editorial. The fear that "bad" music would drive out "good" was unfounded, according to this writer:

The feeling among musicians that the organ performances given in "movie" shows lower the public taste for dignified music seems to be increasing. In regard to the general influence of "movie" organ music a writer in Musical Opinion says: "When the instrument began to take a prominent part in the 'movies,' some of us thought that people, having the organ thus brought to their ears night after night, would esteem it more highly. But this is not likely to provide an exception to the rule that 'familiarity breeds contempt.' We are now beginning to see that the old aloof position of the organ was not a bad thing. True, its public was limited, but if it spoke to comparatively few, the few were devotees. It is not likely to gain new ones from its association with Mr. Chaplin." (*Manitoba Free Press,* 21 September 1918.)

It is astonishing the number of organists we have in this country who are cripples. About one-third of this class of musicians are affected, and the remarkable thing about their particular disease is that it affects both male and female alike. The congregations they play for are more to be pitied than the organist, for he or she has become accustomed to have only the use of one leg. The reader of this may not believe that the organist he listens to every Sunday has only one leg. A sure guide is to listen to the pedaling done next Sunday and afterward go around to other churches, and he will be surprised to find how few organists have a leg attached to the right side of their bodies. (*Winnipeg Town Topics,* 25 July 1903.)

Fair Organist ~ "I am sorry you had to give off blowing for us, Giles."

Giles~ "Yes, Miss; the organ don't sound what it did, do it? Jim, the new blower, be a very good chap, but 'e ain't got no music in 'im. Now, we did used to give 'em summat worth 'earin', didn't we, Miss?"

(*Winnipeg Town Topics,* 28 August 1909.)

An organist says: "My acquaintance with girls and boys as organ pupils is that the former will seat themselves on the bench, look up helplessly and ask 'what stops shall I use?' The boys will promptly pull out all the stops and keep them out until remonstrated with." ("Crotchets," *Manitoba Free Press,* 12 January 1918.)

The Middle Years: *1920-1939*

THE FREQUENCY OF ORGAN INSTALLATIONS in the 1920s almost matched that of each of the preceding two decades, but these events were seldom reported in the newspapers because most organ dedications were part of regular church services, and visiting recitalists were not recruited to perform on these occasions. During the 1930s, however, the number of installations was less than one-half of the preceding decade. Throughout the whole period the great majority of the installations were new instruments, with only a few relocations. The founding of the Winnipeg Centre of the Canadian College of Organists in 1923 was a highly significant event. This was a response to trends that had been developing for some time, such as the arrival in the city of trained organists with their imported musical culture, and the established tradition of visiting recitalists from England, Europe, the United States, and elsewhere in Canada. This coherent group of city musicians now assumed a leading role in the affairs of the organ and church music that would continue throughout succeeding years. In the secular domain, although theatre organs were still active in providing accompaniments to the silent movies, this role was eclipsed by the introduction of sound- and voice-synchronized motion pictures around 1930. A chronological summary of organ installations during this period is given in an appendix: Organ Installations.

Knox Presbyterian Church, Portage la Prairie, 1923

The Karn organ installed in Knox Church in 1904 was destroyed in a tornado that struck the area in the early hours of 23 June 1922. On the same afternoon church officials held a meeting and decided to set about repairing the damage immediately, including replacing the organ. Letters were written to several firms, and estimates and specifications were received. Casavant Frères was awarded the contract for a two-manual, 20-stop instrument at a price of $6,800. Casavant's suggested specifications were reviewed by the church organist and Arnold Dann, one of Winnipeg's leading organists, who recommended some changes that Casavant agreed to include in the contract. At the same time, it was decided to install the organ as a war memorial, thus eliminating the sales tax on the organ.

Almost immediately a problem arose concerning the matter of payment for the organ, due to a shortage of money caused by poor agricultural conditions in the area. The secretary of the Board of Management explained the situation in a letter to the manufacturers:

> In regard to the note which became due on December 1st, 1929 I have been informed that it was quite a struggle for our congregation to meet same on account of the crop conditions which existed here last year.
>
> In order that you might have some idea of the conditions here I beg to advise you that our City is situate in the midst of a farming district and our citizens depend almost entirely on the crops. . . .
>
> During the past eight years we have had very lean years and this year when we had a fair crop the market was so low that many of our farmers did not receive enough from the sale of their grain to pay the costs of harvesting. The result is that it has affected the citizens of our City and the members of our congregation. In fact it would appear that this will be the hardest Fall which our City has ever had and of course it also affects the members of our congregation.
>
> Consequently we may be unable to meet the note due your Company on December 1st next. In the event that we are unable to pay the note on due date would you grant an extension? (Letter from G. R. Shaver to Casavant Frères, 27 October, 1930.)

The reply from Casavant was immediate and affirmative:

> In regard to the note that will come to maturity on December 1st, next, we are pleased to say that if you are not able to settle the note on due date, we will grant you an extension of time of six months, for the payment of the balance, or the total amount of the note. (Letter from Casavant Frères to G. R. Shaver, 3 November 1930.)

The church was successful in paying off the note by the end of December, and new organ was dedicated on 25 March 1923:

> A ceremony of a most impressive nature was performed yesterday morning in Knox Presbyterian Church when the magnificent new organ was dedicated to the memory of the members of that congregation who gave their lives in the Great War for the honor and freedom of their country. . . .

> In the evening the Church was again filled and at the close of the service Arnold Dann, of Winnipeg, gave an organ recital of an hour's duration. It was a real musical treat, and he brought out the fine qualities of the new organ. (*Daily Graphic*, 26 March 1923.)

The new organ was indeed a community project, supported by a member of the congregation who financed the project for several months when the money for the payment was unavailable, and assisted by the women of the congregation whose untiring efforts helped to pay off the cost of the instrument.

Parish Church, Roman Catholic, Ste. Anne des Chênes, 1923

The installation of a new organ in a rural Manitoba town received greater recognition than a similar event in the city. A report of the opening of a new two-manual, 12-stop Casavant organ in the Parish Church in Ste. Anne, at a cost of $4,500, noted the Archbishop's reference to the religious significance of the event as well as the approval of the visiting organist:

> Le 26 juillet au soir, nous avons eu l'inauguration des orgues. Mgr l'Archevêque les a bénites. Sa Grandeur a donné le sermon de circonstance.
>
> "Chantez avec moi, disait le psalmiste, chantez un cantique nouveau. Et il appelait à son aide les instruments de musique: psaltérions, cithares, flûtes, hautbois, cymbales, trompettes. L'orgue est un merveilleux assemblage de tous les instruments. Il chante au Seigneur un cantique nouveau."
>
> "Mais la voix de l'homme est seule digne d'entonner le chant de gloire, parce qu'elle est unie à l'âme immortelle. L'orgue vient à son secours en la soutenant, en l'inspirant."
>
> "Dieu s'est fait homme pour chanter la gloire de son Père. Il s'est fait Eucharistie pour rester avec nous. Le lieu où il réside, c'est l'église. La foi les orne des plus riches productions de la nature. Mais il y manque une voix qui soit la voix de toutes les créatures. C'est l'orgue."
>
> En terminant, Sa Grandeur [a] remercié les paroissiens qui ont enrichi leur église d'un instrument si beau.
>
> M. Georges Dorval, organiste de la cathédrale, [a] nous donné ensuite le concert. Il a été magnifique. Une maîtresse de musique disait après le concert: "Voilà de la vraie musique; j'aurais volontiers écouté encore deux heures." Notre artiste a choisi ses morceaux avec goût. Il ne nous a pas seulement montré la puissance de l'instrument, mais aussi la douceur, la richesse, la variété de ses jeux, et l'heureux effet qu'on peut en tirer en les mélant avec goût. ("Ste-Anne des Chênes, Les orgues," *La Liberté*, 7 August 1923.)

First Federated Church of Unitarians, 1924

When the congregation of the Icelandic Unitarian Church, Winnipeg (its official name was the First Federated Church of Unitarians and Other Liberal

*First Federated Church of Unitarians,
Winnipeg.
Hook & Hastings, 1883, 2/11. Installed 1924.
Typical of a style of moderately priced, small
instruments manufactured by various builders in
the United States in the 1880s.*

Christians, acknowledging the amalgamation of three congregations) moved into its present building in the early 1920s, it obtained tenders for a new organ from two Canadian organ builders, Casavant Frères and Woodstock Pipe Organ Builders, in 1923, but both were rejected. However, with the assistance of a Unitarian Church near Boston, Massachusetts, a small instrument made by Hook & Hastings, Boston, was acquired from a Congregational Church in a Boston suburb, which had just purchased a larger Hook & Hastings instrument. The two-manual, 11-stop, tracker-action instrument was brought to Winnipeg and installed by Blanchard Bros., in 1924. The decorated pipes are typical of those produced by most manufacturers around that time.

GREAT		SWELL	
Open Diapason	8	Stopped Diapason	8
Stopped Diapason Bass	8	Unison Bass	8
Melodia	8	Viola	8
Dulciana	8	Flute	4
Octave	4	Oboe	8
		Tremulant	

PEDAL		Great to Pedal
Sub Bass	16	Swell to Pedal
		Swell to Great Unison
		Swell to Great at 8va
		Bellows Signal

The organ bellows were hand-pumped until 1950, when an electric blower was installed. Unfortunately, the hot dry air drawn from the boiler room where the blower was located caused deterioration of wooden components, and the organ is now barely playable, although the main structure is basically sound. The future of the organ is in question, following the purchase of the church building by another religious group in mid-1997.

The scribbling the bellows boys carved on the inner wooden parts of the organ during the slow parts of the service are of unusual historical interest. The bored pumpers, usually from seven to ten years of age, were responsible for copious graffiti on the inner structures, including some lines of poetry in French, Greek, and Latin. Other notations in English were of a mixed nature:

A.A. Terry '92 Came Oct 20, 1888 Left Jun 28, 1891
Razzle Dazzle, Razzle Dazzle
Sis Boomba
Burah Burah

---

92 92 Run Run Run
Paddy from Ireland
Paddy from Cork
There's a hole in your breeches
As big as New York

"Music hath charms to soothe the savage breast"
Franklin Lobleigh Newton

Seated one day at the organ
I was weary and ill at ease
And my fingers wandered idly
Over the noisy keys
I knew not what I was playing
Or what I was dreaming then
But I struck one chord of music
Like the sound of a great amen

H D Gilbert '94
Served as Pumper
July 5, 1891 - July 8, 1894
Requiescat in Peace
Drowned in the Connecticut River

The tradition of engraved inscriptions was maintained by a later generation:

Dec 14th 1924
This Pipe Organ was installed on the above date and first played
by Paul S. Dalman, Organist of the First Icelandic Federated
Church, Mrs. Engilbrad Dalman being the Soloist.

Winnipeg Organists Organize: The Canadian College of Organists

As early as 1899 the Manitoba Free Press carried a short report on the American Guild of Organists, which was seeking to institute improvements in the standing of organists and choirmasters, with particular reference to their annual contracts and recognition as officers of the church. The music column of this newspaper also printed similar items of interest to organists, such as the method of choosing an organist and the low pay of church musicians (in 1905 organists at the wealthiest Winnipeg churches received about $200 per year for 104 regular services, 52 rehearsals, and other events). In 1910 the paper published an account of the guidelines and membership requirements for the Canadian Guild of Organists, founded in Toronto in the preceding year. Although some Winnipeg organists attended the first National Convention of the Canadian Guild of Organists in 1911, there was no initiative to establish a branch in Winnipeg for over a decade, but some local organists maintained an active connection with the national organization from which they had received their diplomas. In 1918 Ralph Horner and Ernest E. Vinen were appointed local examiners by the Canadian Guild of Organists.

The background of the Canadian organization can be traced to the Royal College of Organists, founded in London, England, in 1864, and to the American Guild of Organists, founded in the United States in 1891. Many of the organists who came to Canada in the early years had received their accreditation from the RCO. The Canadian Guild of Organists was established in 1909, and the name was changed to the Canadian College of Organists in 1920 to bring it into line with the Royal College of Organists and perhaps to strengthen the British connection. At this time the CCO absorbed the Canadian members of the American Guild of Organists.

The formal establishment of a local branch of a guild designed to further the personal and professional development of local organists, as well as to promote the art of organ playing and choir training, was a product of the current conditions prevailing at the time. The second decade of the century was a peak period of organ installations in new Winnipeg churches. Moreover, there were a significant number of well-trained organists on hand to constitute a nucleus for such an organization. Further, the number of organ recitals increased in the early years of the third decade, more than doubling from one year to another. In 1920 more than 10 recitals were played by local organists; in 1921 there were nearly 20, all initiated by the players themselves without the benefit of a sponsoring or coordinating organization. The appearance of visiting recital-ists such as T. Tertius Noble, Joseph Bonnet, and Marcel Dupré in the early 1920s may have provided the stimulus to action. Therefore, the time was right for the emergence of an organization dedicated to the interests of organists and organ music generally.

Late in 1922 a newspaper item predicted that a local branch of the Cana-dian College of Organists would be formed in the following year. The initia-tive for this project was undertaken by the executive members of the Men's Musical Club of Winnipeg. A newspaper announcement invited all city or-ganists and choirmasters to meet on 19 May 1923 to hear about the objectives and activities of the Canadian College of Organists. Formal arrangements for establishing the Winnipeg Centre of the CCO followed.

The first officers of the new organization were Arthur H. Egerton, FRCO, chairman (1923-25); John J. Weatherseed, ARCO, secretary (1923); and Herbert J. Sadler, ACCO, treasurer (1923-25). Others who headed the Cen-tre in its early years included Burton L. Kurth (1925-27); Ronald W. Gibson, ACCO, (1927-29, 1936-37); Wilfred Layton, FRCO, ARCM, (1929-30); Filmer E. Hubble, ACCO, (1930-33, 1935-36); and H. Hugh Bancroft, FRCO, (1933-35); some of these people held other executive positions from time to time, as well. Other officers of the Centre during the same period included Douglas Clarke, Frank C. Colley, Norman A. Elwick (treasurer from 1928 for many years), Wallace H. Gillman, Stanley Hoban, Archibald W. Lee (secre-tary from 1926 for many years), and Hugh C. M. Ross.

The number of members was not large at the outset, yet this enthusiastic and dedicated group generated a high level of activity by sponsoring organ recitals by local and visiting players, by arranging special events designed for the improvement of church music generally, and by arranging program events involving interchanges with members of the clergy. Most of these people also were recitalists and participants in the programs they devised. In the first year, Hugh Ross and Arthur Egerton organized a hymn practice session, involving a massed choir drawn from several Winnipeg churches, to promote the use of fine hymn tunes unfamiliar to most church congregations. Another early ac-tivity of the Winnipeg Centre was the publication in 1926 of a Report on the Conditions of Church Music in Western Canada, which helped to raise the standards of church music.

Between 1926 and 1935 the Winnipeg Centre of the Canadian College of Organists arranged a series of Annual Church Music Conferences (in later years called the Annual Choral Evensong). These events included presentations on such topics as the hymn in public worship, choral demonstrations involving massed choirs from several churches, and organ recitals. The conference held in October 1926, for example, included a report on the state of church music in Canada, a demonstration of the church music of early English composers by a massed choir representing 10 Winnipeg churches, and a recital by three local organists of pieces based on religious themes. These conferences were attended by large numbers of people and received extensive newspaper coverage. This commentary was part of a longer report on the 6th Annual Church Music Conference held on 17 October 1932:

> For since church music is still the form of music in which probably the greatest number of people regularly take part in some way, it is indisputably very important that it should be as vital a thing as possible to them. The organists of the Winnipeg Centre, by arranging these services and by bringing [together] many local, often isolated practitioners of church music, and stimulating them afresh, are performing a valuable service in the cause of church music and of Christian worship in general. (*Winnipeg Free Press*, 18 October 1932.)

Prominent English church musicians visited Winnipeg occasionally, and sometimes they participated in the annual conferences. In 1932 Thomas Nicholson, Exeter Cathedral, talked to members on the conditions of church music in England; on 8 December 1934 Sydney H. Nicholson, founder of the English School of Church Music, addressed members and clergy; and Gordon Slater, organist and choirmaster of Lincoln Cathedral, who was in Winnipeg as a festival adjudicator, played a short organ recital at St. Matthew's Anglican Church following a members' luncheon meeting on 6 May 1935.

The topic of the revision of the hymn books of the United and Anglican churches was a recurrent issue in meetings of the Winnipeg Centre in the late 1920s. Members developed a conservative policy in adopting new tunes, and a liberal attitude towards discarding poor or "infamous" tunes (one of these, Antioch, "Joy to the World," remains untouched to this day, but other targeted tunes were removed). Sometimes these discussions touched on the content of offending hymns, condemning their sentimentalized religious doctrines. A melody edition of the hymnal was also recommended. ("Organists Suggest Changes in Drafted U.C. Hymn Book," *Manitoba Free Press*, 15 June 1929.)

The organists also urged that musicians, not clergy, should serve on hymn tune committees. This latter recommendation was not intended to exclude clergy from all activities of the Centre, for many events explicitly were designed to encourage dialogue and interaction between the clergy and church musicians. For example, members of the clergy were invited to attend the annual conferences on church music, and an annual dinner meeting involving both groups was a major occurrence for many years. Even so, none of the clergy ever became active members of the Centre, although the membership guidelines allowed for their participation.

One of the rituals in the life of a young organist was participation in the Manitoba Musical Competition Festival, held annually in the spring of each

year since 1918. Many of the adjudicators for these events were English organists, brought to Canada especially for similar festivals across the country.
While the number of entries in the organ performance category was never large,
the lack of any entries at all in 1929 was a matter for comment in the music
page of a daily newspaper. At least one of the reasons for the apparent apathy
was that the choice of test pieces—Franck's *Chorale in A Minor* in the senior
class and Vaughan Williams's *Prelude on Rhosymedre* in the intermediate class—
were thought to be too difficult for the average young organ student. Other
deterrents to the preparation of church organists included the scarcity of good
instruments, the difficulty of practicing in cold churches, wearing outdoor
clothing and fingerless gloves in all but three months of the year (heated tents
over the console were impractical), the low salary of church organists, and the
enticement of a position as a theatre organist. While this disinterest in the
Festival was a matter of regret, no immediate solutions were offered. ("No
Entries in the Organ Solo, String Quartette Classes," *Manitoba Free Press*,
27 April 1929.)

As part of their educational and self-improvement activities, members of
the Centre offered short workshops on topics of mutual interest to their colleagues. The series offered in 1931 included illustrated presentations on hymns,
voluntaries and service playing, anthems, vocal solos, and junior choirs. These
initiatives were continued throughout succeeding years.

Local Players

Of all the projects of the Winnipeg Centre of the Canadian College of Organists, perhaps the most significant to the general public was the annual program
of organ recitals, including a Lenten series, played by local organists. Most of
these recitals also included one or two selections by vocal soloists, choral ensembles, or other instrumental soloists or groups. In the peak years of their
popularity in the 1920s, as many as 20 recitals were sponsored during the course
of a year; on some occasions two or three organ recitals were offered on the
same day at different locations in the city. The obvious success of these events
prompted the Centre to recommend that Winnipeg's Celebrity Concert Series, managed by the local organist turned impresario, Fred M. Gee, should
include a visiting organist.

The leaders in the affairs of the Winnipeg Centre were also the busiest recitalists. Until he left Winnipeg in 1927, Arthur Egerton was the most active,
playing about 27 recitals in the preceding six-year period. Other frequent performers included Ronald W. Gibson (about 44 recitals in the 1920s and 1930s,
H. Hugh Bancroft (35 recitals between 1930 and 1936), Herbert J. Sadler (23
recitals in the 1920s and early 1930s), Filmer E. Hubble, Norman Elwick, and
Wilfred Layton, among others. Their recital programs included traditional

pieces from the organ repertoire as well as selections by late 19th- and early 20th-century composers. Transcriptions of orchestral or other instrumental works were much less prominent than in the programs of the earlier generation of organ players. An examination of recital programs offered in the late 1920s and early 1930s reveals a trend to acquaint the general public with more original organ music of all musical periods.

Ronald W. Gibson (1903-1993) came with his family from England to settle in Morden, Manitoba in 1913, later moving to Winnipeg in 1918. His formal organ studies were with Arnold Dann at Wesley College and with Arthur Egerton. He also played the viola and was assistant conductor of the Winnipeg String Orchestra and the Winnipeg Symphony Orchestra in the late 1920s and early 1930s. He served as organist-choirmaster in several of Winnipeg's larger churches (including Holy Trinity Anglican Church from 1934 to 1987), and also conducted the Winnipeg Choral and Orchestral Society during the same period. Returning from overseas service with the Royal Canadian Air Force in 1945, he founded and conducted the CBC String Orchestra in Winnipeg, then returned to England late in 1946 for further musical studies at Manchester University and the Royal Manchester College of Music. Between 1949 and 1963 he was director of the School of Music at The University of Manitoba, where he continued to teach until retiring in 1968, when he began composing works for voice, organ, and choir, chiefly for church use. He also wrote critical reviews of musical performances for the *Winnipeg Free Press* and contributed to *The Canada Music Book* in the 1970s. He played these selections in a program, shared with a vocal chorus, at Westminster United Church on 28 November 1926:

Prelude and Fugue in C Major	Bach
Two Settings of Blessed Jesu,	
We Are Here	Bach, Karg-Elert
On the Song of Symeon	Wood
Chorale: Arise My Soul,	
Adore They Maker	Bach
Adoration	Bingham
Harmonies du soir	Karg-Elert
Fugue	Honegger
Jesu, Joy of Man's Desiring	Bach
Variations and Fugue on	
Our Father Which Art	
in Heaven	Mendelssohn

Herbert J. Sadler (1894-1955), a native of Bristol, England, came with his parents to Winnipeg in 1911, where he continued his organ studies with several city organists, including Hugh Ross and Hugh Bancroft in the late 1920s. During the war he served in France with the Dalhousie University Unit of a

Canadian Stationary Hospital. Before leaving England, he studied organ with H. W. Frogley in London. He had been organist at several Winnipeg churches before filling the vacancy at Westminster Presbyterian Church in May 1920, following the retirement of Ernest Vinen; this became his lifelong post. He was responsible for the tonal design of the large Casavant organ in Westminster Church, which is still the location for most of the recitals by visiting organ virtuosos. Sadler was also a choral conductor, a frequent recitalist, and a teacher of many of Winnipeg's later generation of organists. He was joined by two violinists in his recital at Zion Church on 8 May 1927:

Prelude in F Minor	Bach
Minuet from Concerto in A	Handel
Adagio, Symphony No. 18	Haydn
Concerto for Two Violins,	
2nd Movement	Bach
Festival March	Best
Gethsemane	Malling
Cradle Song	Brahms

Wilfred Layton had been a choir boy at St. George's Chapel, Windsor, before entering the Royal College of Music where he studied with Sir Walter Parratt and Sir Frederick Bridge. His musical career included an appointment as organist and choirmaster at the Royal Naval College, Dartmouth, England, where both the Prince of Wales and the Duke of York sang in his choir when they were cadets at the College. He played at the Royal Albert Hall for the Royal Choral Society and was organist at St. Lawrence Jewry, the official church of the City of London, and also at the First Presbyterian Church in Belfast, Ireland. In 1927 he became the new organist-choirmaster at Augustine United Church, Winnipeg. He participated in the Lenten series of organ recitals at St. Luke's Anglican Church on 26 February 1928, contributing these organ selections in a program shared with a soprano soloist and a violinist:

Toccata and Fugue in D Minor	Bach
Andante and Variations,	
Op. 18, No. 5	Beethoven
Spring Song	Hollins
Adagio, Allegro con spirito	Bridge

Filmer E. Hubble (1904-1969) studied music with Hugh C. M. Ross after moving to Winnipeg from England in 1921, and became Ross' assistant at Holy Trinity Anglican Church. Later he served as organist-choirmaster at other Winnipeg churches, including 24 years at St. Stephen's-Broadway United Church, from 1945 to 1969. During his career he conducted a large number of local choral groups (including the Winnipeg Philharmonic Choir), some of which won awards in Canadian competitions, and directed musical productions at Winnipeg's Rainbow Stage. In addition to adjudicating musical festivals throughout the western provinces and lecturing at the Banff School of Fine Arts, 1958-64, he also taught organ playing to young musicians, sometimes without fees. In an Easter season program at Zion Church on 13 April 1930, shared with a contralto soloist, he played these pieces:

Introduction and Allegro, Op. 5	Harwood
Chorale Preludes:	Brahms
My Inmost Heart Doth Yearn	
O World, I E'en Must Leave Thee	
Good Friday Music, Act 3, Parsifal	Wagner
Chorale Preludes:	
O Man Thy Grievous Sin Bemoan	Bach
Rhosymedre	Vaughan Williams
Chorale in A Minor	Franck

H. Hugh Bancroft (1904-1988) moved to Canada from England in 1929 and became organist-choirmaster at St. Matthew's Anglican Church in the same year. His major post was at All Saints' Anglican Church, where he served during 1937-46 and 1953-57. In the interval he held cathedral positions in Vancouver and in Sydney, Australia. After leaving Winnipeg for the second time, he went briefly to Nassau, The Bahamas, finally settling in Edmonton. While in Winnipeg he was an active choir conductor, composer, organ recit- alist, and teacher of many young organists who later became prominent in the city and elsewhere. He played this program at Westminster United Church on 16 November 1930 as part of a series sponsored by the Winnipeg Chapter of the Canadian College of Organists:

Agitato, Sonata in D Minor	Rheinberger
Cantilène	Rheinberger
Toccatina	Yon
Prelude and Fugue in B Minor	Bach
Prelude on an Old Irish	
Church Melody	Stanford
On Sunset Point	Bancroft
Finale, Symphony No. 2	Widor

Although local organ recitals had not been reviewed in the local news- papers for many years, an enthusiastic member of the audience contributed this commentary:

Rhythmical playing, wonderful registration and a sense of fitness to all moods of the music were features of the organ recital by Hugh Bancroft. . . . Al- though every number on the programme was played in a clean and finished manner, special mention must be made of the Prelude and Fugue in B minor of J.S. Bach. This was real Bach playing and the well thought-out registrations made the performance a delight to any Bach enthusiast. . . . The recitalist's own composition, "On Sunset Point," showed musicianship and was delightfully played. ("Bach Enthusiast Finds Delight in Organist's Work," *Winnipeg Free Press*, 22 November 1930.)

Two years later, there was another contributed commentary following one of Bancroft's recitals that included Reubke's *Fugue on the 94th Psalm*. The impassioned short article, written in a manner characteristic of an earlier decade, expressed impatience with the level of public musical taste. The identity of the writer can be inferred from the credit-line initials; it was an organist-colleague, Archibald W. Lee:

> [Reubke] gave to us one of the greatest organ sonatas of all time. . . . Its performance was the work of an artist.
>
> When will people begin to appreciate the organ works of the great master, Johann Sebastian Bach, the immortal symphonies of Charles Marie Widor, the works of César Franck, Vierne, and many others? When the public does learn to appreciate these great compositions then will music be reaching its rightful place in this city. One wonders when people will tire of the drivel that is played and passes for organ music in some of our churches; the shimmerings and shakings, too, that are sent nightly over the radio, demoralizing public taste for good music and masquerading as organ playing—most emphatically are a curse to the advancement of good organ music and its performance. —A. W. L. ("The Reubke Sonata and Other Matters," *Winnipeg Free Press*, 26 November 1932.)

The declining public attendance at organ recitals by both local and visiting players over the years was a matter of concern to the organizers of these events, and this issue was debated on the music page of local newspapers on one occasion. The dialogue was initiated by a letter to the music editor of one newspaper on the topic, "Are Organ Recitals a Thing of the Past?" One writer replied by referring to the warm public response that had greeted appearances of touring recitalists in earlier days, as well as to the able community of local organists, and urged a return to the enthusiasm of the past:

> Music is advanced and popularized—it needs popularizing—by hearing the best. The organ is at the very foundation of fine music; it is next to the orchestra; it is the only reasonable substitute for the combination of instruments.
>
> And the conclusion is that local organists, for their own sakes, and as contributors to the public's enjoyment, may bestir themselves and revive those former days, which, in some respects, were the better days, musically speaking. (*Winnipeg Tribune*, 10 February 1934.)

Archibald Lee also wrote to the music editor on the topic, referring to the apparent growing disinterest in organ recitals. He pointed out, for example, that attendance at Sunday afternoon recitals by local organists had decreased from an earlier high of audiences of 100 to 150 to the current average of 75 to 100. At the same time, the numbers of people coming out to hear visiting recitalists had fallen off, too. Capacity audiences at Westminster United Church (over 1,000) were no longer the rule, and recitals by Canada's Arthur Egerton in 1926 and by Edwin Seder from the United States in 1929 had attracted only about 400. (An exception was Healey Willan's recital in 1930, attended by a very large audience.) Considering the effort required to present these events, he reported:

> The executive of this centre [Canadian College of Organists] decided that the regular series of Sunday afternoon recitals should not take place this season on account of the very poor attendance during the past two years. . . . It is therefore quite obvious that the public do not want organ recitals and this is the answer to the question "Are organ recitals a thing of the past in Winnipeg." —Archibald W. Lee, Secretary, Winnipeg Centre, Canadian College of Organists. ("Indifference of Public Toward Organ Recitals," *Winnipeg Free Press*, 17 February 1934.)

With the decision of the CCO to cease sponsoring organ recitals, their numbers decreased significantly in the following two years, but individual organists continued to offer programs on their own. Of the relatively few recitals played in city churches in 1934 and 1935, for example, H. Hugh Bancroft at St. Matthew's Anglican Church was responsible for the great majority of these. The CCO resumed its sponsorship activities in 1936, and the number organ recitals in that year increased almost to former levels, aided by the Lenten series at St. Luke's Anglican Church that had been a tradition there for many years. Thus, Archibald Lee's pessimism about public interest in organ recitals may have been slightly premature, for it is reasonable to assume that programs would not continue to be offered in the absence of public support. The number of organ recitals decreased sharply in the years immediately preceding the outbreak of war in 1939, and their frequency would never again rise to the levels of the 1920s and early 1930s.

Visiting Recitalists

In the early 1920s several noted organ recitalists visited Winnipeg. One of these was T. Tertius Noble (1867-1953), the expatriate English cathedral organist who had been living in New York since 1913; his earlier visit to Winnipeg was in 1919. On this occasion many of the organ pieces he played at Holy Trinity Anglican Church on 12 May 1921 were relatively unfamiliar to Winnipeg audiences, compared with those appearing on the recital programs of local organists:

Sonata in A Minor	Borowski
Elizabethan Idyll	Noble
Toccatina	Yon
Solemn Prelude	Noble
Pastorale	H. A. Matthews
Caprice	H. A. Matthews
Prelude and Fugue in B Minor	Bach
Une larme	Moussorgsky

The critical commentary on his recital, although appreciative, was perfunctory at best:

> Mr. Noble has a faultless technique, perfect command of his instrument, and intelligent, sympathetic powers of interpretation. His programme included massive works, technically exacting and gigantic in effect, and lighter compositions calling for delicacy of treatment. ("Tertius Noble Organ Recital," *Manitoba Free Press*, 13 May 1921.)

The most prominent international recitalist to visit Winnipeg in the early 1920s was the French organist Joseph Bonnet (1884-1944). His first instruction in organ was from his father, and later from Guilmant, Tournemire, and Vierne. He took his first position as a church organist at the age of 14. Bonnet was organist at St. Eustache Church in Paris until the start of World War II; his North American tours began in 1916. Acclaimed by the leading critics and musicians of Europe as one of the wonder-artists of his time, Bonnet's repertoire covered the whole of organ literature from the earliest composers to the masters of the late 19th and early 20th centuries; in particular, he was held to be an ideal interpreter of Bach and Franck. He published several collections of early organ music in addition to his own compositions in various styles, ranging from paraphrases of the Gregorian chant to grand concert fantasias. Bonnet received the Legion of Honour in recognition of his accomplishments on behalf of French art. In 1922 it was reported that he intended to enter the priesthood in the order of Benedictines following his return to Paris at the conclusion of a recital tour. His fans were relieved to learn that this report was false, for they had believed that the allegation, if true, would have involved Bonnet's withdrawal from the public world of organ playing. Bonnet eventually settled in Canada, joining the staff of the Conservatoire de Musique de Québec à Montréal in 1943. His grave is in the cemetery of a Benedictine Abbey in Québec.

Bonnet's Winnipeg recitals were preceded by accounts of his phenomenal musical abilities and the ecstatic responses of his European audiences. In 1910, for example, Bonnet gave a series of 40 recitals in Paris, without repeating a single piece and all played from memory. These recitals, which drew immense audiences, were credited with inaugurating a great popular movement in favour of organ music. In of one of his recitals in Prague, he deftly wove the Hungarian national anthem with the Marseillaise in an extemporization. The powerfully excited and aroused audience stormed the platform and carried off the player in a jubilant procession.

On his first visit to Winnipeg on 28 November 1921, arranged by the local organist-impresario Fred M. Gee, Bonnet played this program at Grace Methodist Church:

Trumpet Tune and Air	Purcell
Soeur Monique	Couperin
Prelude	Clérambault
Fantasia and Fugue in G Minor	Bach
Gavotte	Martini
Noël languedocien	Guilmant
Grand Fantasie and Fugue	Liszt
Romance sans paroles	Bonnet
Variations de concert	Bonnet

In addition to the usual descriptive commentaries of the individual pieces in Bonnet's program, Winnipeg's music critics were moved to flights of ecstasy seldom encountered in music criticism:

> The largest audience ever present at an organ recital in Winnipeg . . . gathered to hear Joseph Bonnet. . . . Heralded as king of organists and extraordinary musician, Bonnet faced hearers who expected much; but he more than fulfilled all they hoped for, and left them reluctant to hear the last wonderful note. Possessed of a marvellous technique and dramatic sense of values, he is an artist who uses his materials with unerring judgment and sureness of touch. His effects were those of a master-hand, his pictures clear and distinct. Now dramatic, now tender, he had an amazing versatility of expression, and made his instrument speak every human mood. He played entirely from memory, and did not leave the organ loft until the programme was finished.
>
> The most outstanding composition on his programme was the Liszt "Grand Fantasia and Fugue," a stupendous work occupying fully half an hour. . . . A storm of applause greeted the conclusion of the work, so technically exacting, such a strain on powers of endurance, and so full of marvellous effects. . . . After the artist had played the National Anthem, insistent cries for "La Marseillaise" arose, and his graceful acknowledgement of the compliment was a fitting conclusion to an evening which brought admiration of French art to a point seldom reached before. ("Record Attendance For Organ Recital," Manitoba Free Press, 29 November 1921.)

Although the music of old French masters was not part of the recital programs of local organists trained in the English music tradition, the inclusion of these relatively unknown composers on Bonnet's program was an educational experience for the Winnipeg audience. One critic responded enthusiastically to the unfamiliar sounds:

> As to Mr. Bonnet's playing, comment at second-hand, no matter how brilliant, is hopelessly inadequate in conveying of any realization of its magic. . . . There is really no need, even, to give details of his program. But one may be pardonably permitted perhaps to say this, that his interpretations of the older masters were the purest and most exquisitely cut cameos imaginable—cameos with a surprisingly beautiful surface engraving recreating one of the music's most fragrant and ever-lovely ages. ("Music Lovers Give Bonnet Good Welcome," *Winnipeg Tribune*, 29 November 1921.)

Bonnet's second visit to the city several months later was announced in a newspaper article that commented on the musician's profoundly religious nature, his command of the works of Bach, and his extensive knowledge of English music. This time Bonnet played two recitals on successive days. The first, at Westminster Presbyterian Church on 10 March 1922, consisted of this program:

Grand jeu	Du Mage
Récit de tierce en taille	de Grigny
Fugue in C Major	Buxtehude
Organ Concerto No. 10,	Handel
Pedal cadenza by Guilmant	
Pastorale	Franck
Pièce héroique	Franck
Sonata No. 6 in D Minor	Mendelssohn
Funeral March and Song of the	
Seraphs	Guilmant
Ariel, Berceuse, Rhapsodie catalane	
with pedal cadenza	Bonnet

On the following evening he played:

Sonata in D Minor	Guilmant
Pavane	Byrd
Ricercare	Palestrina
Toccata and Fugue in D Minor	Bach
Poèmes d'automne	Bonnet
Chorale in A Minor, No. 3	Franck
Prelude (new),	
dedicated to Bonnet	Samazeuilh
Sketch in F Minor	Schumann
Toccata, 5th Symphony	Widor

The warm appreciation of Bonnet's performance by the critics matched that accorded to his recital a few months earlier:

A master of the instrument, accepted generally as the greatest living organist, Bonnet could hardly disappoint the expectations of anyone. . . . [The]
impression of controlled strength, of, sometimes, almost untouched resources
of intellectual and emotional insight and of brilliant technique stamped
everything he played as authoritative. There seemed, too, to be a complete
willingness to submerge the personality of the artist in that of the composer
and his work. . . . Three compositions of Bonnet's, "Ariel," "Berceuse," and
"Rhapsodie Catalane," widely different in character, were played with the
intimacy of understanding possible only to their creator, and were delightful
as a consequence. ("Bonnet's Masterful Recital Appreciated," *Manitoba Free
Press*," 11 March 1922.)

With him only one thing counts and that is the music, in, of, and for itself.
He is no specialist. He has no virtuoso skill, exhibited as something for which
it is only a part-means. If he has preference of any kind (and one is sure he is
sufficiently human to have them) he does not intrude them in public. . . .
His programs are an education, and extend over the whole of the immense field
of organ literature. . . . He realizes everything he does in terms of supreme
art, because his soul is in the depths of all the beautiful music which has
been written for the instrument of his choice. ("Why Bonnet is a Magnificent Organist," *Winnipeg Tribune*, 11 March 1922.)

A few months later, Bonnet's fellow-countryman Marcel Dupré (1886-1971)
followed him to Winnipeg under arrangements made by Fred M. Gee. Dupré
was a musical prodigy who exhibited a passion for organs at a very early age.
When he was a child he heard Charles-Marie Widor (1844-1937), the famous
French organist, play a dedication recital at the St. Ouen cathedral in Rouen
(where his father was organist) and decided to become an organist. He played
Bach for Alexandre Guilmant at the age of eight, and became the master's pupil
two years later. At the age of 12 he was appointed organist at St. Vivien, Rouen.
As a young man he was awarded many prizes for his accomplishments, includ-
ing first prizes in piano, organ, and fugue at the Paris Conservatoire, and the
Prix de Rome for a cantata. In 1906 Dupré was appointed assistant organist at
St. Sulpice in Paris, and succeeded Widor, his teacher there, as organist in 1934.

In 1920, at the age of 34, Dupré startled the musical world by playing from
memory the entire organ works of Bach in a series of recitals at the Paris Conservatory, the first time such a performance had ever been given. As this event
unfolded, members of the Parisian artistic community flocked to the performances, along with the professors and students of the Conservatory. Widor addressed the audience at the concluding recital: "We must all regret, my dear
Dupré, the absence from our midst of one whose name is foremost in our
thoughts today—the great Bach himself. Rest assured, if he had been here, he
would have embraced you and pressed you to his heart." The advance notices
of Dupré's visit to Winnipeg reported that American critics had lavished upon

him nearly all the adjectives in the laudatory vocabulary, commenting on his perfection of technique, clarity of performance, and skills in registration and improvisation. Therefore, it was with high anticipation that Winnipeg audiences awaited this recital program at Westminster Presbyterian Church on 7 November 1922:

Fantaisie and Fugue in G Minor	Bach
Soeur Monique	Couperin
Noël avec variations	Daquin
Chorale Prelude: Christ Lay in the Bonds of Death	Bach
Chimes	E. Bourdon
Scherzo, Symphony No. 4	Widor
Prelude and Fugue in F Minor	Dupré
Improvised Symphony in Four Movements on themes submitted by the audience	Dupré

The review of Dupré's performance was a structured and thoughtful piece, but thoroughly critical of the practice of improvisation in general, and of this recitalist in particular.

> M. Dupré appeared in three roles, an interpreter of fine music, a composer, and an improvisator extraordinary, upon the organ. . . . As a composer he merely interested. As an improvisator he must have amazed the majority of his large audience. . . . To hear a tranquil-looking gentleman extemporaneously build up, apparently with as little concern as if it were simpler than shaving, a four-floored edifice of related sounds and rhythm on thematic materials supplied by others and never before seen is something so seldom met by the generality of people that auditors can pardonably gasp with astonishment. . . . However, a thousand performances of this kind do not seem worth a single page from Bach's "forty-eight" or Beethoven's "fifth." Such shows as this of M. Dupré's do not give us anything that counts for much. . . . It is the quality of the creation which counts. . . . This improvisation game, skilful and surprising as it is, seems tinged with too much of the means to an end than an end itself—house building with bricks and no mortar.
>
> As to M. Dupré, the composer with the leisure to pen his thoughts to paper, he played a "Prelude and Fugue in F Minor," in which the preludial movement was much more interesting.
>
> M. Dupré, the interpreter, delighted. His playing was scholarly, not in the sense that it savored of the mustily precise and the pedagogically automatic, but for the loving, unblemished appreciation of the music. ("Dupré Scores Success at Grace Church," *Winnipeg Tribune*, 8 November 1922.)

Joseph Bonnet returned to Winnipeg a year after his earlier appearance. This time he was on a six-week American tour, after conducting master classes at the Eastman Organ School in Rochester, New York. The euphoric advance notices, as before, referred to Bonnet as one of the greatest living practitioners of his art, of the same rank as Casals, Pavlova, Kreisler, Paderewski, and Galli-Curci in their respective fields. Bonnet's standing among other artists was also a matter for comment. It was reported that many famous painters and writers derived inspiration from his playing and dedicated poems, books, sculptures, and pictures to him in gratitude. These people, including some organ builders, would find their way to Bonnet's organ loft after Sunday high mass to listen to his unique extemporizations. Testimonials from prominent musicians were included in announcements of his forthcoming recitals. One of these, the English critic Eaglefield Hull, said:

> I have never known such absolute perfection as Bonnet's playing. During the scores of recitals which I have heard him give in various countries, I have never heard a wrong stop or a wrong note. This is bringing organ play-ing, indeed, to a high level, for he would be a bold man who would say this of many great pianists. ("Joseph Bonnet Has Absolute Perfection," *Manitoba Free Press*, 17 February 1923.)

Bonnet played this program at Westminster Presbyterian Church on 19 March 1923:

Voluntary in D	Purcell
Rondeau	Couperin
Dialogue	Clérambault
Concerto No. 4	Handel, arr. Guilmant
Grand Fantasie and Fugue	Liszt
Song of the Chrysanthemums	Bonnet
Matin provencale	Bonnet
Menuet français	Amadée Tremblay, dedicated to Joseph Bonnet
Toccata	Gigout

The ensuing review found no fault whatsoever with Bonnet's interpretations:

> Last night's programme revealed every side of Bonnet's many-faceted gen-ius, but his dramatic power stood out above everything else. This was prob-ably due to the inclusion of the tremendous Liszt Grand Fantasie and Fugue. . . . The composer's treatment of the original theme compelled wonder and admiration not only of his own genius, but of the performer who had to overcome every imaginable kind of technical difficulty. Yet these feelings were overshadowed by the emotions which the dramatic content of the piece produced, which every listener could fit into an allegory to suit himself. ("Enthusiasm Marks Reception of Bonnet," *Manitoba Free Press*, 21 March 1923.)

On the following evening, 20 March 1923, Bonnet moved to Grace Methodist Church for this program:

Canzona	Gabrieli
Fantasia in Echo Style	Sweelinck
Toccata	Frescobaldi
Prelude, Fugue, and Chaconne	Buxtehude
Chorale in B Minor	Franck
In dulci jubilo	Bach
Prelude and Fugue in D Major	Bach
Psalm Prelude No. 3	Howells
Prelude and Fugue in B Major	Saint-Saëns
Caprice héroique	Bonnet
Romance sans paroles	Bonnet
Finale, Symphony No. 1	Vierne

This time the reviewer thought that Franck's work was the outstanding feature of the program:

> Those who heard Joseph Bonnet play the César Franck Chorale in B Minor in Grace church last night, would find it in their heart to pity anyone who missed it. The music left an impression that had in it profound emotion. It was the peak of a programme that held the Bach Prelude and Fugue in D major moving with compact ease and brilliance.
>
> The recital was remarkable for the same reasons as each of the others; a master mind and the fullest resources at work among some of the most interesting composers for the organ. . . . A Bonnet recital is a lesson in programme building as well as in technique, registration and other things concerned with the purely executive side of the art. ("Profound Impression Produced by Chorale," *Manitoba Free Press*, 20 March 1923.)

Late in 1924 a prominent Canadian musician, Healey Willan (1880-1968), visited Winnipeg. Trained as an organist in England, Willan served as organist-choirmaster in several English churches, as official organist to the St. Cecilia Society, and as an orchestral and choral conductor before coming to Canada in 1913. This move was in response to an invitation to become head of the theory department of the Toronto Conservatory of Music in Toronto; in 1921 he became vice-principal, remaining in that position until 1936, in addition to lecturing at the University of Toronto. In 1921 he began a life-long association with the Anglican Church of St. Mary Magdalene, Toronto, where he introduced an Anglo-Catholic style of service-music. Apparently Willan possessed a facetious brand of wit: he was heard to say that the organ was a dull instrument, that organ recitals bored him, and that he was unable to play his own major compositions. On being elected president of the Arts and Letters Club of Toronto in 1923, he promptly set its constitution to music. Willan came to Winnipeg in connection with the Manitoba Music Teachers Association convention on October 21 and 22. On the first day he addressed the assembly on the topic of plagiarism in music. The next day he played this recital program recital at Fort Rouge Methodist Church:

Prelude and Fugue in C Minor	Bach
Chorale Prelude: Sleepers Wake	Bach
Prelude and Fugue in C major	Bach
Adagio in E	Merkel
Prelude	Clérambault
Minuet, Berenice	Handel
Gavotte	Kirnberger
Rhapsody in A Minor	Saint-Saëns
Rhapsody in D-flat	Howells
Introduction, Passacaglia, and	
Fugue	Willan

As for Willan's own composition, one he had jokingly claimed an inability to play, the reviewer reported a warm audience response:

> The recitalist's Passacaglia and Fugue was received with a very genuine interest and admiration. It proved to be remarkable in its variety of style and mood, its richness of harmonic invention and in the dexterity of its contrapuntal weaving. It is not weighted down with the respectability of the church, despite the fact that there it came into being and has been brought up; it keeps tripping merrily into the open. . . .
>
> Dr. Willan's playing was of the kind that kept one's thoughts on the music; it met the needs of the composers. ("Dr. Willan's Recital Most Keenly Enjoyed," *Manitoba Free Press*, 23 October 1924.)

A year after his first appearance in Winnipeg, Marcel Dupré returned to the city. Advance notices of Dupré's recital described the crowds drawn to his performances in Paris, and how a number of privileged people would ascend to the organ loft after Sunday services to hear him play works by contemporary French masters—Franck, Widor, Vierne, Guilmant—all from memory. Now on his second transcontinental tour, Dupré had played a farewell recital on the Wanamaker Auditorium organ in Philadelphia, said to be the largest in the world. On that occasion his recital was broadcast overseas and was received by the Radio Club of France, as well as by radio listeners in Paris and the suburbs. This event was believed to be the first time that organ music had crossed the Atlantic Ocean by radio. In Winnipeg on 12 November 1923, he played this program at Grace Methodist Church:

Prelude and Fugue in A Minor	Bach
Sonata in E-flat	Bach
Chorale Prelude: Jesus, My Saviour	Bach

Chorale Prelude: Christ Lay in the
   Bonds of Death   Bach
Prelude and Fugue in D Major   Bach
Chorale in B Minor   Franck
Finale in B-flat Major   Franck
Prelude and Fugue in G Minor   Dupré
Noël and Variations   Dupré

Considering the stature of the performer and the enthusiastic accounts of his performances elsewhere that had been conveyed to Winnipeg audiences through advance publicity notices, one short, uninspired review of his recital simply revealed that reviewer was not particularly knowledgeable about organs or organ music:

> The technical criticism of it, the mastery of registration, superlative pedalling and clearness of rapid un-organ-like figures, is left to those who are more familiar with all the details of the instrument. . . . One thing is impressed indelibly on the layman—there seems to be nothing that M. Dupré does not know about it . . . there was no endeavor to put the personality of the player ahead of the music; one point led on naturally to another and everything was part of a big rhythmic scheme. ("Marcel Dupré Gives Fine Organ Recital," *Manitoba Free Press*, 13 November 1923.)

On the other hand, another reviewer, the same one who had attended Dupré's earlier recital, was again inspired to ecstatic heights, although reiterating a disapproval of the artist's improvisations:

> When Marcel Dupré made his first appearance in Winnipeg he indulged in a kind of organ-music-made-while-you-wait business, which some people, though quite cognizant of its inspirational phase, were nevertheless unable to delight in because of its flavor of sensationalism. . . . On Monday night, however, . . . his audience simply sat in wonder at his feet. His program for the occasion was a glorious music intoxication almost throughout. . . .
>
> As to the details of the manner of M. Dupré's playing one fights shy of them beyond a few obvious commonplaces. It was, for instance, a most refreshing experience to listen to an artist who was both austere and always vitally emotional and yet who never vulgarized music by distorting it into blubbering sentimentality. . . . M. Dupré's interpretation of a Franck "Chorale in B Minor" and a "Finale in B Flat Major" were revelations which temporarily took the breath out of the body. . . .
>
> In all, M. Dupré played four of his own compositions. It is an indication of their merits to say that, despite all the fine music that had gone before, it was possible to hear them with considerable pleasure charmed by some of the ideas in them and full of admiration at the skill which they are garbed in the resources of the organ of today. Here and there are occasional superficialities, decked out in plagiaristic utterance, but in the main they

constitute music of splendid standards and which organists must welcome with eager hands. (*Winnipeg Tribune*, 13 November 1923.)

Of all the touring recitalists to visit Winnipeg, one of the most travelled was the blind English organist Alfred Hollins (1865-1942), who held an appointment as organist at St. George's West Church, Edinburgh, for 55 years. Before taking up that position, this extraordinarily gifted musician had performed for Queen Victoria and, as a pianist and student with Hans von Bülow, had astounded the musical public by playing three major piano concertos in one concert. During his career he performed extensively in England and travelled to North America and Australia. During his ambitious tour of the United States and Canada in 1925-26, he visited Winnipeg. The advance notice of his recital promised an exceptional musical experience:

> It is several years since England has sent one of her great keyboard experts in the realm of the organ. Already known . . . by virtue of his charming compositions for the instrument, and preceded by enthusiastic reports of his crisp, sunny, cleancut and rhythmical playing, his remarkable accuracy, his gift of memory and the spirit and melodic grace of his improvisations, the coming of Hollins is arousing great interest. ("English Organist on Third American Tour," *Manitoba Daily Free Press*, 11 January 1926.)

Hollins appeared as a conductor, composer, and player at Grace Church on 26 January 1926. He shared a program with a soloist and All Saints' choir, which sang one of his anthems; his organ solos were:

Sonata No. 1	Mendelssohn
Intermezzo	Hollins
Spring Song	Hollins
Triumphal March	Hollins
Prelude and Fugue in D	Bach
The Answer	Wolstenholme
Minuet Antique	Watling
Scherzo	Turner
Scherzo	Hollins
Improvisations on airs submitted by the audience	
Overture, Oberon	Weber

One reviewer clearly reflected the general public's response, but neglected to comment on the Bach selection, the apex of the recital:

> Winnipeg has heard grander organ playing, but none that showed so much the personality of the player. . . . There was no evidence with big effects; one point simply led on naturally to another; it was all rhythmical but without insistence. Dr. Hollins' own compositions gave a great deal of pleasure— "Intermezzo," "A Song of Sunrise," "Scherzo"—one could not help thinking

of the moving picture houses and wondering if they are ever played there. Dr. Hollins played pieces of Wolstenholme, Watling and an interesting Scherzo by Turner with a "very quaint and pleasing" trio. A feature of the programme was the organist's ingenious and skilful improvisation on the carol, "See Amid the Winter's Snow," in which he brought in all sorts of themes connected with Yuletide. ("Dr. Hollins Pleases With Organ Recital," *Winnipeg Free Press*, 27 January 1926.)

Another critic, however, took a broader approach and reported on an unscheduled "encore":

> Those who listened with enrapt attention to Dr. Alfred Hollins on the organ at Grace Church Tuesday heard more than great music produced in grand style. They came in personal contact with a genius and a very great man.
>
> His conquest of the prestigious technical difficulties that must have beset him tell of the triumph of mind over matter, of the soul over the body. To the many young students of piano, organ or other instrument he is an inspiration, proof that no difficulties can defeat where there is love enough.
>
> Perfectly cool at the keyboard, never hurried or at fault, Dr. Hollins' registration was faultless, and the interpretation best described as spiritual. His program was selected to give pleasure not only to the virtuoso, but to the ordinary boy or girl, man or woman who loves music because it is music.
>
> Of the heavier numbers, the Bach Prelude and Fugue in D was a remarkable performance, and so insistent was the applause that Dr. Hollins followed it with the great Fugue in G Minor, one of the great composer's grandest and most difficult compositions. . . .
>
> Of the Doctor's own compositions, they were in the lighter vein. The spring song, full of bird song and sunshine, the march full of go and ardour. (*Winnipeg Tribune*, 27 January 1926.)

For his part, Hollins was not favourably impressed with Winnipeg's topography or winter weather. In his autobiography Hollins wrote of his experience in the city:

> I thought Winnipeg a flat, uninteresting city, and [we] felt glad that it was not our home-place. . . . Nowhere else have I experienced such penetrating cold as in Winnipeg: 18 degrees below zero [Fahrenheit] is not excessively cold . . . but the biting prairie wind found us defenceless. The thread with which the buttons of my overcoat were sewn on became so brittle that some of them fell off. (*A Blind Musician Looks Back.* Blackwell, 1936, 422.)

Hollins also learned the method that many Winnipeg organists used to cope with cold and drafty churches in winter. He reported this discovery in an article written shortly after his visit:

> I gave a recital on a fine Casavant tubular-pneumatic in Grace Church, Winnipeg. . . . This was a Tuesday, and the heat in the church had been turned off since the previous Sunday night. When I went to practise on the

Tuesday morning they were only just beginning to fire up again. I could not possibly have practised if it had not been for a tent which the organist puts up all around the console in winter with a couple of electric radiators inside it to enable him to do his teaching. I was perfectly snug and warm in my tent, but the poor organ was not, and it showed too, for the valves had got so stiff with the cold that hardly a note would speak. I sent out an S.O.S. for the tuner, who assured me the organ would be perfectly right when the church got warm, and so it was. ("Organs and Organ Building in Canada and the United States," *The Organ*, October 1926.)

However, Hollins did enjoy an "admirably chosen" concert by the newly formed Winnipeg Symphony Orchestra, and he was fascinated with an electric type-writer he encountered for the first time in his visit to the mail-order offices of Eaton's Departmental Store.

Another visiting recitalist was Ernest MacMillan (1893-1973), who now returned to the city after an absence of almost seven years to perform at West-minster United Church on 22 February 1926, assisted by the Knox United Church choir. Although his knighthood for services to music in Canada was still a decade away, MacMillan already had an established reputation as a per-former and educator. Referring to a recital MacMillan had given in Toronto, a newspaper in that city had declared that "this young Canadian is in virtuosity, enthusiasm and authority of style one of the outstanding organists, not merely of Canada, but of North America." In the same year as his visit to Winnipeg, MacMillan became principal of the Canadian Academy of Music, and in 1927 was appointed dean of the Faculty of Music at the University of Toronto. While living in England for a few years in his youth, MacMillan had studied organ study with Alfred Hollins, occasionally substituting for him at St. George's West Church. As in his earlier recital, MacMillan's first selection by Hollins was an acknowledgement of the mutual respect that held between MacMillan and his former teacher:

Concert Overture in F Minor, *dedicated to Dr. Ernest MacMillan*	Hollins
Air, Sarabande and Minuet	Purcell
Le coucou	Daquin
Gavotte	Martini
Prelude and Fugue in G	Bach
Prelude on Eventide	Parry
Scherzo	Hoyte
Epilogue	Willan
Ballet Music, Rosamunde	Schubert
Berceuse	Vierne
Rococo	Palmgren
Scherzo, Symphony No. 4	Widor
Finale in B-flat	Franck

Arnold Dann, former organist at Grace Church, left Winnipeg in 1924 to take up a position in Pasadena, California. While there he was elected sub-dean of the California section of the American Guild of Organists, and gave recitals in various cities in the United States from New York to California. He visited Winnipeg two years later and played this program at Grace Church on 20 April 1926, assisted by an 80-voice choir:

Fantasie dialogue	Boëllmann
Two Chorale Preludes from the	
Little Organ Book:	Bach
Hark, A Voice Saith,	
All are Mortal In Thee is Joy	
Scherzo, Finale, Symphony No. 4	Widor
Two Fireside Fancies:	Clokey
Grandmother's Knitting	
Grandfather's Wooden leg	
Rêverie	Bonnet
Carillon	Vierne

The review of his program was brief, but complimentary:

> The feeling seemed to be . . . that his playing has gained much in artistry and interest since he was heard here before. There was not an item on the program that missed significance, and the organist's vigorous, "salty" style of performance was heartily enjoyed. ("Arnold Dann Recital is Warmly Received," *Manitoba Free Press*, 21 April 1926.)

One of the few American organists to visit Winnipeg in this period was Edwin Stanley Seder, a faculty member at the Sherwood Music School, Chicago. Born in Tokyo, Japan, and educated in Wisconsin and at the University of Mexico, Seder held his first church position at the age of 12. His recital at Westminster United Church on 9 April 1929 consisted of these pieces:

Concert Overture in F Minor	Hollins
Minuet from Suite (ms.)	Walter P. Zimmerman
Come God, Creator, Spirit Blest	Bach
The Walk to Jerusalem	Bach, arr. Griswold
Fugue in E-flat (St. Anne)	Bach
Ave Maria	Schubert
Suite from Water Music	Handel
Dance of the Reed Flutes	Tschaikowsky
Canyon Walls, Mountain Sketches	Clokey
The Chapel of San Miguel (ms. new)	Seder
Scherzo, Sonata No. 2 in C Minor	Mark Andrews
Romance (ms.)	John Kessler
Carillon-Sortie	Mulet

Marcel Dupré made another visit to Winnipeg after an interval of almost six years. At Westminster United Church on 23 October 1929 he played:

Concert Overture	Rogers
Variations, Concerto in G Minor	Handel
Chorale Prelude: Rejoice,	
Ye Christians	Bach
Fugue in C Minor	Bach
Intermezzo, Symphony No. 6	Widor
Pastorale	Franck
Symphony No. 2	
in C-sharp Minor	Dupré
Improvisation on submitted themes	

Dupré's recital must have been impressive, but the reviewer was less than completely enthusiastic regarding the player's own composition:

> Marcel Dupré . . . held his hearers in Grace Church wide-eyed and enthralled before the demonstration of his superlative command of his instrument and his genius in improvising. The whole evening constituted a wonderful refreshment of the spirit. . . . The layman can easily see how he is at once the inspiration and despair of his fellow professionals. Perhaps they could be forgiven then if they felt last night that this astounding artist had still some touch of human frailty about his musicianship; he did not always rise off the earth in his own written composition, a symphony in C sharp minor. . . . There was a mixture of styles that quite operated against unity. Nor did the thought always seem distinguished. But the piece exhibited uniquely the development in technique that has gone hand in hand with the development of organ building. Every other aspect of the recital spelt perfection. ("Marcel Dupré Gives Master Performance," Manitoba Free Press, 24 October 1929.)

Healey Willan returned to Winnipeg on 21 May 1930, after an absence of several years, to play at Westminster United Church. At the time of this visit he was between terms as president of the Canadian College of Organists (later he was made a life member of the RCCO). The choir of Knox Church participated in the program that included his own organ compositions. The reviewer reported that Willan's performance drew one of the largest organ recital audiences ever known in the city and commented on his complete mastery of the organ, but with one misgiving regarding registrations:

> What impresses one most perhaps about both the compositions and the playing is the virility and largeness of thought behind both. There is a touch of austerity, too, in keeping with the tradition of English organ music and playing, which has been absorbed by the recitalist. He had one odd little foible in his playing—a forgivable one surely in the light of all the enjoyment the evening brought forth—an addiction to the tremulant stop, which is not

one of the chief virtues of the fine instrument he played on. Apart from this the musicianship seemed irreproachable as it was distinguished, and if there was not as much color as some visiting organists have given their listeners before, there was plenty of variety and beautifully clean-cut work to take delight in. ("Toronto Organist Gives Programme," *Manitoba Free Press*, 22 May 1930.)

Arthur Egerton received his early training in organ at McGill University in Montréal and later studied on a Lord Strathcona scholarship at the Royal College of Music in London, England, with such notables as Sir Walter Parratt, Charles Wood, and Walford Davies. Upon returning to Montréal he succeeded his former teacher Lynnwood Farnam as organist-choirmaster at Christ Church Cathedral and taught organ and theory at McGill. Even before coming to Winnipeg in 1922 to become organist and choirmaster at All Saints' Anglican Church, he had been rated as a performer in the front rank of Canadian organists. He was elected the first chairman of the Winnipeg Centre of the Canadian College of Organists, established in 1923. A frequent performer during his time in the city, he often gave lecture-recitals on such topics as modern British composers and the organ works of Bach. He left the city in 1927 for the United States, where he remained for 10 years before returning to Canada to reside in Ottawa. On 14 June 1937 he visited Winnipeg and attended a members' dinner of the Centre. Afterwards the group adjourned to St. Matthew's Anglican Church, where Egerton offered his former colleagues an austere program, chiefly of early organ music:

Pro vemium in re	Kotter
From Deepest Woe I Call to Thee	Kotter
Resonat in laudibus	Anon., Sicker's Tablature
Carmen magistri pauli	Hofhaimer
Canzona	Gabrieli
Toccata per l'elevatione	Frescobaldi
Variations on Fortune my Foe	Scheidt
From God I'll Never Turn Me	Buxtehude
My Soul Doth Magnify the Lord	Bach
Fugue in E-flat (St. Anne)	Bach
Larghetto	Wesley

Trends in Repertoire

Although more organs were installed in Manitoba churches in the years up to 1919 than in any other period, the following two decades were marked by the greatest number of known organ recitals. The number of transcriptions amounted to 326, only about 17 percent of the total of the 1,925 selections that comprised these events. In relative terms, this was about one-half of the preceding period. Handel continued to be strongly represented by transcriptions of selections from his operas and oratorios, but the *Hallelujah Chorus* and *Largo* were superseded by arrangements of the *Water Music Suite*. Organ solo versions of instrumental introductions to Bach's cantatas appeared on recital programs for the first time, and *Jesu, Joy of Man's Desiring* was first heard in the early 1930s, following the publication of Harvey Grace's arrangement in 1927. Transcriptions of Elgar's patriotic marches, along with selections from his instrumental and choral works, were also played. Arrangements of selections from Debussy's string quartets and piano works received frequent performances. Wagner's popularity fluctuated from low to high between the early and late years of this period, although the pieces chosen for performance remained much the same. Dvorak, however, occupied about the same relative position on the popularity scale throughout the period. The frequency of performance of organ transcriptions of works by these and other composers during this period is given in Table 4.

Table 4

	Number	Percent
Handel	42	13
Elgar	21	6
Bach	20	6
Debussy	18	6
Purcell	15	5
Wagner	14	4
Dvorak	14	4
Mendelssohn	10	3
Mozart	10	3
Schubert	10	3

The frequency of performance of Bach's original organ works exceeded that of any other composer by a very wide margin, a position that was maintained throughout the following decades. In this period Karg-Elert's chorale preludes, along with some of his descriptive pieces, emerged as frequent elements in recital programs. Composers of the French school were well represented in the programs of leading Winnipeg organists; for example, Franck's *Pièce héroique*, and his *Prelude, Fugue, and Variation*; selections from Widor's symphonies; and standard works by Vierne. Guilmant was less frequently performed than in earlier years, however. Before 1921 the works of Joseph Bonnet were unknown to Winnipeg audiences, but following his recitals in the city between 1921 and 1923, local players immediately began to play his works, and they continued to do so for many years, although not as often later on. The frequency of performance of original works for organ by these and other composers during this period is given in Table 5.

Table 5

	Number	Percent
Bach	333	21
Karg-Elert	91	6
Widor	59	4
Franck	58	4
Mendelssohn	49	3
Guilmant	47	3
Bonnet	39	2
Rheinberger	38	2
Brahms	33	2
Vierne	30	2

Theatre Organs and Organists

The 1920s were the peak years of popularity of cinema organs. Several of the larger movie houses in Winnipeg installed pipe organs in this period, and the arrival of a new instrument was a matter of intense interest on the part of the popular musical establishment and the entertainment industry. When the new Allen Theatre (later renamed the Metropolitan) was opened early in January 1920, the assembled crowd of 2,500, which had lined up for several hours to gain admission, was addressed by an ex-mayor of Winnipeg and entertained by various performers. Although the organ had not yet been installed, it was mentioned in a newspaper account of the opening ceremonies:

> The orchestra is in front, under the proscenium arch, 15 instrumentalists being easily accommodated. The organist will be placed to the side and the pipes go behind the grill work placed over the two large boxes which set off the walls with dignity. . . . This arrangement will make possible beautiful antiphonal effects seldom heard in theatres. It is estimated that this organ will equal in volume and tone color, an orchestra of 200 pieces. ("Thousands Attend Dedication Night at New Allen Theatre," *Manitoba Free Press*, 3 January 1920.)

Later in the year the Lyceum Theatre installed a new Smith Unit Organ, designed by Frederick W. Smith, Chicago. The theatre's advance publicity promised "The Wonderful New Orchestral Organ at Every Performance—An Organ with All the Attributes of a Symphony Orchestra." The arrival of this three-manual, all-electric action instrument received a lengthy coverage in a newspaper story characterized by unusual attention to the mechanical and tonal characteristics of the instrument:

> The Lyceum organ will be the biggest organ of its type in western Canada. . . . The theory is that people go to the theatre primarily to see the picture,

and the organ is there to enhance the value of the picture by giving it the proper musical accompaniment. . . . The construction . . . [consists of] a lightning-like rapidity of action, and extremely high wind pressure, combined with the electric current and the instantaneous magnets make possible a flexibility and rapidity of action not to be found on the piano, let alone organ. The same high pressure also makes possible tonal colors hitherto unknown. . . . The Lyceum organ will be a combination of cathedral pipe organ, symphony orchestra and military concert band. Its registration includes strings, flutes, piccolos, clarinets, bassoons, trumpets, tubas, and all other church and orchestral stops, including xylophones, orchestral bells, cathedral chimes, castanets, tambourines, Chinese blocks, snare drums, bass drum, tympani, triangles, and crash cymbals, etc.

It will be a revelation to music-loving theatre patrons, and totally unlike any other pipe organ in the city. ("Lyceum Organ Wonderful in Construction," *Manitoba Free Press*, 9 October 1920.)

The film featured at the opening of the organ was *Huckleberry Finn*.

When the Capitol Theatre opened early in 1921, its pipe organ was described as "one of the finest in the Dominion." The College Theatre, a smaller motion picture house, followed in the same year with the installation of a two-manual pipe organ supplied by Warren & Son, Woodstock, Ontario, at a cost of $10,000. It had all the latest attachments, including chimes, harp, xylophone, and various orchestral stops, along with the much-loved vox humana. The two divisions of the organ were placed behind grill work on opposite sides of the stage, and both were enclosed in swell boxes.

The installation of a "Monster Giant Wicks Symphony Pipe Organ" at the Garrick Theatre in Winnipeg on 8 September 1928 received significant attention in the press. The opening ceremonies, which included an address by the city mayor, were broadcast on a local radio station. The 150-stop instrument—actually 12 ranks with much unification, and the usual bells, chimes, drums, and other percussion effects—was advertised as "Canada's Most Modern Pipe Organ" and "the largest direct-electric controlled 3-manual theatre organ in the country." It was installed by J. J. H. McLean and Company, Winnipeg, agents for the Wicks Pipe Organ Company, Highland, Illinois. The instrument took three months to assemble at the factory and six weeks to install. Extensive structural changes to the theatre were required to accommodate the instrument, which was said to occupy the space of a six-room apartment. The console was beautifully finished in ivory, decorated in gold and shaded with brown. A unique feature was a telephone located at the console for communicating with a technician in the organ chamber during tuning or maintenance procedures. At the opening, the visiting theatre organist Margaret Earl accompanied the screening of *Passion*, starring Emil Jennings and Pola Negri. As for the organ, a newspaper report remarked that "no conception of its powers is possible from the previous hearing of organs in this city, as nothing like it has been installed before. Under the control of an experienced organist the effects are equal to a symphony orchestra of more than 100 musicians." (*Manitoba Free Press*, 8 September 1928.)

The Garrick Theatre organ was dismantled by inexperienced personnel in 1953, suffering considerable pipe damage in the process, and it remained in storage under the theatre stage for a time. In 1975 it was purchased and stored by an organ enthusiast in the Vancouver area who intended to rebuild it and install it in his home, a project that was not fulfilled. In the early 1990s it was acquired by the British Columbia Theatre Organ Trust, which intended to restore the instrument completely and install it in a new civic theatre in the Vancouver suburbs.

The Tivoli Theatre, a smaller cinema across the street from Westminster United Church that housed the grandest Casavant organ in the city, installed a two-manual, 12-stop Casavant organ in December 1927; the event was reported briefly in the daily newspapers. Recitals of popular music played by the long-time incumbent organist Alan Caron—he also served at St. Mary's Roman Catholic Cathedral and played at the Garrick Theatre—were broadcast on a local radio station for several years. When the Tivoli Theatre closed in 1958, the organ was acquired by Broadway First Baptist Church.

Theatre organists were practitioners of an art quite different from that of a church organist. In addition to a sound keyboard technique, the players needed a thorough working knowledge of musical harmony and the ability to "orchestrate" their repertoires of hundreds of melodies, drawn from the orchestral, band, or piano literature, through constant changes in registration. They also required the ability to improvise freely and at length, in response to the events unfolding on the silver screen. Harold St. John Naftel, organist at Winnipeg's Capitol Theatre since 1921, and former organist at Young and Holy Trinity churches before spending a year in the United States, provided some insights into his personal approach to the task in an interview-article published in a daily newspaper. Unlike some theatre organists whose accompaniments consisted exclusively of improvised performances, Naftel adopted a more structured system. First he previewed the film, taking notes on the style of music required for each individual scene, making alterations after the initial performance. This ideal was not always adhered to, particularly when the theatre showed several different films during a week. Synchronization of dramatic and musical events was paramount, of course, so the screen must be watched continuously. Naftel's style apparently favoured the use of transcriptions of familiar orchestral or popular music, rather than purely impressionistic and unstructured improvisations:

> Some organists think it necessary to pound out what I suppose they would call an organ recital with the film as background, instead of the music being a background for the film. I do not personally believe in improvisation to

pictures, except in rare cases where a change of music has to be made, and I question whether the average audience cares to be inflicted with a succession of meaningless chords or with sounds like that of a cat chasing a mouse up and down the keys. . . .

There is plenty of good music published that will fit most scenes, if the trouble is only taken to find it. Effects are good when they are absolutely called for by the screen action, but chiefly for comedy purposes. ("Does Organist See the Picture?" *Manitoba Free Press*, 15 September 1928.)

Other professionally trained theatre organists also endeavoured to bring arrangements or transcriptions of music from well-known operas to the movie audiences. Walter Dolman, at the National Theatre, used selections from *Cavalleria Rusticana, Il Trovatore, Faust,* and other similar works to accompany the action on the screen, in addition to other original pieces:

Mr. Dolman received this week a large assortment of compositions of James Colman, vicar choral of Litchfield Cathedral, England, a personal friend of Mr. Dolman's brother Fred, who is a leading tenor of England and a student with Mr. Colman. These are a class of musical works which have not been heard here and will be of interest to a large number, in particular when played with the skill of Mr. Dolman. ("Dolman at the Organ," *Manitoba Free Press*, 26 March 1921.)

The manuscripts apparently were arrangements for organ of songs by English composers that Dolman played soon after, along with other staple numbers, such as the *Pilgrim's Chorus* from Wagner's *Tannhaüser*. Dolman's playing was much admired by his audiences at various movie theatres where he performed, as this short editorial comment testified:

Listening to the concert organ in the Dominion theatre and the fine playing to the pictures of the organist, Walter Dolman, one cannot help be convinced that the genius of this artistic musician is responsible for a large number who attend this theatre daily. Mr. Dolman has never shown his musicianly qualities to a more telling extent than since he has been at the Dominion, where, on a smaller instrument than the ones he has been accustomed to, he is securing such pleasing results. ("Organ Playing at the Dominion," *Manitoba Free Press*, 2 September 1922.)

Dolman's popularity among theatre goers was no doubt heightened by the constant attention the newspapers paid to his career, which involved frequent moves from one theatre to another. The account of his appearance at the Starland Theatre also provided an opportunity for a brief review of the new organ:

It will be greeted as very enjoyable news to patrons of the Starland theatre . . . that the management of Starland has secured an organist fitted to play the grand orchestral organ which has been installed in this beautiful and commodious Main Street theatre. . . . The instrument is one of the costliest ever brought to this city. It is equal in power and equipment to an orchestra of fifteen pieces, having such brilliant stops as the xylophone, chimes, drums, cymbals, castanets, violin, tubers [sic], vox humana, flute, piccolo and snare drums, and possesses over 40 stops, making it fully equal to any exacting musical score placed before the one who will preside. ("Walter Dolman to Play at Starland," *Manitoba Free Press*, 18 November 1922.)

While at the Starland Theatre, Dolman inaugurated the practice of community singing on Friday nights, and these proved to be extremely popular. He also played special organ scores provided by the motion picture makers for accompanying their silent films. In May 1923 Dolman played one such accompaniment prepared under D. W. Griffith's supervision for his film, *One Exciting Night*.

The role of the theatre organist and the place of organ music as an accompaniment to motion pictures generally was aptly summarized in this brief article:

Music is an invaluable and necessary aid to the success and enjoyment of moving pictures. But the accompanying, or illustrating, music must be of the right kind or else its very aim will be defeated. Unfortunately, the right kind of "picture music" is something that is not universally understood, and the organist, no matter how trained he may be in his trade is beset by a great many problems when he attempts to follow and illustrate in music the fast moving film.

The music of the concert hall and church stands upon a very high plane catering to a musically highly educated audience. Neither has nor will consent to lower its standard in order to exert a more general appeal, and until the advent of picture music good [music] has been a closed book to the majority of people.

The picture organist must have psychological insight—or, if you will, common sense. His music must have universal appeal, his programmes must contain neither all classical music nor all jazz, and most of it should also be melodious and easy to grasp, as the audience hears it usually for the first time and then only once. Since this audience contains the millionaire and professor, as well as the tired day laborer and uneducated person, he must remember that his chief purpose is to entertain.

To the picture organist, knowledge of orchestration is also essential, not only to assist in solo playing, but as most organists at some time must play with the orchestra in order that the organ may be maintained in correct relationship to the other instruments, filling in missing parts, reinforcing any weakness, permitting solo voices to progress unhampered, and above all to maintain the correct strength and color. Although absolute pitch is not essential, the organist should be able to recognize all keys in order to be prepared to continue the musical thought unbroken wherever the orchestra leaves it.

In speaking about "theatrical values" the organist should always remember that he is not playing an organ recital but that he is furnishing theatrical music for a theatrical production. Tragedy and comedy are built on the basis of ancient and well recognized rules. As the play progresses, gains impetus, presents problems and intrigues, gradually reaches its climax and leads to the solution, so should the music advance and follow the march of events with an ever increasing intensity.

The greater number of pictures seek mainly to entertain, the music consequently being in a lighter vein. The organist will therefore place in his mental storeroom a sufficient [supply] of the latest popular hits—in short be up-to-date.

To summarize as briefly as possible, organ playing in a picture show is a new art demanding a greater development of interesting qualifications with the addition of many hitherto unused attributes. ("The Theatre Organist," *Manitoba Free Press*, 27 January 1923.)

In the early months of 1927 there were several letters to the editor of a local newspaper on the topic of the training and compensation of church organists; eventually the interchange touched on the position of theatre organists. The debate was sparked by this complaint from a clergyman:

To the Music Editor—Did it ever strike you how inadequate is the supply of competent organists and choir masters—especially so when we realize how much money is spent on the musical education of our young folk? They seem to stop their training at some point before reaching the practical stage. . . . True, the remuneration is rather small—only fifty dollars a month—yet it would be a nice addition to the salary of some one who was already engaged in some other occupation. . . . —[Canon] D. T. Parker, Rector [Portage la Prairie]. (*Manitoba Free Press*, 26 March 1927.)

The patronizing tone of this letter generated an immediate response from several readers. H. St. John Naftel, who had been a church organist for several years before joining the ranks of theatre organists, spoke from a position of authority on this topic, drawing attention to the time and expense involved in gaining proficiency in organ playing and choir leading:

Competency deserves its proper recognition, which it does not always get, and organists' salaries in churches generally are much too small to be any recompense for their labors. Those churches that are able to pay well do not always do so, and those who cannot afford it should be content to engage some younger member of the profession, who is wishful of gaining experience, unless they are fortunate enough to get hold of a competent man who cannot at the moment obtain a position his talent may demand. In some cases I have known organists to give their services gratis to churches who are financially able to pay a reasonable salary, and this to my mind should not be tolerated. . . . The Canadian College of Organists are employing very worthy efforts in improving church music generally, and perhaps, in the course of time, may be able to achieve results which will benefit the profession materially as well as artistically. Remember that the laborer is worthy of his hire, and this applies none the less to organists. —H. St. John Naftel, Associate Organist, Capitol Theatre. ("Takes up Cudgels in Defence of Organists," *Manitoba Free Press*, 2 April 1927.)

Another correspondent replied to the same letter, drawing attention to the relatively privileged status and treatment of clergymen, who were "received" by church congregations with full salary and housing, while organists were "hired" on a low-paying, part-time basis. The opportunities for employment as a theatre organist, with its accompanying higher income, were considered serious competition for the talents of trained musicians. Compared with the heavy responsibilities and insufficient remuneration of the church organist, the job of theatre organist had its attractive aspects:

The theatre musician has a modern organ with all up-to-date conveniences of voicing and mechanism, kept constantly in perfect order; he plays to audiences frankly seeking entertainment, therefore is free from the limitations imposed by the Church of God, and can play the type of music demanded by young 1927, as well as the more dignified compositions of traditional organ works.

As the theatre organist probably earns more in a week than the church organist does in a month, and is without the constant small worries of choir leading, is it any wonder that our best men are turning to theatre positions?

The congregations hold the solution. When they realize that praise and prayer embodied in music are as much a power for good as oratory in the common tongue, and make it possible, by adequate payment, for their leaders to devote a clearer mind to individual training of choristers, they will induce many of the best musicians to return work of breadth and dignity in the church. —Albert G. Crawley, Organist and Choirleader, Knox Church, Souris. ("Attitude of Clergy Partly to Blame for Organists' Inefficiency," *Manitoba Free Press*, 9 April 1927.)

The first sound-synchronized "talkies" were shown in the Metropolitan Theatre in Winnipeg on 26 October 1928; the film *The Street Angel*, starring Charles Farrell and Janet Gaynor, had only an integrated orchestral sound track, but the accompanying short film, *The Treasurer's Report* with Robert Benchley, featured all-synchronized human voices; animal voices were introduced in 1930. In the following years other theatres followed the trend and installed "Movietone" or "Vitaphone" sound systems to take advantage of the new developments in motion picture technology. From this time onward, the role of the theatre organist began to change. With the gradual demise of silent motion pictures, cinema organists still continued to provide musical entertainment before picture showings and during intermissions, but these practices eventually were discontinued as the talking movies came to be regarded as self-sufficient entertainments in themselves.

———◆•◆•◆———

A Period of Recession: *1940-1949*

THIS PERIOD, which encompassed several of the war-time years, was relatively inactive in most respects, as compared with earlier times. When some of the members of the Winnipeg Centre of the Canadian College of Organists entered military service, the Centre ceased formal activities for almost a decade, although recitals continued to be offered by both local and visiting players, particularly in the postwar years. Organ manufacturing was curtailed due to the shortage of construction materials; for example, the few wholly new Casavant organs installed in Manitoba churches were unit organs of small dimensions indeed, with one exception. Of the nine installations during the 1940s, two were relocations from other buildings. A chronological summary of organ installations, relocations, and renovations during this period is given in Appendix 1: Organ Installations.

St. Matthew's Anglican Church, 1948

St. Matthew's was the only church to install an organ of substantial size during the period of restricted activity in organ building during the war years.

The story of St. Matthew's goes back to 1896 when a group began meeting in the home of two members; a small building was put up in 1897, followed by a larger one in 1909. The present large building was built on the a new site in 1913 (information on the organs up to this time and for almost two decades afterwards has been lost). Following the resignation of the church organist in 1929, the rector, while in England, arranged with H. Hugh Bancroft, then

St. Matthew's Anglican Church, Winnipeg.
Casavant, 1948, 3/40.

assistant organist at Grimsby Parish Church, to come to Winnipeg to fill the vacancy. Immediately upon his arrival in September 1929, Bancroft wrote the specifications for a new three-manual, 40-stop organ, which was installed by Casavant Frères in 1930 at a cost of $18,325; it was considered to be one of the most complete three-manual organs in Western Canada. It was at the church and on this organ that Bancroft commenced his active musical career as an organ recitalist in Winnipeg. The church became known throughout the prairies through radio broadcasts of Sunday services that began in 1934 and continued without interruption until 1964.

Disaster struck the church in 1944 when an extensive fire razed the building completely, and not a scrap of the organ was left. Volunteer workers cleared the debris and salvaged only a few items. Within two weeks, the congregation had established a pledge objective to replace the building; this was achieved by 1947. At the same time, negotiations were undertaken with Casavant Frères to replace the lost organ by a new instrument having the same specifications. Casavant gave this response:

> The list of stops and accessories has been copied from the signed agreement form of the organ which was destroyed and which bears the date of November 27th 1929. You will note, however, that No. 4 of the Great Organ on our new copy is typed "Dopple Flute [sic] (or Hohl Flute)". The Doppel Flute is considered by many organists and lovers of organ music to be less useful in regular Church work than the Hohl Flute, so either may be chosen without change in price.
>
> Then again amongst the couplers, No. 55 Great Sub is considered by most people today as a useless accessory and one which is decidedly harmful to the ensemble when used for that purpose. We offer in place of it an extra combination piston to either the Great, Choir or Pedal. (Letter from Stephen Stoot, Casavant Frères, to The Venerable G. R. Calvert, St. Matthew's Church, 14 January 1946.)

The installation was delayed for almost a year due a shortage of materials, described by the company in this way:

> In fact we have not been able to start work on this instrument, and even more have not been able to secure the necessary raw material for the building of this organ. It is due to the fact that the restrictions on tin have not yet been lifted, and we are allowed to buy only a few pounds per month. We are therefore making a very limited production and only on small models which do not need too much metal. Should we attempt to build your organ we would not have enough metal to complete it. We have therefore postponed indefinitely the possibility of manufacturing your organ until there is a possibility to purchase this metal. (Letter from J. L. Laframboise, Casavant Frères, to The Venerable G. R. Calvert, St. Matthew's Church, 24 September 1946.)

In view of this uncertainty and the possibility of the eventual cancellation of the Casavant contract, the Church obtained a price quotation for a new instrument from Hill, Norman & Beard, London, England. The firm proposed that a Canadian builder would receive, erect, and finish the instrument, or arrangements would be made for one of their representatives to accompany the instrument and to supervise the work of local technicians. This proposal was set aside when Casavant was successful in securing supplies of the scarce metals in 1947, even though the new prices of essential materials increased the cost of the organ by nearly one-third the amount of the original contract. The organ was installed early in 1948.

The Winnipeg Centre of the Canadian College of Organists Dissolves

In the late 1930s attendance at regular members' meetings of the Winnipeg Centre of the Canadian College of Organists diminished to small numbers, and the activities of the Centre weakened accordingly. In retrospect, the signs of impending deterioration were evident in the relatively low attendance at recitals of local and visiting organists in the late 1930s. This low point in the history of the Centre was reached in a special meeting held on 26 October 1940, when the crisis was explicitly recognized. After much discussion, the members decided that some attempt would be made to carry on the work of the Centre by sending a letter to every organist and choirmaster in the city, inviting them to indicate their support by attending a special meeting. This attempt to revitalize the Centre was unsuccessful. Since some of the members entered military service, it was foreseen that the effectiveness of the Centre could not be sustained throughout the war years. The Centre then lapsed into a period of inactivity lasting almost a decade.

Local Players

Although the Winnipeg Centre no longer officially existed, several of its members continued to give recitals on their own. Although the programs for these events were published in advance, none of the recitals were reviewed; they had been ignored by the critics for many years. The most likely explanation for this neglect was that these short concerts were given before or after regular church services, occasionally on Sunday afternoons, and usually involved the participation of another instrumentalist, a vocal soloist, or small choral group. Also, some of these events continued the tradition of Lenten organ recitals, offered in earlier years under the auspices of the Winnipeg Centre of the CCO. Perhaps because of their religious context and focus, these recitals were no longer regarded by the music critics as musically significant events, even though they often included organ music of a purely secular nature.

This display of disinterest on the part of local music critics in the activities of Winnipeg organists was partly offset by the place given to organ recitals in radio broadcasts. A regular feature of Sunday radio programming in this period was the presentation of short recitals of organ music by players across Canada. The prominent Winnipeg organist Hugh Bancroft played this program over the national network of the Canadian Broadcasting Corporation on 7 December 1940:

Agitato, Sonata in D Minor	Rheinberger
March, Scipio	Handel
Fidelis and Divertimento	Whitlock
Allegro vivace, Symphony No. 5	Widor

In March of the same year Hugh Bancroft, Frans Niermeier (who would receive his doctorate in music from the University of Toronto in June), and Harold J. Lupton were winners of the annual compositions contest sponsored by the Winnipeg women's musical club, Wednesday Morning Musicale. This group was established in 1933 to enrich the musical life of the community and to encourage young artists. The adjudicator for this competition was Healey Willan, teacher of counterpoint and composition at the University of Toronto and university organist.

The year 1940 was one of accomplishment for another organist, Eila Buchanan, who was the first Winnipeg organist to receive the diploma, Licentiate of Trinity College London.

Among the local organists offering recitals in this period, Norman O. Smith was the most active; Dr. Smith played frequent programs at St. John's Anglican Cathedral where he was the incumbent organist (his full-time professional occupation was that of a faculty member in the chemistry department at The University of Manitoba). Hugh Bancroft was a frequent performer at All Saints' Anglican Church and occasionally elsewhere, before leaving the city in 1946 to accept a position as organist at Christ Church Cathedral, Vancouver. Other local players who presented programs of organ music included Douglas Bodle, Allan Borbridge, Fred M. Gee, Donald Hadfield, Clayton Lee, Frans Niermeier, Fred Walker, and Helen Young. Most of these recitals were fund raisers for patriotic or religious causes, such as the Red Cross, church choir projects, or organ funds.

While most of these recitals took place in larger churches having adequate pipe organs, an exception was a recital played by Melvin Yeo on the new Hammond electric organ at Chalmers United Church on 27 September 1942. The Lieutenant-Governor of Manitoba attended to unveil an honour roll commemorating members of the congregation who had enlisted in the armed forces. On that occasion the recital program was:

Sonata No. 2	Mendelssohn
On Wings of Song	Mendelssohn
Chorale Prelude on Melcombe	Parry
Rococo	Palmgren
Intermezzo	Stanford
Introduction, Variations,	
and Fugue on Tallis Canon	Percy Fletcher

Ronald W. Gibson, who had headed the Winnipeg Centre of the CCO for several terms in its early years, served overseas with the Royal Canadian Air Force during the war. Upon his return to Winnipeg he resumed recital activities immediately with this program at Holy Trinity Anglican Church on 20 January 1946, specifically identified as inaugurating his return to musical life:

Allegro, Sonata No. 1	Mendelssohn
Blessed Jesu, We Are Here	Bach
Blessed Jesu, We Are Here	Karg-Elert
Scherzo, Symphony No. 4	Widor

Processional	Dubois
Fugue	Honegger
Chorale No. 3	Franck

Gibson did not remain in Winnipeg for long, for later in the year he returned to England for further musical studies, where he stayed until 1949. Then he returned to Winnipeg and became director of the School of Music at The University of Manitoba, a position he held until 1963.

Although claims for the organ as an orchestra substitute were heard less frequently than in the early days when orchestral transcriptions were frequent items on organ recital programs, an exception was found at the end of this recital program of standard organ repertoire pieces played by Norman O. Smith at St. John's Anglican Cathedral on 27 April 1947:

Passacaglia and Fugue in C Minor	Bach
Trumpet Tune and Air	Purcell
Fantasia, Sonata in D-flat	Rheinberger
Evening Song	Bairstow
Scherzo	Whitlock
Finale, Symphony No. 1	Vierne
Piano Concerto	Schumann
Douglas Bodle, piano,	
Orchestral part played on the organ	

Several young Winnipeg musicians began their careers as organists in the mid-1940s. One of the youngest to be appointed as a regular Winnipeg church organist was Hugh McLean, who assumed his duties at St. Luke's Anglican Church in September 1945 at the age of 15, while still a high school student. McLean had been a choir boy at All Saint's Anglican Church and had studied piano with a local music teacher for 10 years, and organ with Hugh Bancroft in Vancouver for two years, before taking his new position. As early as 1947 he gave his first recital on one of CBC radio's Sunday organ programs. In 1949 he went to England on an organ scholarship to the Royal College of Music, then continued his training at King's College, Cambridge, on an organ scholarship, between 1951 and 1956. Following his return to Vancouver he served as an organist-choirmaster, founded a choral society, and conducted a Baroque music instrumental group. In addition to extensive performances in North America and Europe, McLean was a productive musicologist, editing and publishing works by Purcell, Krebs, Blow, Felton, Mozart, and other 18th-century composers. McLean became a prominent figure on the Canadian musical scene as a recitalist, organ consultant, musicologist specializing in 17th- and 18th-century studies, composer, arranger, editor, writer, lecturer, and radio commentator, in addition to travels to other countries. In 1973 he accepted a seven-year appointment as dean of the Faculty of Music at the University of Western

Ontario, where he remained until 1995. In recognition of his contributions to the artistic life of the country, he was made a Fellow of Royal Society of Canada and was named a Member of the Order of Canada 1987.

Another organist who began his career in Winnipeg was Douglas Bodle, who was appointed organist at St. George's Crescentwood Anglican Church, Winnipeg, at the age of 22, in September 1945. Two years later he accepted a similar post at St. Luke's Anglican Church. While in Winnipeg, Bodle studied organ with Hugh Bancroft, in addition to piano and general music with other local teachers. His career as a teacher included appointments at the Royal Conservatory of Music in Toronto, beginning in 1959; at the School of Music at The University of Manitoba, 1966-68; and at the Faculty of Music, University of Toronto, 1969-89, including part-time service at that institution in succeeding years. He also has served as organist-choirmaster at St. Andrew's Presbyterian Church and Holy Blossom Temple in Toronto. As a recitalist, he has performed on the organ and harpsichord on CBC radio and on tours to major cities in Canada, the Eastern United States, and Europe.

Another youthful appointment as organist-choirmaster was Donald Hadfield, a fellow choirboy of Hugh McLean, who assumed such a position at St. James Anglican Church, Winnipeg, in 1946 at the age of 15. He began studying organ with Douglas Bodle at the same time, and engaged in concentrated organ studies in Manchester, England, for six months in 1950. Apart from a short sojourn in Montréal in the mid-1960s, Hadfield served as organist-choirmaster in several of Winnipeg's Anglican churches (St. James, St. Aidan's, St. John's Cathedral, All Saints') through the years and gave frequent public recitals and on CBC radio. Choirs he conducted made four singing tours of England between 1979 and 1989, and the choir at All Saints' Anglican Church, Winnipeg, recorded various anthems and service music under his direction. He is now organist at Holy Trinity Anglican Church, Winnipeg.

Visiting Recitalists

Several visiting recitalists came to Winnipeg during the 1940s, and two of them were world-renowned organists of their generation. The outstanding event of the early part of the decade was the recital by the famous French organist Joseph Bonnet, who returned to Winnipeg in 1941 after an absence of 19 years. Bonnet and his family had succeeded in leaving Paris safely just a few hours before the advancing German army entered the city, and now he was free to resume his touring activities. His recital program at Grace Church on 13 March 1941 consisted of these selections:

Offertoire upon Vive le Roi	Raison
Cancion religiosa	Cabezón

Toccata and Fugue in D Minor	Bach
Gavotta in F Major	Martini
Noël sur les flûtes	Daquin
Pièce Héroique	Franck
Noël languedocien	Guilmant
Marche des Rogations	Gigout
Scherzo in E Major	Widor
Berceuse	Bonnet
Ariel	Bonnet
Rhapsodie catalane	
(with pedal cadenza)	Bonnet

The critics' responses to Bonnet's recital were extremely general in nature, rather than dealing with specific aspects of his recital program. Nevertheless, they were unanimous in their praise:

> There have been tragic changes in Mr. Bonnet's world since his last visit, but his art has the same characteristics as before of quiet confidence, faultless taste, largeness and delicacy. He has the technical means for perfect performance with wonderful fluidity of movement, and everything on his programme was so exhaustively and simply treated that one sat blissfully, not wishing anything different. The music seemed to be receiving its complete fulfillment. ("Joseph Bonnet Gives Recital That Stirs," *Winnipeg Free Press*, 14 March 1941.)

> There was a deep spirituality about the playing which exactly expressed the personality and humility of the artist himself. . . .
> The brilliance of Bonnet's technique and his genius for phrase, always poetic and sometimes marvellously prophetic, making the almost commonplace sound like a voice from another world, and the richness of his coloring (called registration), were things to marvel at. ("Bonnet Genius of Organ Tone," *Winnipeg Tribune*, 14 March 1941.)

Another visiting recitalist was Alexander McCurdy, a member of the Curtis Institute of Music, Philadelphia, who performed this program at Westminster United Church on 7 October 1947:

Chorale Preludes:	Bach
All Praise Be Unto Thee	
Our Father Who Art In Heaven	
Hark! A Voice Saith, All are Mortal	
Prelude and Fugue in A minor	Bach
Meditation on the Bells	McCurdy
Greensleeves	Purvis
The Legend of the Mountain	Karg-Elert
Now Thank We All Our God	Karg-Elert
A Lovely Rose is Blooming	Brahms

Open Fifths	Flora Greenwood
Four Antiphons	Dupré

Dr. McCurdy's composition attracted the reviewer's attention, for the church recently had installed a Schulmerich carillon in the main tower (the performer was on retainer with the manufacturer at the time):

> Organ recitals are all too few in Winnipeg, and it was a distinct pleasure, as well as a novelty, to have one of the kind given . . . by Dr. Alexander McCurdy of Philadelphia. Not only was the recital featured by some playing of distinctly virtuoso order, but it marked the Canadian premiere of the use of carillonic bells. . . . Used by themselves, and in conjunction with the organ, they had a marvellous tone, and when they emerged, in the climactic moments, in full crescendo passages, they evoked a storm of applause from the audience. ("Dr. McCurdy Recital Appealing," *Winnipeg Free Press*, 8 October 1947.)

During this period H. Lowery, London, England, was in Winnipeg as an examiner for the Trinity College of Music. Dr. Lowery's recital at St. Matthew's Anglican Church on 6 June 1948 was announced, but not reviewed:

Overture in G	Stanley
Chorale Preludes:	Bach
My Soul is Filled With Longing	
O Whither Shall I Fly	
Canzona	Karg-Elert
Toccata and Fugue in D	Reger
Soliloquy	Alec Rowley
Liturgical Improvisation	George Oldroyd
Theme, Variations, and Finale	James Lyon
Irish Tune from County Derry	Traditional
Festival Piece	George Aitken

Marcel Dupré, the French organist believed to be the greatest organist of his time, returned to Winnipeg 26 years after his first appearance in the city. Dupré's recital at Westminster United Church on 12 November 1948 included these selections:

Fantasy and Fugue in G Minor	Bach
Concerto No. 8 in A Major	Handel
The Stations of the Cross	Dupré
Sonata No. 5 in D Major	Mendelssohn
Prelude on a Theme in	
Gregorian Style	Eric Delamarter
Pièce symphonique	Franck
Variations on an Old Noël	Dupré
Improvisation on a Given Theme	

The reviews of the event were wholly enthusiastic in their praise of his abilities as a player and improviser:

> In Marcel Dupré there is an inseparable blend of technical virtuosity and beauty of spirit. . . . Too many organists regard their instrument as a stop-gap for a symphony orchestra. Mr. Dupré is content to treat it as an organ, and it sounds gloriously as an organ.
>
> In Dupré's hand there is no thick, muddy masses of sound. The strands of the music stand out or are interwoven with the utmost grandeur or delicacy of effect. His tonal palette is boundless and discriminating, his taste is fastidious, and his heart is always in company with his head.
>
> It was an evening to remember for years to come, and it made one hope that Mr. Dupré will visit us more often than he has in the past. ("Dupré Superb at Organ Before Capacity Audience," *Winnipeg Free Press*, 13 November 1948.)

> His sure handling of large volumes of tone was linked with a keen sense of musical architecture, so that the design of the music seemed a growing organism. His colors were clear and unmuddied, his melodic line sharply contoured, his accents both subtle and incisive. . . . The exceptional gifts of M. Dupré were made manifest by his constructing at a moment's notice what was veritably a symphonic poem on two themes. . . .
>
> It may be said that M. Dupré took these themes and built them up into a symphony of elaborate structure, so developed that if one did not know the piece was improvised, the listener could take it for granted as carefully composed and written out for publication in the orthodox manner.
>
> The audience was so loud in demonstrating approval that upon the completion of the printed program, M. Dupré played three encores. They were Fileuse from Le Suite Bretonne, by Dupré; Toccata, Widor; and Prelude and Fugue in D Minor, Bach. ("Dupré Shows Glory of Pipe Organ," *Winnipeg Tribune*, 13 November 1948.)

The last visiting recitalist to visit Winnipeg in this decade was Harold Darke, St. Michael's Church, Cornhill, London, England, who was in Winnipeg as an examiner for the Associated Board of the Royal Schools of Music. Dr. Darke played this program at Westminster United Church on 25 May 1949:

Overture, Athalia	Handel
Chant de Mai	Jongen
Fantasie in F Minor	Mozart
Prelude and Fugue in A Minor	Bach
Meditation on Brother James' Air	Darke
Pièce héroique	Franck
Psalm Prelude No. 1	Howells
Toccata	Gigout

Although the ensuing review was brief, it recognized the player's restrained musicianship:

> Dr. Darke is a musician to whom clarity of style, of lucidity of execution are paramount. There is never, in his playing, an excess of emotional stress at the expense of the basic outlines of the music, and yet he is capable of the most poetic thought, and his feeling for "bigness" of tone enables him to build towards surging climaxes without recourse to forcing. ("Dr. Harold Darke Gives Distinguished Recital," *Winnipeg Free Press*, 26 May 1949.)

Trends in Repertoire

The practice of including transcriptions in organ recital programs declined even further in this recessionary period. Only 24 such pieces were included in the 26 known recitals of this period, about 11 percent of the total of 221 selections. Most of the selections were arrangements of simple tunes, light in texture, and technically undemanding. Adagio or andante pieces, such as Bach's *Air on the G String* and *Be Thou But Near*, Handel's *Largo*, Purcell's *Evening Hymn*, Saint-Saëns' *The Swan*, and Tchaikovsky's *Andante cantabile*, seemed to express in musical terms an air of peaceful detachment characteristic of this postwar period. The frequency of performance of organ transcriptions of works by these and other composers during this period is given in Table 6.

Table 6

	Number	Percent
Bach	5	21
Handel	4	17
Purcell	3	13
Saint-Saëns	2	8
Wagner	2	8
Couperin	1	4
Elgar	1	4
Mendelssohn	1	4
Mozart	1	4
Schumann	1	4

The standard Bach repertoire of toccatas, preludes and fugues, and chorale preludes again led the list of most frequently performed compositions, far ahead of the same familiar pieces by Widor and Franck heard by audiences of preceding periods. Mendelssohn's sonatas, when performed, were presented in their entirety. Guilmant's works, now heard less frequently than before, consisted mainly of his lighter pieces, occasionally juxtaposed with the more vigorous *March on a Theme by Handel*. While works by such English composers as Bairstow,

Whitlock, and Parry had been presented to audiences in earlier periods, they achieved slightly greater prominence in recitals of the 1940s. The frequency of performance of original works for organ by these and other composers during this period are given in Table 7.

Table 7

	Number	Percent
Bach	40	20
Widor	11	6
Franck	9	5
Mendelssohn	9	5
Handel	8	4
Karg-Elert	8	4
Vierne	7	4
Bairstow	6	3
Whitlock	5	3
Bonnet	4	2
Guilmant	4	2
Mozart	4	2
Parry	4	2

A Time for Renewal: *1950-1959*

THE DRAMATIC RESURGENCE of activity in the 1950s was exemplified by the increased number of organ installations and renovations that almost matched that of the peak periods of the first three decades of the century. Even so, there were only a few wholly new instruments; most of the installations were renovations or revisions of existing instruments. The Winnipeg Centre of the Canadian College of Organists, given the "Royal" designation in 1959, initiated several new projects in addition to sponsoring recitals by local members and others from eastern Canada and elsewhere. A chronological summary of organ installations, renovations, and relocations during this period is given in Appendix 1: Organ Installations.

St. Luke's Anglican Church, 1953

The English organ builders William Hill & Son and Norman & Beard extended their postwar Canadian operations into Winnipeg in the 1950s, when they were engaged in new installations and renovations. Their renovation of the three-manual, 30-stop Casavant organ, installed in St. Luke's Church in 1910, involved a new four-manual console and additional ranks of pipes, making a complete instrument of 61 stops. It was thought that the instrument was modelled in part on the organ in Westminster Abbey in London, England. According to the church organist:

> What wanted was an instrument capable of three functions: (1) adequately to accompany the liturgical services; (2) to be adequate for the whole range

of organ music from the early seventeenth century, through the Romantic School, to the present day; (3) to suit the acoustics and the difficulties peculiar to our own building. Emphasis has been placed upon the latter two requirements and the results have by no means robbed the instrument of meeting the first requirement. It is an organ which is unique in Winnipeg and in Western Canada. (Herbert D. White, Program Notes, Inaugural Recital, 26 October 1953.)

Severe problems developed in the renovated instrument in the following years, however; some of them were attributed to the severe winter climate, while others were alleged to have been inherent in the design and mechanism of the installation itself. Early in 1967 the rector wrote to the company, pointing out that the poor state of the organ made it difficult to hire a new organist. His vigorous complaint continued:

The major overhaul we contracted for seems to have done us more harm than good. No one from William Hill & Son and Norman & Beard appears much interested in giving us either service or explanation. You will be aware what this does for the reputation of your firm. (Letter from the rector to Hill, Norman & Beard, 17 March 1967.)

The ensuing interchange between church and company representatives continued for two years and covered matters relating to the effects of temperature changes in the church on tuning and regulation, and on questions about potential weaknesses in the console. Two prominent local organists also offered written opinions: one thought that the renovated 1953 instrument was in reality a reconstituted 1910 organ, since the company used two-thirds of the old instrument; another believed that the old Casavant was a better organ, given the problems of uneven keyboard touch, nonfunctioning stops, and defective manual controls in the new console. Twenty-five years later, the deficiences of the organ were still being discussed. In connection with a proposed revision prepared by Lawrence Ritchey, School of Music, The University of Manitoba, the church organist wrote:

When this organ was rebuilt in 1953, there was some unfortunate placement of ranks. This results in a lack of clarity. The sound is too heavy and too dark in color for proper support of singing, both of the congregation and the choir. The lack of clarity also makes it more difficult to play many of the standard works from traditional organ repertoire. With this improper design, it is almost impossible to develop the different tonal families on each division. Many of the required stops are there, but they are all mixed up between the front and the back [west swell or echo] organ. [The proposed revision] is an attempt, in other words, to restore the instrument to its former glory. Since the work in 1953 was, according to Professor Ritchey, "poorly done," these modifications would restore the proper balance in each of the separate families: diapasons, flutes, strings, and reeds. . . .

It is Professor Ritchey's opinion that, without adding any new pipework, this organ could be twice as good as it is, with these proposed changes. When you consider that this is now a $200,000 instrument—or more—a 5% improvement with these results is pretty impressive! (Letter from Martha Graham to Rector and Wardens, St. Luke's Church, 5 July 1979.)

The contract for the revision, involving the recommended relocation of pipes and other alterations, was given to the local technicians Buck & Mantle in 1979, and the results were quite satisfactory to everyone. The present four-manual, 59-stop organ is still the largest instrument in Winnipeg. Its West Organ, with separate great, swell, and pedal divisions mounted over the interior entrance to the church, also makes it unique in this respect.

The Winnipeg Centre of the Canadian College of Organists Reorganizes

During 1949 Herbert J. Sadler, the first chairman of the Winnipeg Centre of the Canadian College of Organists, had been making quiet inquiries among local organists to ascertain the extent of interest in reforming the group on a formal basis. He wrote to his former associate John J. Weatherseed, now at the Royal Conservatory of Music in Toronto and president of the Canadian College of Organists, for advice. Weatherseed's encouraging reply suggested that public interest and support might be attracted by the Centre's participation in a national project, the British Organ Restoration Fund, to finance the construction of a new organ in Coventry Cathedral, destroyed during the recent war. He enclosed the necessary application forms with his letter:

> I need hardly say that there is no idea in my mind of taking money out of Winnipeg to help an effete East live up to its obligations, but Coventry makes a wide public appeal, and I think you will find that an immediate definite objective will not only touch the hearts of those organists, clergy, and musicians, and choristers whom you contact in order to reopen the Centre, but it will also attract the members of the public to support the Recitals, Lectures, Hymn sing songs, which you put on in aid of the Fund. (Letter from John J. Weatherseed to Herbert J. Sadler, 2 January 1950.)

Sadler immediately sent his personal application and $3 membership fee to Weatherseed by return mail, then called a meeting of prospective members to proceed with the reorganization. On 27 February 1950 a motion "that the Winnipeg Centre of the Canadian College of Organists be re-established forthwith" was approved. A newspaper item announced the reorganization and invited all city church organists and other interested persons to assemble 10 April 1950 in Westminster Church to elect an executive and to discuss future plans. At the meeting attended by 11 organists, Sadler was again elected chairman. Other officers included John W. Clarke, vice-chairman; Clayton Lee, secretary; and Gertrude Newton, treasurer. Weatherseed visited Winnipeg in July to meet with the members and addressed them on the topic, "Music in Worship."

In May 1950 the Red River overflowed its banks in a damaging flood of historic proportions, covering farmlands, inundating several small towns in southern Manitoba, and invading many low sections of Winnipeg. For several weeks Winnipeg's music makers became both flood victims and flood fighters. Many homes were flooded, some churches were surrounded by water and suffered flooded basements, and citizens worked on building dikes. Some church services were cancelled or curtailed due to the lack of heat and electricity; thus many church organs were not used during this period. Church concerts and recitals were cancelled or delayed during this crisis period in the history of the province.

Local Players

Former levels of activity of the newly re-established Centre were not achieved immediately. However, in 1951 the Centre launched a new project, the Young Organists Recital, which was to continue for many years. The three chosen recitalists, previously auditioned by Ronald W. Gibson, now director of the School of Music at The University of Manitoba, would assume prominent positions in Winnipeg's community of organists in later years. This program for the group recital at All Saints' Anglican Church on 13 May 1951 included a male soloist:

Elwyn Davies	
Suite in F Major	Corelli, arr. Noble
Elegy	Thalben-Ball
Toccata, Gothic Suite	Boëllmann
Barry Anderson	
Chorale Improvisation	
on Nun danket	Karg-Elert
Prelude, Fugue, and Variation	
in B Minor	Franck
Carillon	Vierne
Winnifred Johnston	
Fugue in E-flat Major (St. Anne)	Bach
Harmonies du soir	Karg-Elert
French Clock	Bornschein
Epilogue	Willan

This event was described as the highlight of the season in the secretary's report of activities to the Toronto headquarters. Moreover, it was seen as a way of ensuring the continuation and growth of the Winnipeg Centre by involving promising younger organists in its activities at an early stage in their careers. Shortly afterward, young organists were admitted to membership at a reduced fee of $3 up to the time of their appointment as church organists, but they were not to undertake the CCO examinations during this period.

In 1952 the scale of activities of the Winnipeg Centre increased, although not to the former level of intensity of the 1930s. Ronald W. Gibson led off a series of four organ recitals in aid of the British Organ Restoration Fund; his program at Holy Trinity Anglican Church contained several selections with the dedication, "In Memoriam—George VI," in tribute to the king who had died. Other performers in the same series were John W. Clarke at All Saints' Anglican Church, Helen F. Young at Gordon-King Memorial United Church, and Herbert J. Sadler at Westminster United Church. The contributions of the Winnipeg Centre assisted in the attainment of the national objective, and eventually the new organ was installed in the rebuilt Coventry Cathedral as the gift of the Canadian College of Organists.

The forthcoming royal coronation of Queen Elizabeth II in England received recognition in a series of short Noon-Day Coronation Organ Recitals played in Holy Trinity Anglican Church in June 1952 by four different organists who had received their early musical training in England; their programs consisted wholly of music by British composers. A typical recital, played by Herbert D. White on 4 June 1952, consisted of these pieces:

A Purcell Suite	arr. Fricker
Concerto in B-flat	Arne
Folk Tune	Whitlock
Sonata in G, 1st Movement	Elgar
Crown Imperial	Walton

In the early 1950s members of the Winnipeg Centre devoted more attention to the development of the next generation of organists and to the quality of church music generally. The absence of members of the clergy at meetings continued to be a matter of concern, so it was realized that the responsibility for high standards in church music ultimately resided with organists themselves. Because enthusiasm for the earlier annual choir festivals had faded, the Centre redirected its energies to more focused activities, such as suitable music for weddings and a competition to encourage young organists. In October 1953 an organ prize was given to the School of Music at The University of Manitoba for the first time, and it was recommended that an organ category should be included in the Manitoba Music Teachers' scholarship series, to correct a long-standing omission.

A number of new organ installations or reconstructions took place in this decade, and the regular meetings of the Winnipeg Centre often were scheduled at the respective churches. Members combined business meetings with inspections of the new instruments and discussions with organ technicians or builder's representatives, followed by short organ recitals. The British organ building firm Hill, Norman & Beard was responsible for a number of organ installations or renovations in the 1950s; instruments by this company in St. Luke's Anglican Church and St. George's Anglican Church were examined by local organists. In connection with these projects, Herbert Norman, the head of the firm, and his chief voicer both discussed the matter of organ pipe voicing on two different occasions. Casavant's consultant, Edwin D. Northrup, also met with members to discuss the tonal design of the modern organ. Other instruments examined in these lecture-demonstration-recital meetings included the city's finest Casavant instruments in St. Stephen's Broadway United Church, St. Boniface Cathedral-Basilica, and All Saints' Anglican Church. In one meeting the group examined a recently rebuilt 1891 Warren organ that had been moved from All Saints' to St. Alban's Anglican Church in 1917. A diversion from the exclusive concentration on pipe organs was provided by a comparative demonstration of a new Conn electronic organ and the large Casavant organ in Westminster United Church.

Apart from organ inspections and demonstrations, the regular monthly meetings throughout the decade featured reports, lectures, and discussions on a variety of topics of current interest: the lack of young people preparing to become church musicians, methods for encouraging the development of young organists, and the impact of television on church attendance. On the practical side, members discussed such topics as organ accompaniments in church services, improvisation, the quality of hymns, choir training, the shortcomings of church music generally, and clergy-organist relations. In December 1955 the Festival of Carols was initiated; this was intended to become an annual event, but after 1956 it was displaced by other activities.

In March 1957 Hugh Bancroft, organist at All Saints' Anglican Church, left the city for Florida. The newspaper report of his departure from Winnipeg commented specifically on the achievements of two of his students from the 1940s, Douglas Bodle and Hugh McLean, as well as on the careers of several others who were occupying key positions as organists in Winnipeg churches. Of Bancroft the judgment was that he was "probably the only organist in Winnipeg whose repertoire and record of performance justify the name 'concert organist'," considering his mastery of all the major works of Bach, the organ concertos of Handel, the sonatas of Mendelssohn, and the important works of Franck, Widor, Vierne, as well as the organ concerto of Poulenc. ("Bancroft Leaves for Sarasota," *Winnipeg Free Press*, 23 March 1957.) Bancroft's stay in Florida was only brief, for within an few months he went on the Nassau, The Bahamas, for an equally short period. He returned to Canada in 1958—the climates in both places were "too hot for an organist," he said—to take a position at All Saints' Cathedral in Edmonton, where he remained until his death in 1988.

Bancroft's successor at All Saints' was Henwood Jewell, LTCL, GTCL, ARCM, FRCO, who had been recruited from England, where he had served as organist in several London churches following his training at Trinity College. Thus the order of succession in English church music at All Saints' was ensured. His inaugural recital at the church on 29 October 1957 consisted of these selections, with adequate representation of the English school of organ composition:

Prelude and Bell Allegro	Stanley, arr. Williams
Adagio, Trio Sonata No. 3	Bach
Sonata No. 2	Hindemith
Prelude in the Form of a Toccata	Stanford
Chorale, Op. 37, No. 4	Jongen
Elegy	Thalben-Ball
Meditation No. 2 in F-sharp Minor	Guilmant
Prelude in A	Bairstow

In 1959 the designation "Royal" was added to the name of the Canadian College of Organists by permission of Queen Elizabeth in commemoration of the 50th anniversary of the founding of the College. There were 42 members in the Winnipeg Centre at the time.

Visiting Recitalists

The first organist with an international reputation to visit Winnipeg in this decade was the Belgian musician Flor Peeters. Acclaimed by music critics as a master of the technique and resources of the organ, Peeters was organist at Metropolitan Cathedral in Malines, Belgium, and professor of organ at the Lemmens Institute in the same city; he was also professor of organ at the Royal Conservatory in Antwerp. In addition to extensive concerts in Europe, he performed in the United States and Canada in 1946 and 1947. Peeters' compositions included works for organ, piano, voice, orchestra, and chorus. This was the program for his recital on 28 November 1950 at Westminster United Church, sponsored by the church choir:

Passacaglia and Fugue in C Minor	Bach
Preludio	Corelli
Giga	Loeillet
Grand pièce symphonique	Franck
Greensleeves	Purvis
Étude symphonique	Bossi
Elégie	Peeters

    Chorale Preludes: Peeters
        How Lovely Shines the Morning Star
        Now Rest Beneath Night's Shadow
    Lied to the Sun   Peeters

The critics of both newspapers commented specifically on the recitalist's own compositions, in addition to complimentary descriptions of the other pieces. The two fragments are perhaps more indicative of the divergent imaginative reconstructions on the part of the critics than informative about the music itself:

> Mr. Peeters' playing was in turn grandiose, sprightly and serene as his selections demanded.
>
> One of the highlights of the concert was his brilliant playing of his own composition Lied to the Sun. Here Mr. Peeters captured the sparkling effect of sunlight in a lively toccata dedicated to the source of light. ("Visiting Belgian Organist Master of Interpretation," *Winnipeg Free Press*, 30 November 1950.)

> Mr. Peeters' technique at the console, pedal and in registration made even Bach seem "all in a day's work."
>
> The opening Bach Passacaglia and Fugue performance was of grand dimensions, spacious in outline and clear and forceful in its contrapuntal weaving. Melody steady and sweet sang its way through reed tones, sometimes in upper octave, sometimes in tenor repetition. Bach's poetic instinct and religious fervour were revealed in varied tonal beauty. . . .
>
> The fifth and final section of Mr. Peeters' Lied (Hymn) Symphony, composed after his visit to America in 1947, concluded the printed program, in bursts of splendor and rich sonorities. Some passages had the scintillating animation of crisp wavelets glinting in the sun. ("Flor Peeters Brings to Life Organ Voice," *Winnipeg Tribune*, 30 November 1950.)

Charles Peaker, organist at St. Paul's Anglican Church, Toronto, visited Winnipeg twice during 1951. Early in his musical life he was a theatre organist before assuming his lifelong association with various churches in Ontario. He became one of Canada's foremost concert organists, whose performing career included tours in England and the United States. Peaker taught at the Toronto Conservatory of Music for 40 years, serving briefly as director. He also served as president of the CCO in 1944-45. In 1964 he was appointed university organist at the University of Toronto. On his first visit to Winnipeg his recital was the opening event at the Canadian Federation of Music Teachers' annual convention; he played this program at Westminster United Church on 3 July 1951:

    Fantasia and Fugue in G Minor   Bach
    Aria   Peeters

Diferencias	Cabezón
Pavane	Byrd
Auf Mein Lieben Gott	Hanff
Pastorale	Old French Carol
Communion	Purvis
Naiades	Vierne
Prelude	Bales
Ecce jam noctis	Willan
Urbs Hierusalem beata	Willan
Introduction, Passsacaglia, and	
Fugue in E-flat Minor	Willan

Later in the year, on 26 September 1951, he was sponsored by the choir of Westminster Church; this was the first recital to be given on the new console and reconditioned organ at the church. His program was:

The Cuckoo	Daquin
The Swallow	Ireland
The Bee	Schubert
Mr. Ben Jonson's Pleasure	Milford
Prelude and Fugue in B Minor	Bach
Chorale in A Minor	Franck
Ayre, Minuet	Clarke
Ecce jam noctis, Andernach,	
Puer nobis nascitur	Willan
The Musical Clocks, 7 pieces	Haydn
Prelude and Fugue in G Minor	Bach

Late in 1951 the Icelandic National League sponsored an organ recital by Pall Isolfsson, director of the Reykjavik Conservatory of Music and at organist the Cathedral of Iceland. Following musical training in Iceland, Isolfsson studied in Leipzig, where he was an assistant to Karl Straube at St. Thomas' Church in the city; in 1925 he studied with Joseph Bonnet in Paris. He played this program at Westminster United Church on 9 November 1951:

Passacaglia in D Minor	Buxtehude
Lobt Gott, ihr Christen allzugleich	Buxtehude
Prelude and Fugue in E-flat	Bach
In dulci jubilo	Bach
Toccata and Fugue in D Minor	Bach
Chorale Prelude: Old Icelandic Tune	Hallgrimur Helgason
Chorale Prelude: Old Icelandic Tune	Jon Leifs
Chorale Prelude, Chaconne:	
Old Icelandic Theme	Pall Isolfsson

A short, purely descriptive review reported that a small but appreciative audience heard several of the player's "virile full-bodied compositions" and that his performance generally "was distinguished by its consummate mastery of the organ and crystal clarity of tone." ("Icelandic Organist Gives Impressive Recital Here," *Winnipeg Tribune*, 10 November 1951.)

William Neil McKie, organist and master of the choristers at Westminster Abbey since 1941, was in the city in 1952 in his capacity as an examiner for the Royal Schools of Music. A native of Australia, Dr. McKie studied on a scholarship at the Royal College of Music, London, before occupying posts as organ scholar at Worcester College, Oxford, and director of Music at Clifton College, Bristol. In 1938 he accepted a position as organist in Melbourne, Australia, then returned to England in 1941 to take up an appointment at Magdalen College, Oxford. In connection with his Winnipeg visit, local newspaper articles reported that he had played at the wedding of Princess Elizabeth and the Duke of Edinburgh in 1947, and described preparations for the coronation in 1953 of Queen Elizabeth II in Westminster Abbey where McKie would conduct a choir of 400 singers, an orchestra of 60 players, and trumpeters. During his current tour McKie gave organ recitals at several locations in the United States and in six Canadian centres. He offered this program of mainly English music at Westminster United Church on 30 May 1952, under the auspices of the Winnipeg Centre:

Overture to Athalia	Handel
Musette, Minuet, from Berenice	Handel
Ostinato, from a Concerto	Handel
Prelude and Fugue in A Minor	Bach
Pastorale	Franck
Rhapsody No. 3	Howells
Larghetto	S. S. Wesley
Fantasia and Fugue	Parry

At the time of his visit to Winnipeg, Frederick Silvester was principal of the Toronto Conservatory of Music summer school. This organist, recitalist (sometimes over CBC radio), conductor, composer, and administrator was national president of the CCO, 1945-47, and served as registrar of the Royal Conservatory of Music for twenty years, until 1966. He presented this program in connection with the 65th anniversary celebrations at Augustine United Church on 1 October 1952:

Suite from Bonduca	Purcell
Larghetto, Clarinet Quintet	Mozart
Minuet and Musette	Handel
Concerto No. 2 in B-flat	Handel
Andante	Stametz
Allegro, Violin Sonata	Corelli
Toccata and Fugue in D Minor	Bach

Two Preludes on Plainsong Melodies:	Willan
Ecce jam noctis	
Urbs Hierusalem beata	
Scherzo for the Flutes	Crawford
Introduction and Passacaglia	
in D Minor	Reger

The brief review was respectful but superficial, and completely lacking in insight into the musical structures or the refinements of organ playing. Instead, it remained safely within the realm of common platitudes, referring to "a well-planned and beautifully executed recital," one which "displayed fine technique and musical style." As for the pieces performed, the Mozart was "beautifully expressive," the Handel was "played brightly," and the Reger was "performed with many expressive dramatic touches." ("Recital Marks Augustine's Anniversary," *Winnipeg Free Press*, 2 October 1952.)

Another visitor from Toronto was the organist and recitalist Muriel Gidley Stafford. In addition to her duties as a church organist, she was a recitalist at the Casavant Society in Toronto and a frequent performer at annual conventions of the Canadian College of Organists there. A former examiner for the Royal Conservatory of Music, she also served as a member of the board of examiners for the CCO. She was the first woman to head the Toronto Chapter of the Royal Canadian College of Organists, and served as the first woman national president of the RCCO, 1957-59. Her program at Westminster United Church on 16 January 1956 included these pieces:

Sonata No. 2, 1st Movement	Hindemith
Elévation	Couperin
Paspy, A Concerto Movement	Felton
Fantasia in F Minor	Mozart
Pastorale	Bancroft
Three Choral Preludes:	Bach
Glory to God in the Highest	
When We Are in Greatest Need	
Come, Holy Ghost, Lord God	
Le banquet céleste	Messiaen
Spinning Song	Dupré
Prelude and Fugue in C Minor	Willan

About this time, a former Winnipeg organist, Rodolphe Pépin, who had been absent from the city for 37 years, returned to give a recital at his former church. Born in New Hampshire, Pépin came to St. Boniface in 1911, at the age of 19. His development as a student of Fred M. Gee was so rapid that he gave his first recital after six months of study. Pépin became organist at St. Boniface Cathedral in 1914, where he remained for five years before leaving to take an appointment at the New England Conservatory of Music in

Boston. In 1925 he went to Paris to study with such notables as Dupré, Bonnet, and other teachers. From 1944 he was organist at Mission Church, Boston, and played frequent recitals in the eastern United States and Montréal. Pépin played this program at St. Boniface Basilica on 22 April 1956:

Suite gothique	Boëllmann
Das alte Jahr	Bach
Jesu, Joy of Man's Desiring	Bach
Fantasia and Fugue in G Minor	Bach
Berceuse	Vierne
Prelude and Fugue in G Minor	Bach
For Easter	Quef
First Movement, Symphony No. 5	Widor

In 1956 two former students of Hugh Bancroft who had commenced their musical careers as church organists in Winnipeg in their youth, and who later achieved international recognition, returned to Winnipeg to perform at Bancroft's church, All Saints' Anglican. Douglas Bodle came from Toronto to play this program at All Saints' Anglican Church on 16 September 1956:

Prelude and Fugue in G Minor	Buxtehude
Come Redeemer	Bach
Prelude and Fugue in G Minor	Bach
Pastorale	Franck
Capriccio on the Notes of a Cuckoo	Purvis
Legend of the Mountain	Karg-Elert
Three Pieces	Bancroft

A year later, almost to the day, when he was vacationing in Winnipeg, he gave a similarly structured recital program that balanced five Bach selections by pieces by four contemporary composers.

The other returning recitalist in 1956 was Hugh McLean. He had just made his debut in 1955 with the London Philharmonic orchestra under Sir Adrian Boult in the premiere performance of Malcolm Arnold's *Organ Concerto*; the occasion was a command performance for Queen Elizabeth II. He played these selections at All Saints' Anglican Church on 2 October 1956:

Fantasia for Double Organ	Gibbons
Prelude and Fugue in C Major	Bach
Andante in F for Mechanical Organ	Mozart
Pastorale	Franck
Introduction, Passacaglia, and Fugue	Willan

During the 1950s both local newspapers displayed a consistent indifference to the performances of visiting organists (recitals by local organists had been ignored for decades). Apart from the detailed accounts of Flor Peeters' recital in 1950, the reviews of several other recitals amounted to merely perfunctory descriptions of the various pieces on the program; some performances were ignored entirely. In the case of a recital by Lady Susi Jeans at St. Luke's Anglican Church on 12 April 1955, although the announcement of the forthcoming visit of this distinguished English organist consisted of a fairly detailed biographical sketch describing her musical studies with Karl Straube in Leipzig and briefly with Widor in Paris, along with her extensive concertizing throughout the United Kingdom and Europe, her program was not printed (perhaps it was not available in advance), and her free-admission concert was not reviewed. Whether this general neglect reflected a deliberate policy of the newspapers or the incompetence of their staff critics cannot be known with certainty. What is clear, however, is that most of the reviews during this period, when they occurred at all, were unskilled efforts at musical reporting.

Trends in Repertoire

The relatively low proportion of transcriptions to original compositions increased only slightly during this period. A total of 59 such pieces were included in the 58 known recitals, about 14 percent of the total of 414 pieces. The patterns of the previous period continued; with few exceptions, these soft-textured adagios provided relief for both players and listeners alike from the longer, more demanding pieces from the repertoire of original organ compositions. The less musically knowledgeable members of audiences probably regarded many of these arrangements as genuine organ compositions and welcomed their recurrence on recital programs. The frequency of performance of organ transcriptions by some major composers during this period is given in Table 8.

Table 8

	Number	Percent
Bach	10	17
Handel	10	17
Purcell	10	17
Corelli	3	5
Couperin	3	5
Byrd	2	4
Mendelssohn	2	4
Saint-Saèns	1	2
Wagner	1	2

In addition to the large number of works by Bach that still were performed with great frequency, original works by several contemporary composers achieved prominence in this period. Visiting Canadian recitalists and local players alike championed the works of Healey Willan, particularly his preludes and fugues, and the *Introduction, Passacaglia, and Fugue*. One local organist presented compositions by the American composer Richard Purvis in eight of his recitals. Works by the modern Belgian organist Flor Peeters were played by several local organists a few years after his recital in Winnipeg in 1950. Compositions by representatives of the French school continued to occupy a prominent place in the recitals of this period. Such perennial favourites as Franck's *Pièce héroique*, his *Prelude, Fugue, and Variation*, and various chorales; Guilmant's *March on a Theme by Handel*; Widor's marches and the *Toccata* from his *Symphony No. 5*; and Vierne's *Carillon* continued to be heard by local audiences throughout this period. The compositions of Bonnet, Karg-Elert, and Mendelssohn maintained modest but consistent positions on recital programs, as in preceding periods. The frequency of performances of original works for organ by these and some other composers during this period are given in Table 9.

Table 9

	Number	Percent
Bach	65	18
Willan	27	8
Purvis	13	4
Franck	12	4
Peeters	12	3
Vierne	11	3
Widor	10	3
Guilmant	7	2
Schumann	7	2
Whitlock	7	2
Bonnet	6	2
Howells	6	2
Karg-Elert	6	2
Mendelssohn	6	2

Recent Times: *1960-1997*

IT IS APPARENT that the number of pipe organs in Manitoba has stabilized, for after the postwar resurgence of activity in the preceding 10-year period, the numbers of installations in each of the decades from 1960 onward were among the lowest in the century. Even so, the pattern of organ installations since 1960 has exhibited considerable diversity: installations of new Casavant organs and instruments representative of several new Canadian organ builders, several historic instruments from the United States, a major import from Germany, and relocations of instruments of Canadian builders of earlier times. Some of the local work was in the form of community projects involving skilled parishioners working under the supervision of local organ technicians. Musical activity, on the other hand, was intense: the number of visiting recitalists during the 1960s, both from Canada and other countries, exceeded that of any other period. Although members of the Winnipeg Centre of the Royal Canadian College of Organists were less active as performers, they undertook some demanding new projects that broadened the scope of their influence in the musical community generally. A chronological summary of organ installations, renovations, and relocations during these recent years is given in Appendix 1: Organ Installations.

First Presbyterian Church, 1963

The most important event of this period, from the point of view of contemporary organ design, was the installation of a new two-manual, 30-stop von Beckerath organ in First Presbyterian Church. The church's first organ, a three-

First Presbyterian Church, Winnipeg.
von Beckerath, 1963, 2/30.

manual instrument, was originally in the home of a wealthy resident of Walkerton, Ontario, and later was installed in Winnipeg's Province Theatre by C. Franklin Legge, the Toronto builder, around 1930. In spite of the economic depression at that time, the women's group of the church succeeded in raising the purchase price of $2,000. The organ sustained serious damage during the Winnipeg flood of 1950, and although some repairs were carried out, the results were disappointing. After local organists Ronald Gibson and Filmer Hubble heard the decrepit organ and pronounced it dead, it was decided that the cost of restoring an instrument of that type could not be justified. In 1960 the decision was made to replace it with a new instrument, and the future purchase was approved.

A member of the congregation proposed the idea of a von Beckerath organ around 1961, and a Montréal organ consultant was retained to assist in the decision. Casavant Frères entered a bid for a tracker instrument, but the contract had already been given to von Beckerath. The decision to locate the organ in the rear gallery of the church was controversial, for it would obstruct the view of the Cameron Highlanders stained-glass window, but the window was relocated when the organ was installed. Built in the tradition of Silbermann and Schnitger organs in the time of Bach, the von Beckerath organ featured straight mechanical action, using modern materials for lightness of touch and unnicked pipe mouths for clarity of speech. The visible pipes, all functional, were installed in boxed towers for directional sound projection. The instrument was designed to be an adequate accompanying instrument for vocal solos, instrumental ensembles, choir, and congregational singing. It was also well suited for the performance of early organ music. The organ was revoiced and adjusted by Gerhard Brunzema in 1990. The stoplist was as follows:

HAUPTWERK		RÜCKPOSITIV	
Quintadena	16	Gedackt	8
Prinzipal	8	Quintadena	8
Rohrflöte	8	Prinzipal	4
Spitzflöte	8	Rohrflöte	4
Oktave	4	Oktave	2
Gemshorn	4	Nasat	1 1/3
Nasat	2 2/3	Sifflöte	1
Oktave	2	Sesquialtera	II
Waldflöte	2	Scharf	III-IV
Mixtur	IV-VI	Krummhorn	8
Trompete	8	Tremulant	
PEDAL		COUPLERS	
Subbass	16	Rückpositiv to Hauptwerk	
Prinzipal	8	Rückpositiv to Pedal	
Rohrgedackt	8	Hauptwerk to Pedal	
Oktave	4		
Nachthorn	2		
Mixtur	V		
Fagott	16		
Trompete	8		
Schalmei	4		

The installation was reported in detail, partly because of the uniqueness of the organ, the first modern mechanical-action instrument to be installed in the city, and because the organist for the inaugural recital was the noted American organist Robert Noehren, from the University of Michigan. The article included information about the mechanical aspects of the organ, its historical predecessors, and other similar installations in Canada. There were also some chatty lines about the relationship between the builder and the recitalist:

To Rudolf van Beckerath every organ he builds is like a child. He now has nine in North America.

This week in Winnipeg's First Presbyterian Church, the 56-year-old organ builder from Hamburg, Germany, put the finishing touches to his latest "child," a 2,000-pipe medium-size instrument, then sat back and said "she sounds wonderful."

"About the best organ west of Montreal," said music professor Robert Noehren, who came here from Michigan University's music school in Ann Arbor to give the first recital.

It's a mutual admiration society between the two friends.

The organ builder thinks Noehren is about the best organist this side of the Atlantic—"better than many an artist in Europe; when I hear him play I can sit back and breathe freely." The organist likes von Beckerath's work and was responsible for it coming to this country.

The two met in the old northern German city of Luenenburg 10 years ago, when Mr. von Beckerath was restoring a famous old organ in the cathedral there.

Prof. Noehren was so convinced of von Beckerath's skill and approach to music and instrument, that three years later the first Beckerath mechanical organ went up in Cleveland, Ohio.

Since then, the German craftsman and his 26 helpers have built instruments in Richmond, Va., Bloomington, Ind., the DeLand University in Florida, the Pittsburgh Cathedral.

There are four Beckerath organs in Canada, three (including an $80,000-instrument at St. Joseph's Oratory) in Montreal. (Manfred Jager, "New Church Organ 'Best in West'," *Winnipeg Tribune*, 2 December 1963.)

The inaugural recital by Robert Noehren was attended by about 500 music lovers, including Sir Ernest MacMillan, who was in the city for recording sessions with the CBC. Noehren, university organist and professor of organ at the University of Michigan, toured extensively in the United States, Canada, and also in Europe on ten different occasions. His organ recordings were well known to the listening public, and he was one of only two organists outside France to win the coveted Grand Prix du Disque. His program on 3 December 1963 included these selections:

Variations on Mein junges Leben hat ein End	Sweelinck
Prelude, Fugue, and Chaconne	Buxtehude
Benedictus, Dialogue	Couperin
Noël: Grand Jeu et Duo	Daquin
Variations on the Chorale Vater unser im Himmelreich (Sonata No. 6)	Mendelssohn
Sketch in D-flat	Schumann

Chorale Prelude on	
Es ist ein Ros' entsprungen	Brahms
Fugue in D Major	Bach
Chorale Preludes:	Bach
Wachet auf!	
Alle Menschen müssen sterben	
Toccata and Fugue in D Minor	Bach

University of Manitoba, School of Music, 1967

In conjunction with the completion of a new building for the School of Music
on the University campus in 1965, plans were made to install a pipe organ in
the concert hall. The Men's Musical Club of Winnipeg strongly supported the
project and offered to contribute to the University Organ Fund. The Club's
fund-raising activities included the sponsorship of a production of Handel's *Acis
and Galatea* in Augustine Church and a Symphony Pops Concert; additional
funds provided by the Women's Auxiliary supplemented individual subscriptions and contributions by the government. A sum of $8,000 was given to the
University in December 1965 to offset the total cost of the $30,000 instrument.

The contract with Casavant Frères for a two-manual, 21-stop instrument
stated that "the general display of the pipe organ shall make use of the natural
shapes of the pipe work to form an artistic and contemporary design dictated

*The University of Manitoba, School of Music, Winnipeg.
Casavant, 1967, 2/21.*

by the internal planning of the building." The organ was installed in mid-1967, followed by dedication ceremonies in September that included a short recital by Conrad Grimes, a staff member of the School of Music. His program included pieces by Clérambault, two chorale preludes by Brahms, and Bach's transcription of the Concerto in D minor by Vivaldi.

Knox United Church, 1968

The 1906 Casavant organ had served the church congregation for sixty years, first in a previous sanctuary, and since its reinstallation in the new, larger edifice in 1917. In the intervening years the instrument had become slow in operation, noisy, and in need of repair, and it was feared that further deterioration would prejudice the high standard of musical worship in the church. The purchase of a new instrument was made possible, in part, by funds accruing from substantial gifts from two visitors from Iowa who first attended the church on World Communion Sunday in 1945. They were sufficiently impressed with the service on that day that they made a contribution on the spot. The couple made other donations during their visits to the church in later years, including a gift of 960 acres of Saskatchewan farm land in 1952. These and other gifts were administered by the DuVal Foundation, which allocated them to various church projects over the years.

The plans for the new organ involved a careful comparison of the specifications of other large organs in Augustine Church, St. Andrew's Church, and Zion Church. The intention was to preserve the original hand-carved walnut woodwork surrounding the existing pipe facade that would now be replaced by speaking pipes. The new three-manual, 40-stop Casavant organ was installed and dedicated on 10 November 1968. Virgil Fox, the American organ virtuoso and organist of Riverside Church, New York, played the inaugural recital on 16 November 1968, a year that also marked the 100th anniversary of Knox Church. His program on that occasion is listed later in this chapter.

Gloria Dei Lutheran Church, 1977

The oldest historic organ in Manitoba, a two-manual, 16-stop instrument made by the American builder George Stevens in 1850, was installed in the balcony of Gloria Dei Church, Winnipeg, in 1977. The early history of the organ up to 1894 is unknown, but from that date until 1973 it resided in the Universalist Church, Rumford, Maine. John Shortridge, an organ builder in Rockport, Maine, purchased the instrument and later offered it for sale through the Organ Clearing House.

When this suburban congregation erected its new church building in 1977, some members of the congregation wanted an electronic instrument, but the

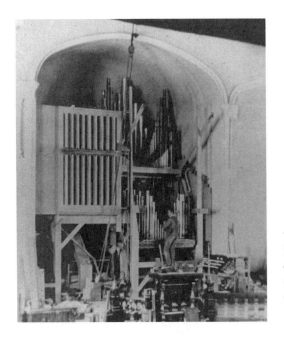

The reinstallation of Knox United (Presbyterian) Church, Winnipeg, in 1917. First installed by Casavant, 1906, 3/32.

Knox United (Presbyterian) Church, Winnipeg. Casavant, 1906, 3/32. Installation completed 1917. Photo from Casavant archives.

Gloria Dei Lutheran Church, Winnipeg.
George Stevens, 1850, 2/16. Installed 1977. The oldest historic
organ in Winnipeg.

pastor at the time, an American who was interested in church music and organs, knew the sources in the United States where used pipe organs could be obtained, and influenced the congregation in that direction. Some of the men of the congregation retrieved the organ from its location in Maine, transported it to Winnipeg, set it up, and maintained it until a local organ technician took over its care. The Stevens organ remains intact and unaltered in its conservative tonal disposition and is an excellent example of the builder's small organ design.

GREAT		SWELL	
Open Diapason	8	Open Diapason	8
Dulciana	8	Viola da Gamba	8
Clarabella	8	Stop Diapason	8
Stop Diapason Treble	8	Stop Diapason Bass	8
Stop Diapason Bass	8	Principal	4
Principal	4	Oboe	8
Flute	4	Tremolo	
Twelfth	2 2/3		
Fifteenth	2		

PEDAL		
Sub Bass	16	Couple Great and Swell
		Couple Pedals to Swell Bass
		Blowers Signal

The inaugural recital was played by Lawrence Ritchey, School of Music, The University of Manitoba, on 12 June 1977. The program consisted of a selection of pieces by German, English, and American composers.

First Mennonite Church, 1991

When the new Mennonite church building was erected in 1950, provision was made for the eventual installation of a pipe organ in the design of the chancel area. Even though a pipe organ fund was established at that time, the church used electronic instruments until the church debt was retired and the purchase of a pipe organ was approved in May 1989. The church acquired a 13-rank, two-manual instrument from St. Jude's Anglican Church, originally built around 1915 by the Canadian Pipe Organ Company. Winnipeg technicians Richard Buck and Bruce Mantle renovated and installed the organ early in 1991; the augmented version has 20 ranks, with some unification, yielding 37 stops. The organ dedication recital, designed to illustrate the various tonal divisions of the organ, was played by the church's five organists. The First Mennonite Church (and Burrows Bethel Mennonite Church) are among the few Mennonite churches in Canada with a pipe organ.

First Mennonite Church, Winnipeg.
Canadian Pipe Organ, c.1915; Buck & Mantle reconstruction,
2/37 from 20 ranks. Installed 1991.

Community Organ Projects

Crestview United Church, a small suburban Winnipeg congregation, is the only known instance where an electronic instrument was replaced by a pipe organ, thanks to the initiative of the church minister and the contribution of many hundreds of hours of work by dedicated volunteer members who favoured the pipe organ. In the early 1980s the church obtained a C. Franklin Legge organ, Opus 84, 1930, from a private residence near Belleville, Ontario; the instrument formerly was in St. Andrew's Presbyterian Church in that city. The organ was installed by skilled members of the congregation and completely redesigned in a manner different from its traditional layout. The open pipework was mounted in a symmetrical array over the enclosed windchests and other mechanisms in a case at the rear of the church, with the console at the front. The older electrical parts were replaced by some solid-state components. The total cost of the installation was about $7,200, including the $5,200 purchase price of the original instrument. There is much unification in the two-manual instrument: six ranks of pipes yield 27 stops. The organ was dedicated on 16 May 1982.

Although St. Thomas Anglican Church, another small suburban church, was built in 1923, it did not obtain a pipe organ until 1932, when it received

St. Thomas Anglican Church, Winnipeg.
Karn, 1910, 2/14. Installed 1932.

a two-manual, 14-stop Karn organ from St. Peter's Anglican Church. This 1910 instrument was rebuilt in the 1950s by F. Radcliffe, a Winnipeg organ technician, but progressive deterioration of the decrepit tubular-pneumatic action in subsequent years required immediate attention in the late 1980s. The decision to rebuild was the product of discussions among members of the church vestry on the relative merits of a pipe organ versus an electronic instrument. Although the rector was reported as having opposed the renovation project, the opinion in favour of the pipe organ prevailed. Richard Buck and Bruce Mantle, local organ technicians, proposed a figure for the restoration of the organ, including conversion to electric action, that was beyond the resources of the parish. Nevertheless, the estimated reconstruction cost of $15,000 was reduced to one-third with the use of volunteer labour by some men—carpenters, electricians, machinists, painters—of the congregation, along with help from nearby Sparling United Church. Working long hours over a period of many months under the supervision of Buck and Mantle, the renovation was completed and celebrated on 11 December 1989. This event consisted of a musical concert with a Christmas content involving soloists and a high school choir conducted by Barry Anderson, organist at Knox United Church, who opened the event with a performance of William Albright's narrated musical offering, "The King of Instruments." Ronald W. Gibson, the prominent Winnipeg organist who had learned to play the organ while a choir boy at St. Peter's Church 70 years earlier, was in attendance.

The story of the two organs in Calvary Temple, a downtown Winnipeg church, also illustrates how pipe organs can be acquired, installed, and maintained using volunteer labour. The two-manual, 23-stop organ now in the Temple Chapel was manufactured by the W. W. Kimball Company, Chicago, for a movie theatre in Kansas City; it was later installed in Winnipeg's Orpheum Theatre before being acquired by the Temple in the 1940s. When the old church building was demolished in 1985 and replaced by an education building in the following year, the organ was relocated in the chapel of the new edifice. The decorated pipe facade of the instrument is misleading, for these original pipes are simply arrayed against a front wall to provide a visual focus; the functioning pipes of the organ are enclosed in a chamber high on an adjoining wall. The organ was installed by Keates-Geissler Pipe Organs, Acton, Ontario, and some work was done by a volunteer member of the congregation. A few years later, the Temple acquired parts of a Casavant organ previously used in a Toronto church and other components; these were intended to comprise the organ for the main auditorium of the Temple. Since the architectural design of the new auditorium had not included an adequate space allowance for the 16-foot organ pipes, the same volunteer technician of the congregation took several of the pipes to his basement workshop, cut them back, and resoldered the ends back on at 45-degree angles to provide the necessary

Calvary Temple - Chapel, Winnipeg.
Kimball, c. 1910, 2/23. Installed 1986. This organ was
first in a movie theatre in the United States, then in
Winnipeg's Orpheum Theatre before it was acquired by
the Temple in the 1940s.

clearance under the auditorium ceiling. A new console was supplied by Keates-Geissler in 1991 to complete the installation of the three-manual, 34-stop instrument. Both organs are now maintained by the man who knew nothing about pipe organs only a few years earlier.

The congregation of the Roman Catholic Parish Church in St. Norbert, a southern suburb of Winnipeg, had to wait about five years from the time when the organ built by Edward Lye in 1906 was removed from its former location—the second in its history—in Sacré-Coeur Church by Winnipeg organ technician James Musselwhite in 1992 and finally installed in its new home. Originally the instrument was intended for a parish church in Ste-Geneviève, a nearby rural town, but the plan had to be abandoned because of the opposition of the parish priest. A city organist's aunt, who lived in a residence adjoining the St. Norbert Church, persuaded its parish priest to store the organ in the balcony of the church until the necessary funding for its installation could be secured. (The church building, erected in 1929 following the destruction by fire of the original Parish Church that contained the first Casavant organ installed in

Manitoba, first housed a two-manual Thomas reed organ, then an electronic instrument for the last 25 years.) The money for the retored pipe organ was raised through a series of five bingo games that raised $25,000. Working under the supervision of James Musselwhite, 30 volunteers of the congregation set up a workshop in the church balcony and worked together in groups of four or five on daily shifts to complete the extensive renovations involved in the installation of the organ, finished in the spring of 1997. Their efforts made it possible to acquire a pipe organ that otherwise would have cost about $85,000.

Local Players

Local organists continued to give public recitals in their own or other churches, although none of these were presented under the auspices of the Winnipeg Centre of the RCCO. The performers were among a new generation of musicians who would be active in the affairs of Winnipeg's church music community in subsequent years: Barry Anderson, Conrad Grimes, Donald Hadfield, Donald Menzies, and Winnifred (Johnston) Sim. At the same time, the annual student organist recitals, featuring between 8 and 12 performers, continued to be offered in the spring of each year. These events became adjudicated competitions in 1967. In 1969 the competitors were judged in junior and senior service playing, as well as in performance categories.

Recitals by local organists also were not as frequent as in earlier years. On 14 November 1971 Ronald Gibson played a recital on the modern three-manual Casavant organ that had just been installed in the new St. Stephen's Broadway United Church, rebuilt after a destructive fire in 1968; a week later he was granted a lifetime membership in the Winnipeg Centre of the RCCO. St. Stephen's was the site for recitals by other members as well: in 1972 Lawrence Ritchey, School of Music, The University of Manitoba, played an all-Bach program; Winnifred Sim played a recital there also. In the fall of the same the year, a series of noonday recitals were offered at the church by other members of the Winnipeg Centre.

Visiting Recitalists

Although members of the Winnipeg Centre of the Royal Canadian College of Organists offered relatively fewer public organ recitals during the 1960s than in preceding years, the number of visiting recitalists coming to Winnipeg in this decade was greater than in any period before or since. Half of these touring organists were from the United States, several were from Europe and England, but only two Canadians were invited. Some of these performers also offered master classes for local organists and church musicians. Several of the most prominent organists of the day were among these visiting recitalists, already known to the musical public through their recordings. Some of them held full-time positions as church musicians, others were faculty members in university music departments, and a few were sufficiently successful to be free of church or academic duties altogether. The RCCO sponsored only about half of these visiting recitalists; the remainder were brought to the city by the larger churches in connection with new organ installations or other significant events.

1960	February 23	George Markey	USA
	May 12	Peter Hurford	England
1961	May 17	Susi Jeans	England
1962	April 12	Marilyn Mason	USA
	October 2	Hugh J. McLean	Canada
1963	February 19	Gerald Bales	USA
	May 14	Peter Hurford	England
	December 2	Robert Noehren	USA
1964	February 18	Gerald Bales	USA
	February 2	Paul Jenkins	USA
	April 6	Kenneth Gilbert	Canada
	August 25	Heinrich Fleischer	Germany
	August 26	Hugh J. McLean	Canada
	November 24	Martin Foerstemann	Germany
1965	May 9	Jan Bender	USA
	September 23	Anton Heiller	Austria
1967	October 21	E. Power Biggs	USA
1968	November 16	Virgil Fox	USA

In 1960 the English organist Peter Hurford embarked on a tour in aid of the restoration of the organ at St. Alban's Cathedral, where he had been organist since 1958. His recital in Winnipeg on 12 May 1960 was jointly sponsored by St. George's Anglican Church and the Winnipeg Centre of the RCCO. He played this program on the three-manual instrument installed in the church by Hill, Norman & Beard six years earlier:

Prelude and Fugue in F-sharp Minor	Buxtehude
Chorale Preludes:	Bach
Allein Gott in der Hoh sei Ehr	
Valet will ich dir geben	
An Wasserflüssen Babylon	
Trio Sonata No. 2 in C Minor	Bach
Chorale Preludes:	Pepping
Wie soll ich dich empfangen	
Gelobet seist du, Herr Jesu Christ	
Vom Himmel hoch	
Five Verses on a Melody from the	
Paderborn Gesangbuch (1765)	Hurford
Variations sur Lucis Creator	Alain
Suite modale	Peeters

Hurford returned to Winnipeg on 14 May 1963 to play the opening recital on the four-manual organ at Holy Trinity Anglican Church, recently renovated by Hill, Norman & Beard.

The visit by Marilyn Mason, head of the organ department at the University of Michigan, was one of the highlights of this period. She played this program at Westminster United Church on 12 April 1962:

Concerto in F Major, Op. 4, No. 5	Handel
Miniature (1958)	Langlais
Epilogue, for pedal solo	Langlais
Prelude and Fugue in D Major	Bach
Pastorale (1909)	Roger-Ducasse
Two Preludes:	Searle Wright
Greensleeves (1950)	
Brother James' Air	
Suite for Organ (1957)	Paul Creston

The subsequent reviews were highly enthusiastic regarding the diversity of the program and the performer's musical prowess:

> There has been nothing to suggest a resurgence of interest in organ music for several years, but the recital presented by Dr. Marilyn Mason . . . should pave the way for such a renaissance.
>
> This was the most memorable organ recital given here since the middle 1940s when Marcel Dupre was heard in the same edifice. . . .
>
> Dr. Mason commands a highly developed technique, at the service of no less developed musicianship. Her mastery of the organ's immensely complex vocabulary was evident from the start. . . .
>
> The high point of the recital came with the performance of Bach's most dazzling virtuoso work, the Prelude-Fugue in D major. The interpretation was one of taste and imagination, joined with a hand-and-foot dexterity which served the bidding of a discerning musicianship. (S. Roy Maley, "Recital An Evening to Be Remembered," Winnipeg Tribune, 13 April 1962.)

> If the sound old saying "Once bitten, twice shy" holds true, then "Many times bitten, many, many times shy" must do likewise. And in view of the many times I've been bitten (that is to say, betrayed, bullied and bored) by organ recitals, I have become increasingly reluctant about attending them.
>
> Imagine my surprise and delight, then, when Miss Mason's recital Thursday turned out to be one of the musical pleasures of the season. . . . And the Bach Prelude and Fugue, highpoint of my evening, had the life it has been denied so often.
>
> There was none of the sanctimonious monotony that, for me, has come almost to represent the main stuff of organ recitals. There was only the surge of living music which, for me, has come to represent the great Bach revealed. It was music, and playing, of the best kind, in which structures and

efficiencies were the toys of musical intelligence and musical feeling. (Ken Winters, "An Organist Par Excellence," *Winnipeg Free Press*, 13 April 1962.)

In connection with her visit, sponsored by the Winnipeg Centre of the Royal Canadian College of Organists, Dr. Mason also conducted a master class for organists, covering the technique of organ playing, the art of registration, music in worship, and the literature of the organ from pre-Bach times to contemporary music in Europe and America.

The Winnipeg Centre also arranged for the visit of the Viennese organist, harpsichordist, and conductor Anton Heiller on 23 September 1965. Although his program lacked the tuneful crowd-pleasers common in recitals by other artists, it was well suited to the tonal capabilities of the contemporary von Beckerath organ installed in First Presbyterian Church two years earlier:

Prelude and Fugue in E Minor	Bruhns
Passamezzo (12 variations)	Scheidt
Fantasy and Fugue in G Minor	Bach
Fantasy and Fugue in D Minor	Reger
Improvisation	Heiller

Heiller's visit to Winnipeg was his only Canadian excursion during a three-month tour of North America. In the course of an interview he expressed amazement at the increased interest in old classical organ music among North Americans, particularly on the part of the younger generation. He attributed this enthusiasm to the large number of modern mechanical organs recently imported into Canada and the United States. He added that "with the electric or pneumatic instrument the organist was more or less operating a machine, that's all. Albert Schweitzer used to call them the factory organs." Both reviews of his performance mentioned the mechanical-action, Baroque-style organ in First Presbyterian Church, because of its uniqueness among other large organs in the city.

> To me, the most intriguing aspect of the Anton Heiller recital of organ music at First Presbyterian Church Thursday night was the highly unusual quality of the Beckerath instrument that is installed in the church.
>
> There is a full range of tone-quality combinations available to the player, and Anton Heiller made the most of this. He is a performer of remarkable talents, particularly in this aspect, and manages to give the listener a consistently engaging tonal interplay. . . . I felt that, as amazed as I was at the possibilities of this instrument, the fine treatment it got from this performer could not hide the fact that so much of the music was played in a manner that revealed a lack of rhythmic cohesion.
>
> Certainly this is of basic musical importance and no resort to the delights of color should take precedence over it. (Dirk Keetbaas, "Remarkable Recital by Organist Heiller," *Winnipeg Tribune*, 25 September 1965.)

While the second review also drew attention to the relation between the organ and its appropriate musical literature, it included some broader speculations about the nature of improvisations. Written by an organist, it contained a message for other organists:

> The organ recital by Anton Heiller Thursday night in the First Presbyterian Church was undoubtedly one of the best I have heard in Winnipeg for some time.
>
> Mr. Heiller's improvisation proved to be somewhat of an anticlimax. Perhaps the reason was that the choice of Vaughan Williams' magnificent tune Sine Nomine as the first of two submitted themes proved unsatisfactory. It is a long tune—too long for this use. It is associated with words in the minds of all who know it, and the treatment of the tune offered certain problems of style. . . . It left me with mixed feelings about themes for improvisation. Perhaps shorter, more contrasted themes are needed—one smooth, one athletic. Even so, one must admire the adroit manner in which Mr. Heiller was able to manipulate these themes and work up to a thrilling finish.
>
> The organ of the First Presbyterian Church still holds great interest. It was especially suited to the Bruhns, Scheidt, and Bach, though in this latter I could wish for a bigger 16-foot sound on the pedal, and in the Reger, we could have done with another manual. In spite of this, it remains a unique and fine instrument. (Ronald Gibson, "Anton Heiller Scores Success," *Winnipeg Free Press*, 25 September 1965.)

E. Power Biggs was one of the few organists of recent times who made a full-time living as a concert recitalist. Born and educated in England, Biggs settled permanently in the United States in 1930, where he set about developing a career as an independent organist. He was also an influential proponent of contemporary organ design, a passion that emerged from his experiences with European organs; he also promoted an appreciation for historic American organs. Biggs toured extensively in North America, Europe, and Australia, mainly to promote the sale of his many recordings (almost 150 during his lifetime). His visit to Winnipeg in 1967 became the focus of attention for local organists and members of the knowledgeable musical community. A committee of the Winnipeg Centre of the RCCO arranged the event in recognition of the 75th anniversary of Westminster United Church, where the recital was held on 21 October 1967. Biggs concentrated on early Spanish organ music in the first part of his program:

The Emperor's Fanfare	Soler
Sonata, For the Clarines	Soler
Concerto No. 3 in G Major	Soler
Air in D Minor	Angeles
Batalla Imperial	Cabanilles
Sonata No. 1 (1937)	Hindemith

Pièce héroique	Franck
Toccata in F Major	Bach
From the Little Notebook	
for Anna Magdalena Bach:	Bach
Wer nur den lieben Gott	
lässt walten	
March and Three Minuets	
Passacaglia and Fugue in C Minor	Bach

The critics were not wholly impressed, for a variety of reasons, and they disagreed on the design of the program as a whole. Clearly, they were attending to different aspects of the same performance. One critic, while generally appreciative, had a few misgivings:

> So the artistry—or wizardry—of an organist lies, apart from considerable keyboard and pedal technique, in knowing how to impart individuality of color by manipulating the stops and mixtures available to him. This is a mystique appreciated by few except other organists.
>
> His staccato style in [the] Spanish music would likely be suitable, necessary even, in a huge, reverberating Spanish cathedral, but in the smallish hall of Westminster United with its well-filled pews it seemed jerky and uncertain. . . .
>
> The first half closed with the 19th century Belgian César Franck's Pièce Héroique. Organ music pure and simple, this is the kind of thing that gives an organ virtuoso best chance to show off the talents of his instrument, and this Mr. Biggs dutifully did.
>
> After intermission it was all Bach, and a section of the audience settled in their seats as though this was what they had really come out to hear.
>
> The F major toccata, arch upon arch of canonic structure soaring magnificently over those deep-held pedal notes, is a never-failing source of joy, and Mr. Bigg's choice of pedal registration for the deep passage work had a crystal brightness and definition.
>
> The concert ended with one of Bach's longest, stateliest and most austere pieces of music, the C minor Passacaglia and Fugue. It was a grand windup to an evening which, while uneven in some ways, nonetheless gave Winnipeg organists a rare chance to hear one of the leading men of their craft. (M[ichael] O[lver], "Finale Highlights Organ Concert," *Winnipeg Tribune*, 23 October 1967.)

Another critic found much to complain about. Biggs' technical abilities he thought left much to be desired, blaming some of the minor slips and faults on "the seemingly slow action of the organ at Westminster Church." He viewed the program as a whole "not an exciting one except for the Bach selections in the second half," and had critical words for Hindemith's score as "arbitrary, dull and unspontaneous" and "harmonically sour and emotionally dry." As for Franck's well-known piece, he wrote that "behind the fluster and pretentiousness of the cloying chromaticisms there is precious little of real musical worth or much of thematic distinction." The later part of the program was more sat-isfying, however:

> At last we got to Bach, and naturally it was at once the more rewarding part of the recital. The dazzling brilliance of the F Major Toccata was largely realized. . . . The introductory passage over a pedal point is followed by a long drawn out pedal solo. Here came an indication of a certain hesitancy, some hurried playing coupled with signs of rhythmic uncertainty; later inner voices tended to be smudged. It was good playing but not free of anxiety. . . .
>
> The artist's performance was hardly laborious but I failed to appreciate fully the surging momentum of the Passacaglia one has heard in other performances. . . . The fugue was better, the entries had a chirper quality to them, and Mr. Bigg's suave sense of phrasing was heard here at its best. (Jeffrey Anderson, "E. Power Biggs Not At His Best," *Winnipeg Free Press*, 23 October 1967.)

Another American organ virtuoso, Virgil Fox, visited Winnipeg in the fol-lowing year in connection with the 100th anniversary of Knox United Church, and immediately following the installation of the new three-manual, 40-stop Casavant organ. After serving as organist of New York City's Riverside Church for 19 years, Fox devoted all of his time to concert work from 1965 onward, touring the world. His program on 16 November 1968 consisted of these works:

Prelude and Fugue in G Minor	Brahms
Trio Sonata in E Minor, No. 4	Bach
In dulci jubilo	Bach
In dulci jubilo	Liszt
Sonata in C minor on the 94th Psalm	Reubke
Giga	Bossi
Sonata No. 1 in F Minor	Mendelssohn

Fox's performance received a thoughtful review from an organist's point of view; it covered both the scheduled program numbers and the improvisation:

> I first heard Virgil Fox in 1933 at a convention of the National Association of Organists in Chicago, when as a youth of 17 years, he shared a program with Clarence Eddy, the 80-year-old dean of American organists. The im-pression created by the very young Mr. Fox was one of a highly gifted player with all the technical endowments, and just waiting for the experience of a few years to crown.
>
> The years have passed, and Virgil Fox is probably at the height of his powers. He remains, however, a strange paradox. The same player who made the first movement of the Bach Trio Sonata in G an exciting tour de force, and the Reubke Sonata into a towering monument, could also distort the rhythm of the opening of the Mendelssohn F minor Sonata so that it seemed almost unrecognizable.
>
> The other Bach piece was Mr. Fox's arrangement of a melody, a fussy,

over-romantic affair which must have made some serious organists squirm.

Mr. Fox's registration veers between the effective and the bizarre. The effective kind was found in the Reubke and the Bossi; the bizarre in the recitative of the Mendelssohn, where we had two acid quality reeds in duet, and the chorale section played on the swell oboe.

Stripped of all the circus trappings, he remains an impressive player, with a stupendous dexterity, but a showman rather than a scholar, and whose appeal to the public in general seems irresistible. (Ronald Gibson, "Paradox Presented in Musician's Work," *Winnipeg Free Press*, 18 November 1968.)

If the decade of the 1960s provided a veritable feast of organ music provided by visiting recitalists, the 1970s were years of relative famine. In the early years of the decade there were very few organ recitals, either by visitors or by local organists. In 1970 Wolfgang Dallman, professor at the Institute for Church Music, Heidelberg, Germany, lectured on German Church Music and played a recital at First Presbyterian Church. In the following year Bernard Lagacé, Conservatoire de Musique, Montréal, came to Winnipeg under the auspices of the Winnipeg Centre of the RCCO and played a recital at Knox United Church. Virgil Fox returned to play at Knox United Church on 19 September 1972, four years after his earlier appearance there, to present this program:

Passacaglia and	
Double Fugue in C Minor	Bach
Trio, Praise to the Lord	Bach
Come Sweet Death	Bach
Fantasy and Fugue in G Minor	Bach
Variations on America	Ives
Andantino in D-flat	Lemare
Fantasy and Fugue on the Chorale,	
Ad nos, ad salutarem undam	Liszt

Fox the showman, with his crimson-lined cape and flamboyant personal style, had the capacity for making instant contact with his audiences everywhere by introducing each selection on his program. His Winnipeg recitals were no exception:

Mr. Fox does not talk down to the audience in presenting his program, although he is quite informal about it all. He has a gift for stimulating interest before he sits at the console. He can turn anyone into an organ fan . . . a rare power. (Madeleine Bernier, "Organ Recital Majestic," *Winnipeg Tribune*, 20 September 1972.)

Other visiting organists who came to Winnipeg included the extroverted American recitalist Carlo Curley, who played on a recently installed Allen Digital Computer Organ at St. Alphonsus Catholic Church on 19 May 1986, and the English organist Gillian Weir, who performed Paer's *Concerto for Or-*

gan and Poulenc's *Concerto for Organ, Strings and Tympani* with the Manitoba Chamber Orchestra at Westminster United Church on 15 October 1986. The Harpsichord Association of Manitoba ventured into the organ field by sponsoring a program of Baroque organ works recital by John Grew, head of the organ and harpsichord area of the Faculty of Music, McGill University (and also chairman of the Competitions Committee of the RCCO), at First Presbyterian Church on 11 April 1989. The RCCO sponsored a recital by Christoph Lorenz from Germany in 1993, and Joyce Jones, from the United States, played the inaugural recital on the new Létourneau organ in Young United Church late in 1993.

Some of the initiative in planning organ recitals by visiting performers was assumed by Westminster United Church, when the incumbent organist, Donald Menzies, inaugurated the Westminster Concert Organ Series in 1989, with the cooperation of the Winnipeg Centre of the RCCO. This program became the fastest growing musical series in Winnipeg and was a major fund-raiser for the church. The location was ideally suited for organ recitals, for the removable screen around the front-and-centre console allowed audiences an unobstructed view of the player of the four-manual Casavant organ, one of the grandest in the city. Since its beginning, internationally acclaimed organists such as Christopher Herrick, Peter Hurford, Simon Preston, and John Scott from England; Marie-Madeleine Duruflé and Olivier Latry from France; Kei Koito from Switzerland; and Diane Bish, Clay Christiansen, David Higgs, Thomas Murray, John Rose, and John Walker from the United States performed for large audiences. Local organists Barry Anderson and Donald Menzies shared a recital program in the same series in 1990.

Royal Canadian College of Organists Activities

The 1960s were also busy years for members of the Winnipeg Centre of the RCCO. Their meetings included presentations by both visiting and local church musicians, and also by a few members of the clergy, on a variety of topics of current interest. The Centre held a special meeting on 5 May 1960 to hear Gerald Knight, director of the Royal School of Church Music, London, England, talk on the activities and aims of that institution. Church music often provided a focus for many specific presentations, and the members participated in lecture-discussions on topics such as Lutheran liturgy; new sounds in the sanctuary; music suitable for weddings (secular songs were forbidden in some churches); hymn, anthem, and solo accompaniment; the Anglican chant; music for children; techniques for rehearsing junior choirs; and choral conducting. The annual choir festival, involving 350 participants in 16 church choirs conducted by Filmer Hubble, was resumed in 1966.

The Centre's regular meetings still included inspections and demonstrations of recent organ installations (now given the racier designation, "Organ Crawls"). Smaller two-manual instruments and unit organs were given their share of attention, and electronic instruments in newer suburban churches or chapels were examined along with the more imposing pipe organs in prestigious churches. Sometimes the demonstrations of electronic organs took place in dealers' showrooms. On one wintry evening in 1966, as part of a "Carillon Crawl" to several churches with electronic carillons, some of the hardier members ascended the tower of St. Luke's Anglican Church to examine its eight genuine bells, cast in England by the historic firm of Mears and Stainbank and installed in 1911.

The most demanding responsibility assumed by the members of the Winnipeg Centre was the National Convention of the Royal Canadian College of Organists, held in Winnipeg in August 1964. The event included an opening recital by Heinrich Fleischer, the German organist then living in Minneapolis, and other performances by the Canadian recitalist Hugh McLean, Vancouver, and George Black, chapel organist at Huron College, London, Ontario, who played the 1965 RCCO diploma examination pieces. Local organists Barry Anderson, Ronald Gibson, Conrad Grimes, and Donald Hadfield also participated. The 199 registrants (including 42 from the United States) visited several Winnipeg churches for organ demonstrations, attended choral workshops, and previewed new music for the Advent and Christmas seasons. The financial surplus of the event was distributed between the national office of the RCCO, a fund for a regional convention, and the University of Manitoba Organ Fund.

Occasional organ recitals by members, organ demonstrations and church tours, choral concerts and festivals, church music workshops on various topics, organist-clergy dinner meetings, and annual social events in the summer and at Christmas comprised the yearly round of activities of the Winnipeg Centre of the RCCO in the 1970s. The number of registered members of the Centre varied from about 45 to 60 throughout this period.

A major disappointment was the failure of a project to support the installation of a pipe organ in Winnipeg's new Centennial Concert Hall. The matter had been discussed in meetings of the Winnipeg Centre on several occasions, along with a plan to raise funds through sponsored choir festivals. This was followed by a resolution in 1970 to approach the Centennial Centre directly on the matter. The idea eventually was thwarted by the negative decision of the Centennial Centre committee, based primarily on financial considerations. Performances in the Hall requiring organ accompaniment have been held from time to time, using a rented electronic instrument.

The general pattern of the activities of the Winnipeg Centre of the RCCO did not change significantly in the following years; nevertheless, there were variations on common themes, strengthened by the participation of new members of the association. While the traditional organ crawls, church music workshops, and choir festivals continued on a regular basis, some of the meetings held in the 1980s featured more specialized and innovative topics. These included an organ workshop on Bach's *Art of Fugue*, a sing-along using anthems by Canadian composers, a workshop on the mechanics of the organ, a presentation on harpsichord construction, a St. Cecilia evening of serious and lighter music in honour of music's patron saint, and compact disc listening sessions to hear recent organ recordings.

Among the organ programs sponsored by the Winnipeg Chapter were a series of nine recitals on the new Casavant organ at Elim Chapel in 1980, and three recitals in recognition of the Diamond Jubilee of the Royal Canadian College of Organists early in 1983. Into the 1990s organ recitals included performances by both visiting and local players: there was a César Franck Festival by nine local organists, and a weekly recital series during the month of August became an annual occurrence.

In 1983 the Winnipeg Centre commenced the publication of a regular newsletter that informed members about forthcoming events and also provided commentaries on other matters of interest and concern. Besides admonishing members for their lack of attendance at recent events, the editorial content ranged over such topics as the contribution of electronic organs to the continued viability of church music, the working conditions of organists and the need for guidelines on hiring and salaries, sources of funding for activities, and the need for growth and creative musical programming.

Late in the 1980s the Winnipeg Centre formulated for the first time an explicit statement of its goals for the forthcoming year: to encourage organ recitals by both big-name players as well as by local organists; to support the Westminster Concert Organ Series; to improve its financial position by a variety of fund raising activities; to cooperate with other local music groups like the Manitoba Harpsichord Association, the Manitoba Choral Association, the Winnipeg Bach Festival, and the Manitoba Music Educators Association; to promote education about organs through the schools and teachers; and to prepare for the National Convention to be held in Winnipeg in 1991.

All of these intentions were consistent with the aims of the national association. Today the Royal Canadian College of Organists is Canada's oldest musical organization, with headquarters in Toronto and local centres across the country. It is primarily an examining body that grants Associateship (ARCCO) or Fellowship (FRCCO) diplomas in organ performance, choir training, and service playing. In addition to promoting organ music and improving members' skills, the RCCO encourages organ recitals and other public musical events designed to increase an understanding and appreciation of church music generally. Recently the RCCO developed a code of ethics governing the behaviour of members; a Professional Concerns Committee was available for help in resolving disputes. Annual general meetings include reports and dicussions on a variety of topics related to RCCO activities: examinations, education, awards, competitions, scholarships, conventions, publications, and liaison with theological schools. In 1996 there were 1283 members of the RCCO throughout Canada; 43 were registered with the Winnipeg Centre.

———————◆•◆•◆———————

The Future of the Organ

THE PLACE that the organ will occupy in the musical culture of the 21st century is not easy to predict, given the number of factors involved and their possible interrelationships. However, an awareness of these influential conditions will assist in understanding the probable outcomes of recent trends.

Organ Installations

Most of the organs installed in Manitoba churches in the early years, although their tonal design was quite conservative by contemporary standards, escaped the pernicious tendencies to excessive romantic-symphonic sound palettes that affected organ building elsewhere at the time. Although few of these organs exhibited economy or effectiveness in tonal design, they were adequate for rendering Handel choruses or other transcriptions of orchestral compositions that crowded the organ recital programs of both visiting and local players in the early years. Similarly, none of the more recent organ installations could be described as "screaming neobaroque boxes," those superficially conceived instruments that appeared in the early years of the Organ Reform Movement in the late 1960s. This early and late conservatism simply reflects the primary liturgical requirements of the accompaniment of congregational hymn singing and the support of church choirs. Until comparatively recently, the tonal design of new organs reflected the rather homogeneous musical tastes of organists and church music committees, as well as the usual financial restrictions on expenditures for elaborate instruments. With the few exceptions of the larger organs in prestigious and wealthy churches, none of the organs in

Manitoba churches were conceived of as recital instruments capable of handling a wide repertoire of organ music.

New organ installations since the mid-1960s have been the products of Canadian or European builders whose tonally integrated instruments reflected neoclassical concepts prevalent in Europe and the United States. Although these instruments are not entirely suitable for the performance of all schools of organ music, they are probably more versatile than the earlier generation of organs for general liturgical and performance purposes. Changing styles of organ building and tonal design are based upon the rediscovered qualities of universally admired older instruments of the 17th and 18th centuries, without blindly copying them. The uneasy hybrid designs of earlier years largely have been abandoned. In recent years several of Winnipeg's Lutheran congregations have chosen to install small pipe organs representative of modern tonal ideals, and these instruments have proved to be remarkably stable in tuning and reliable in mechanical operation.

Whether this trend will be manifested in the future is uncertain, for there are no anticipated installations of completely new pipe organs in Manitoba churches in the foreseeable future. The purchase of a two-manual, 29-stop Létourneau organ by Young United Church in 1993 at a cost of almost $300,000 was made possible by adequate insurance that compensated for the loss of a 1907 Casavant instrument in the disastrous fire of 1987. Pipe organs have always been expensive. Nevertheless, although the unit or standard-design pipe organ of an earlier era has disappeared, today's buyers have another choice in the less expensive electronic organ.

Electronic Organs

Advances in the technology of electric sound production in the early part of the 20th century made it possible to create musical sounds from electronic vibrations, using loudspeakers powered by electric amplifiers. These inventions provided the means for the development of the Hammond Electric Organ, manufactured in the United States in the mid-1930s. The original Hammond technology was primitive by present-day standards. It consisted of small iron discs on a spindle rotating at constant speed past the cores of activated electromagnets to produce the electronic vibrations required to generate various sound pitches. Because their perfect sine-shaped vibrations were entirely pure, Hammond organs never went out of tune, their speech was precise, and there

(Right) Young United Church, Winnipeg.
Létourneau, 1993, 2/29. This organ replaced the 1907 Casavant instrument lost in the fire that destroyed the original church building in 1987.

were no problems caused by changes in temperature or humidity. Their small consoles and unobtrusive speakers created no installation problems. For many small churches, the chief advantage was their relatively low cost (under $2,000), only a fraction of the price of a small pipe organ.

Further advances in electronic organ technology included the introduction of electronic oscillators and the use of vacuum tubes as tone generators in 1939, and the replacement of oscillators by transistors in 1959; both by the Allen Organ Company in the United States. The expectation that electronic oscillator organs would, with enough time, effort, and the right combination of components, produce sounds indistinguishable from pipe organs, proved groundless. The results of this method were only approximate at best, and organs using oscillator technology are now a thing of the past.

Highly advanced digital technology for tone generation and control was developed by Allen in the world's first Digital Computer Organ, introduced in 1971. This system allows for the storage in digital form of musical waveshapes—often from a "bank" of actual windblown organ pipes—and their retrieval and reproduction as musical tones, using sophisticated microcircuitry. Although this system of tone generation is free of extraneous noise and nonharmonic sounds produced by actual organ pipes, the idiosyncracies of some ranks of pipes and other transient phenomena are available when desired for certain installations.

These design innovations provide permanent and accurate control over all aspects of sound production, including custom tuning, graduated attack and release of individual notes, voicing, speech delay, reverberation, and adjustment to different installation environments. For several years a library of computer cards was available to add stops to the organ. Special features available in Allen organs in the mid-1990s include a transposer to shift the pitch of the entire organ, a programmable capture action to pre-select combinations of stops, automatic recording and playback systems, orchestral sounds, and MIDI interface that makes it possible to play synthesizers or sound modules from the organ's keyboards, all augmented by advanced digital sampling technology. Early Allen organs were two-manual instruments, but the company has manufactured larger instruments, up to five-manual organs exceeding 200 stops, custom-designed for particular environments.

When reed organs in small suburban or rural churches outlived their usefulness, they were replaced by electronic instruments of different kinds, with or without pedals. The Hammond organ was the instrument of choice in many Manitoba churches over a period of 30 years from the late 1930s onward. Organs by other makers, such as Conn, Gulbrandsen, Lowry, Minshall, Saville, Wurlitzer, and Yamaha were chosen by some churches. Most of these smaller instruments were installed in the years between 1950 and 1970. Larger electronic church organs embodying more advanced technology became available in Manitoba in the 1960s. Instruments made by Baldwin were the first to appear, followed by Allen organs in the mid-1970s. Rodgers instruments, which have the capability of combining ranks of genuine organ pipes with the loud-speakers of electronically-generated sound systems, entered the regional market more recently. A few churches have chosen newer Hammond organs that employ up-to-date digital technology, or Galanti instruments from Europe. Of these, Allen organs are the most numerous; about 250 instruments were installed in Manitoba churches, chapels, and residences during a 20-year period since 1975, when they were first introduced into the area. For the most part, electronic instruments did not supplant pipe organs; they simply replaced other outdated electronic instruments or reed organs.

The respective merits of pipe organs and electronic instruments have been debated since the latter were first introduced. The arguments have centred around the capability of electronic instruments to produce authentic pipe organ sounds, their cost, and their longevity. Some people have argued that since electronic circuits fall short of reproducing all the responsive nuances of pipe organ sound, the best that a "loudspeaker organ" can do is to sound like a recording of a pipe organ. Others have pointed out that these alleged shortcomings can be overcome through the use of properly designed stops, multichannel sound generating systems, and the use of additional and larger loudspeakers. As for cost, a comparable pipe organ costs about three times as much as a high quality electronic instrument; however, maintenance costs for pipe organs may amount to about four times that of electronic instruments. As for longevity, the worst-case scenario for electronic instruments may be that advances in technology will render many of today's gadget-oriented instruments obsolete in a decade or two. On the other hand, many well-designed and con-structed pipe organs having historic significance have been maintained and successfully restored over the years.

Apart from these considerations, at the present time there is an obvious answer, based on musical criteria, to the question, Which is preferable: a poorly designed, badly maintained pipe organ, or a high quality electronic instrument? Electronic instruments have a place in locations where pipe organs are out of the question, whether for space or budgetary considerations. The increasing aceptance of electronic instruments, with their improved technology, further diminishes the probability of even a small number of pipe organ installations in future years. Electronic organs have proved adequate for the liturgical re-quirements of many small or medium-size churches with limited budgets, and these instruments have provided competition for more costly pipe organs.

Organists

The question of the availability of trained organists can be regarded as one of interrelated supply and demand, sometimes mitigated by musical considera-tions. On the supply side, the two major sources of church musicians of professional calibre have been university schools of music in the two provincial universities or elsewhere, and private instruction. The greater majority of the present generation of organists obtained instruction from other highly trained church organists and received their certification from various examining agencies, such as the Royal Conservatory of Music in Toronto, the Royal Canadian College of Organists, the Western Board of Music, or Trinity College, London. About one-quarter of the members of the Winnipeg Centre of the Royal Canadian College of Organists in 1994 were products of university-level music programs. Moreover, the possession of RCCO certification is not a requirement for membership in the guild. It is not known whether professionally designated members specialized in organ training during their formal musical studies or whether they adapted their training in piano technique to the organ, through private instruction, at a later date.

On the demand side, a church having an adequate pipe organ and financial provision for a salaried organist will endeavour to secure the most highly qualified musician available. Conversely, trained organists ordinarily prefer appointments to churches with pipe organs, and often wait for several years for an opportunity to apply for an opening commensurate with their training and aspirations. Once hired, their presence encourages the continuation of the pipe organ tradition and its music. This situation applies not only in prestigious churches having large pipe organs, but also in smaller suburban congregations. These organists seldom move on to other posts, except for denominational preferences, the opportunity to move upwards in the musical hierarchy of their particular denomination, the chance to play and perform on a better organ, or perhaps on account of disputes over liturgical practices or other dissatisfactions.

In a few of the smaller churches equipped with pipe organs today, the presiding organ player may be a volunteer member of the congregation with training in piano technique only, or perhaps simply an amateur piano player who was invited to take over in the absence of a professionally trained and unaffordable church musician. These players, however dedicated and necessary they may be, are limited to accompanying congregational or choir singing. For reasons of cost, such churches would likely replace a decrepit pipe organ with an electronic instrument, rather than incur escalating maintenance or restoration costs for a troublesome instrument. Exceptions to this possible trend are found in those churches that have managed to preserve older pipe organs with the help of volunteer labour working under the supervision of an experienced organ technician.

On the other hand, if a church considering the purchase of a new organ already has a fully trained organist, this person, working with a musically educated and supportive pastor or worship committee, can influence the decision of an only moderately affluent congregation in favour of a small pipe organ in preference to an electronic instrument, providing that a realistic fund-raising objective can be achieved.

Changing Religious Liturgies

Changes in the liturgical practices of some religious denominations in recent years have rendered the use of pipe organs redundant in a few churches. For example, when the choirs in some Catholic churches moved out of the balcony to join the congregation in hymn singing on the main level, in accordance with provisions in Vatican II, the organs became silent and fell into permanent disuse. In other denominations, youth-oriented liturgical practices have favoured the use of guitars and other instruments associated with folk music or religious rock groups; for these reasons a large pipe organ at the front of a Winnipeg Baptist church is seldom used, except for weddings and funerals. Even some mainstream denominations have special youth-segregated services exhibiting similar musical preferences. These subcongregations often create their own music and compose their own hymns, quite independently of traditional practices involving the organ. The effect of these changes is to produce a generation of worshippers unfamiliar with the organ, its musical heritage, and its literature.

A much broader issue is the question of the future of institutionalized religion and its possible decline due to the growth of science, education, and secularization, on the one hand, or its theological transformation in engaging in ameliorative or charitable action, locally or globally, on the other. In recent years, various "New Age" cults influenced by Eastern religions and philosophies have encouraged individualistic expressions of spiritual development, without any unifying concepts. These prospects, along with a future possible megasynthesis of the major world religions, undoubtedly will take many centuries to resolve. In the near future, however, the closure of many of the larger churches of the major religious denominations does not seem likely. But if that should occur, their organs would be preserved, providing that the church buildings were designated as historic sites and converted to concert halls. In these cases, the protected instruments would be preserved for many years as cultural resources, and would continue to be used for recital purposes, thus maintaining the musical traditions associated with them.

Population Demography

Some suburban churches located in stable neighbourhoods now have congregations comprised largely of aging members, many of them in or near retirement and living on limited incomes. Fewer younger, fully employed members are joining such congregations. These churches are finding it difficult to maintain their church buildings and organs on their diminishing financial resources. Although many of these groups are surviving through increased volunteer activity to reduce costs, including the job of organ maintenance with advice from experienced technicians, they cannot continue to do so indefinitely. The inevitable result will be the amalgamation or dispersal of congregations, the closure of some church buildings or their conversion to other uses, and the removal or possible relocation of their pipe organs. All of these trends have been taking place in Manitoba churches for about the past 40 years. The general implication is that many of the organs remaining in these churches will be lost unless they can be relocated elsewhere. The more affluent churches with a wider spread of ages among the members of their congregations, and which encourage the full participation of younger members in their musical programs, are the only ones where pipe organs likely will escape this fate.

Organ Technicians and Builders

The renovation, rebuilding, maintenance, and tuning of existing organs has provided full-time employment for relatively few people in Manitoba. For example, members of the Blanchard family were the only organ technicians active in the region for about half a century from the mid-1920s onward. The names of the Blanchard brothers, Edouard and Albert, official Casavant representatives, first appeared on a contracts for the installation of organs in Winnipeg in 1926. Albert's son René, who had worked in the Casavant factory for a time, covered Manitoba, Saskatchewan, and Northwestern Ontario. An elder son, Robert, worked throughout Alberta. Another technician, F. Radcliffe, renovated instruments in Winnipeg in the 1950s. Edwin Foidart, who apprenticed with René Blanchard and with Casavant Frères in St. Hyacinthe, Québec, succeeded the Blanchards in Winnipeg; his first installation for Casavant was St. Stephen's Broadway United Church in 1971. Organist-technician Richard Buck and his associate Bruce Mantle have rebuilt and serviced pipe organs in the area since 1977; their territory now includes Manitoba, Northwestern Ontario, and Saskatchewan. They moved a Casavant organ from St. John's United Church, Winnipeg, to Central United Church, Brandon, in 1988, and reconstructed an instrument manufactured by the Canadian Pipe Organ Company that they removed from St. Jude's Anglican Church, Winnipeg, and installed in the First Mennonite Church in the city in 1991. A major project of James Musselwhite, who moved to Winnipeg from British Columbia in 1991, was the renovation and installation of an Edward Lye tracker instrument in the Roman Catholic Parish Church, St. Norbert, in 1997.

In this respect there seems to have been a stable balance between the supply of available technicians and the number of organs requiring routine maintenance and occasional rebuilding or relocation. The arrival of a new technician in the area may upset this delicate balance temporarily, for the relatively few new installations in recent years do not require sustained attention. On the other hand, the replacement of departing technicians is an uncertain matter. If the demand for technicians should exceed their available numbers in the future, the costs of organ maintenance undoubtedly will rise in accordance with the economic realities of supply and demand. This may be both aggravating and risky for churches with pipe organs, particularly if trained maintenance personnel must be brought in from other provinces on a visiting basis. Perhaps the manufacturers of new pipe organs that might be installed in future years will offer service contracts, filled by visiting technicians, as part of the purchase arrangements. Whether this will discourage the purchase of pipe organs in favour of electronic instruments is unpredictable.

Public Awareness

Although organ recitals do not occupy the prominent position in the musical life of the community today as they did in former times, the instrument is still brought to public awareness by the annual programs of organ recitals by visiting and local performers, sponsored by the Winnipeg Centre of the Royal Canadian College of Organists and by Westminster Church's Concert Organ Series; the latter programs attract audiences of several hundred people. Radio programs of the Canadian Broadcasting Corporation sometimes include recordings of organs, either solo or in orchestral combinations. For many years the CBC scheduled a weekly Organists in Recital program, featuring performances by Canadian organists, until its cancellation in 1986; a weekly afternoon program devoted almost exclusively to organ music was withdrawn in 1996 upon the retirement of the program host. For several years an American public television station whose broadcasts were received in Winnipeg offered a weekly program of organ music recorded chiefly in European churches by the prominent American organist, Diane Bish; the series then was continued on another television station. Winnipeg record stores display a modest assortment of recordings of organ music, and organ music fans have a wide choice of organ recordings made in Europe or the United States that can be ordered through international sources. Interest in the organ music is still relatively strong, considering the various musical and performing arts alternatives, as well as the other forms of cultural involvement or entertainment available in the concluding decade of the 20th century. There is no reason to suppose that this trend will be reversed in the coming years.

Educational Opportunities

To ensure that the next generation has an awareness of the organ, an appreciation of the instrument and its music should be developed early in the lives of children, preferably in the elementary school grades. Information about the organ should be part of regular music instruction, along with the attention now given to the piano and other orchestral instruments. A typical comprehensive educational program would include informative in-service sessions for school music teachers, preparation of classroom learning materials, inspection trips to local pipe organs, participation of piano students in brief on-site demonstration and recitals, and concerts by and for school children involving the organ and choral or instrumental groups. The objectives of such a program would be to satisfy the curiosity of young people about the organ, to inform students about the history of the instrument and the variety of sounds it can produce, and to present organ music in a context and at a level that students can understand and enjoy. A successful program embodying these objectives was launched by the Wichita Chapter of the American Guild of Organists in the early 1990s.

This kind of educational program would complement those other avenues to raising public awareness mentioned earlier, and would contribute to the development and maintenance of an appreciative audience for the organ and its literature through coming decades. Taken together, these various factors contribute to an optimistic outlook on the future of the King of Instruments well into the 21st century.

———◆◆◆———

Appendix 1: Organ Installations

The following lists summarize the known organ installations, renovations, and relocations in Winnipeg and rural Manitoba in each of the historical periods. Organs still in existence at their listed locations, although perhaps modified, are marked "X".

The Golden Age of the Organ: 1875-1919
Winnipeg / St. Boniface

1875	St. Boniface Roman Catholic Cathedral	Louis Mitchell (removed, divided and relocated 1909)
1878	Holy Trinity Anglican	Warren 2 manuals/24 stops
1882	Knox Presbyteria	maker unknown, from USA
1882	Zion Methodist	maker unknown 1/??
c. 1883	Central Congregational	Warren 2/??
1883	First Baptist	Bolton 2/11
1883	St. Mary's Roman Catholic	Louis Mitchell 2/18
1884	Victoria Hall	maker unknown 2/11
1885	Grace Methodist	Warren 2/??
c. 1885	Knox Presbyterian	Warren 2/?? (to Knox Presbyterian, Regina 1906)
c. 1886	Christ Church Anglican	Bolton 2/??
1891	All Saints' Anglican	Warren 2/16 (to St. Alban's 1917)
1894	Grace Methodist	Williams 3/34
1894	St. George's Anglican	Warren 1/??
1894	Westminster Presbyterian	Warren (from Grace Methodist)
1896	Immaculate Conception Roman Catholic	Eusèbe Brodeur 2/19
1899	Westminster Presbyterian	Karn 2/24
1902	St. John's Anglican Cathedral	Compensating Pipe Organ 2/14

1903	St. Stephen's Presbyterian	Toronto maker unknown 2/??
1904	St. Andrew's Presbyterian	Casavant 3/28 (fire 1968)
1905	Augustine Presbyterian	X Karn 3/28 (revisions 1994, 2/31)
1905	Zion Methodist	Casavant 3/37
1906	First Lutheran	Casavant 2/22 (to St. Boniface Cathedral 1921)
1906	Fort Rouge Methodist School	Casavant 2/17
1906	Knox Presbyterian	Casavant 3/32 (to new building 1917)
1906	St. Stephen's Presbyterian	Casavant 3/26
1906	Trinity Lutheran	Edward Lye 2/10 (to Sacré-Coeur 1968)
1907	Broadway Methodist	Casavant 3/36
1907	Grace Methodist	Casavant 4/46 (fire 1917)
1907	Young Methodist	Casavant 2/18 (fire 1987)
1908	Wesley Methodist	Casavant 2/17 (to First Church of Christ, Scientist 1919-20)
1909	St. Mary's Academy	X Casavant 2/10
1910	St. Luke's Anglican	Casavant 3/30 (Echo 1912, 3/36)
1910	St. Peter's Anglican	Karn 2/14 (to St. Thomas Anglican 1932)
1911	Fort Rouge Methodist	X Casavant 3/33
1911	Trinity Baptist	Karn 3/23
1912	Holy Trinity Anglican	Canadian Pipe Organ 4/50
1912	La Maison Vicariale	Casavant 2/11
1912	Westminster Presbyterian	X Casavant 4/49
1913	St. Giles Presbyterian	X Canadian Pipe Organ 3/25
c. 1915	Dominion Theatre	maker unknown
c. 1915	St. Edward's Roman Catholic	X Canadian Pipe Organ 2/23
c. 1915	St. Jude's Anglican	Canadian Pipe Organ 2/14 (to First Mennonite 1991)
c. 1915	St. Margaret's Anglican	Canadian Pipe Organ 2/7 (to St. Paul's Anglican, Dauphin, 1974)
1915	Bijou Theatre	Fotoplayer
1916	Christ Church Anglican	Casavant 2/16 (fire)
c. 1916	Holy Ghost Roman Catholic	Casavant (?) 2/20
1917	All Saints' Anglican	X Casavant 3/37
1917	Grace Methodist	Casavant 4/47 (to S. Kolbinson 1955)
1917	Province Theatre	C. Franklin Legge 3/??
1917	St. Alban's Anglican	X Warren 2/16 (from All Saints' Anglican)
1918	St. Mary's Roman Catholic Cathedral	X Casavant 2/18
1919	First Church of Christ, Scientist	X Casavant 2/17 (from Wesley Methodist)
1919	First English Evangelical Lutheran	X Canadian Pipe Organ 2/7

Rural Manitoba

1887	Presbyterian Church, Birtle	Bolton & Baldwin 1/5
1899	Parish Church, Roman Catholic, St. Norbert	Casavant 2/12 (fire 1929)

c. 1900	Christ Church Anglican, The Pas	maker unknown 1/?? (from England)
c. 1900	First Baptist, Portage la Prairie	X Karn 2/11 (to new building 1968)
c. 1900	St. Mary's Anglican, Portage la Prairie	X Karn 2/10
1903	First Methodist, Brandon	Casavant 2/15
1904	Knox Presbyterian, Portage la Prairie	Karn 2/20 (tornado 1922)
1904	Parish Church, Roman Catholic, Ste. Anne des Chênes	maker unknown
c. 1906	St. Matthew's Anglican Cathedral, Brandon	Karn 2/??
1907	Carman Methodist	maker unknown
1912	St. Augustin Roman Catholic, Brandon	X Casavant 2/20
1916	Parish Church, Roman Catholic, St. Pierre-Jolys	Casavant 2/9
1917	Knox Presbyterian, Souris	Casavant 2/12 (to St. Paul's United 1946)

The Middle Years: 1920-1939

Winnipeg / St. Boniface

c. 1920	Home Street Presbyterian	Woodstock 2 manuals/15 stops
c. 1920	National Theatre	maker unknown
c. 1920	Allen theatre	maker unknown
1920	Lyceum Theatre	Smith 3/?? unit organ
1921	Capitol Theatre	maker unknown
1921	College Theatre	Warren 2/??
1921	First Lutheran	Canadian Pipe Organ 3/??
1921	St. Boniface Roman Catholic Cathedral	Casavant 2/22 (from First Lutheran)
1922	Starland Theatre	maker unknown
1924	First Federated Church of Unitarians	X Hook & Hastings, 1883 2/11 (from USA)
c. 1925	St. James Anglican	X Woodstock 2/14
1926	St. George's Crescentwood Anglican	Casavant 2/7
1927	St. Andrew's River Heights United	Casavant 2/7 (to Harrow United 1958)
1927	Tivoli Theatre	Casavant 2/12 (to Broadway First Baptist 1958)
1927	St. John's Anglican Cathedral	X Casavant 2/19
1928	Garrick Theatre	Wicks 3/150 from 12 ranks
1928	King Memorial United	X Casavant 2/25
1928	St. Philip's Anglican	X Casavant 2/7
1929	St. Ignatius Roman Catholic	X Casavant 3/29

1930	St. John's United	Casavant 2/25 (to Central United, Brandon 1988)
1930	St. Matthew's Anglican	Casavant 3/40 (fire 1944)
1931	Greenwood United	Casavant 2/7
1932	St. Thomas Anglican	X Karn 2/14 (from St. Peter's Anglican 1932)
1933	Gardiner Funeral Home	Möller 2/20 from 5 ranks
1934	Clark Leatherdale Funeral Home	X Casavant 2/7
1934	First Presbyterian	C. Franklin Legge 3/25 (from Province Theatre)
1936	Greenwood United	Casavant 2/7 (to University of Manitoba, St. John's College 1983)
1937	Sparling United	X Kilgen 2/13 (from Grace Methodist, Portage la Prairie)

Rural Manitoba

c. 1920	Strand Theatre, Brandon	maker unknown
c. 1920	Grace Methodist, Portage la Prairie	Kilgen 2/13 (to Sparling United, Winnipeg 1937)
1921	Neepawa Methodist	Warren (from Ontario church)
1923	Knox Presbyterian, Portage la Prairie	X Casavant 2/20
1923	Parish Church, Roman Catholic, Ste. Anne des Chênes	X Casavant 2/12
1927	Crystal City United	X C. Franklin Legge 2/16 from 5 ranks (to new building 1979)
1928	First Presbyterian, Brandon	X Casavant 2/19
1939	Roman Catholic Cathedral, The Pas	Casavant 2/22 from 3 ranks

A Period of Recession: 1940-1949

Winnipeg

1940	Mordue Funeral Chapel	Wicks 2 manuals/20 stops from 4 ranks (to University of Winnipeg Chapel 1982)
c. 1945	Calvary Temple	Kimball 2/23 (from Orpheum Theatre)
1945	St. Aidan's Anglican	Casavant 2/27 from 7 ranks
1947	Robertson Memorial United	X Casavant 2/25 from 5 ranks
1948	St. Matthew's Anglican	X Casavant 3/40
1949	Knox United	X Casavant 3/34 (console, additions)

Rural Manitoba

1941	First United, Dauphin	X Casavant 2/25 from 4 ranks (to new building 1962)
1946	St. Paul's United, Souris	X Casavant 2/12 (from Knox Presbyterian/United)
1947	Neepawa United	T. Eaton Co./Legge 2/21

A Time For Renewal: 1950-1959
Winnipeg

1950	Holy Trinity Anglican	Casavant 4 manuals/53 stops (console, additions)
1951	St. John's Anglican Cathedral	X Casavant 3/39 (additions 1951, 1953, choir 1955, 1980)
1951	Westminster United	X Casavant 4/52 (console, additions); 4/54 (revisions 1985, 1986)
1952	Elim Chapel	Casavant 3/32 (fire 1974)
1952	St. Stephen's Broadway United	Casavant 3/39 (console, renovations; fire 1968)
c. 1953	St. Alban's Anglican	X Radcliffe 2/24 (rebuilt Warren 1917 2/16)
1953	St. Luke's Anglican	X Hill, Norman & Beard 4/61
1954	Our Saviour's Lutheran	X W. Legge 2/35 from 7 ranks
1954	St. George's Crescentwood Anglican	X Hill, Norman & Beard 3/36
1954	Trinity Baptist	X Hill, Norman & Beard 3/26 (reconstruction)
1955	First Church of Christ, Scientist	X Hill, Norman & Beard 2/25 (console, reconstruction)
1955	St. Boniface Roman Catholic Cathedral-Basilica	Casavant 3/47 (console, additions; fire 1968)
1957	St. Mary's Roman Catholic Cathedral	X Casavant 2/26 (console, additions)
1958	Broadway First Baptist	X Casavant 2/12 (from Tivoli Theatre; revisions 2/14)
1958	Harrow United	X Casavant 2/7 (from St. Andrew's River Heights Anglican)
1958	St. Andrew's River Heights Anglican	X Casavant 3/39 (pipes relocated 1981)
1959	All Saints' Anglican	X Casavant 3/48 (console, reconstruction)
1959	First Lutheran	X Hill, Norman & Beard 3/26 (console, reconstruction)

Rural Manitoba

1952	Parish Church, Roman Catholic, Ste. Agathe	X Casavant 2/7
1955	St. Paul's United, Brandon	Casavant 3/38 (fire)
1959	St. Matthew's Anglican Cathedral, Brandon	X Casavant 3/39

Recent Times: 1960-1997
Winnipeg

1962	Holy Trinity Anglican	X Hill, Norman & Beard 4 manuals/59 stops (renovation, additions)
1962	St. Aidan's Anglican	X Casavant 2/25

1963	First Presbyterian	X von Beckerath 2/30
1967	University of Manitoba, School of Music	X Casavant 2/21
1968	Knox United	X Casavant 3/40
1968	Sacré-Coeur Roman Catholic	Edward Lye 2/10 (removed 1992)
1968	University of Manitoba, School of Music Studio	X von Beckerath 2/3
c. 1970	Knox United, Chapel	X Casavant 2/16 from 5 ranks (from private residence)
1971	St. Stephen's Broadway United	X Casavant 3/31
1973	Young United	Casavant (console, additions; fire 1987)
1974	Messiah Lutheran	X Wilhelm 1/7
1975	Calvary Temple, Main	X Hybrid-Casavant 3/33 (parts from Toronto church)
1977	Christian Reformed	X Foidart 2/19 from 6 ranks
1977	Gloria Dei Lutheran	X George Stevens, 1850 2/16 (from USA)
1978	Elim Chapel	X Casavant 3/20 (renovations, additions 1983, 1985, 1987, 1988; now 3/26)
1980	Christ Lutheran	X Hutchings-Stuart 1897/1979 2/17 (from USA)
1982	Crestview United	X C. Franklin Legge, 1930 2/28 from 6 ranks (from residence, Hamilton, Ontario)
1982	St. James Lutheran	X Brunzema 1/10
1982	University of Winnipeg Chapel	X Wicks 2/20 from 4 ranks (from Mordue Funeral Chapel)
1983	University of Manitoba, St. John's College Chapel	X Casavant 2/7 (from Greenwood United Church; renovations, E. Foidart)
1986	Calvary Temple, Chapel	X Kimball 2/23 (from previous building)
1991	Calvary Temple, Main	X Keates-Geissler (console)
1991	First Mennonite	X Canadian Pipe Organ 2/37 from 20 ranks (from St. Jude's Anglican, c. 1989; rebuilt, augmented by R. Buck & B. Mantle)
1993	Young United	X Létourneau 2/29
1997	Parish Church, Roman Catholic, St. Norbert	X Edward Lye 2/10 (from Sacré-Coeur; renovations, J. Musselwhite)

Rural Manitoba

1974	St. Paul's Anglican, Dauphin	X Canadian Pipe Organ 2/7 (from St. Margaret's Anglican, Winnipeg 1974)
1981	Cistercian Abbey, Holland	X Guilbault-Thérien 2/12
1988	Central United, Brandon	X Casavant 2/25 (from St. John's United, Winnipeg)
1989	Brandon University, School of Music	X Gabriel Kney 2/9

Appendix 2: Specifications of Organs

This section consists of an inventory of the specifications of all known organs installed in Manitoba churches, educational institutions, halls, theatres, and funeral establishments from the earliest date to 1997, derived from inspections of existing instruments, records of organ builders, church archives, and newspaper reports. The specification codes following the installation dates refer to the number of manuals/number of speaking stops. Current church names and denominations are used throughout; former names or denominations are in parentheses. Addresses are given for locations containing existing pipe organs.

ALL SAINTS' ANGLICAN CHURCH, Broadway & Osborne, Winnipeg.
1. Warren, 1891, 2/16. To St. Alban's Anglican 1917.

GREAT		SWELL		PEDAL	
Open Diapason	8	Horn Diapason	8	Bourdon	16
Dulciana	8	Aeoline	8		
Melodia	8	Stopped Diapason		COUPLERS	
Stopped Diapason		(Treble)	8	Great to Pedal	
(Bass)	8	Stopped Diapason		Swell to Great	
Principal	4	(Bass)	8	Swell to Pedal	
Fifteenth	2	Traverse Flute	4	Tremolo	
Trumpet	8	Mixture	III		
		Oboe & Bassoon	8	Bellows Signal	
		Cornopean	8		

2. Casavant, Opus 705, 1917, 3/37.

GREAT		SWELL		CHOIR	
Double Open (ext.)	16	Bourdon	16	Geigen Principal	8
Open Diapason I	8	Open Diapason	8	Melodia	8
Open Diapason II	8	Stopped Diapason	8	Dulciana	8
Doppel Flute	8	Viola da Gamba	8	Lieblich Gedeckt	8
Gemshorn	8	Voix Celeste	8	Suabe Flute	4
Principal	4	Aeoline	8	Flageolet	2
Harmonic Flute	4	Principal	4	Orchestral Oboe	8
Fifteenth	2	Flauto Traverso	4	Clarinet	8
Mixture	III	Harmonic Piccolo	2	Tremulant	
Trumpet	8	Mixture	III		
		Cornopean	8		
		Oboe	8		
		Vox Humana	8		
		Tremulant			

PEDAL		COUPLERS			
Open Diapason	16	Great to Pedal		Choir to Great Unison	
Bourdon	16	Swell to Pedal		Choir to Great Sub	
Gedeckt (Swell)	16	Choir to Pedal		Great Super	
Violoncello	8	Swell to Great Unison		Swell Sub	
Stopped Diapason		Swell to Great Sub		Swell Super	
(ext.)	16	Swell to Great Super		Choir Sub	
Trombone	16	Swell to Choir Unison		Choir Super	
		Swell to Choir Sub			
		Swell to Choir Super			

3. Casavant, Opus 2508, 1959. Console, reconstruction of Opus 705, new pipes,* 3/48.

GREAT		SWELL		CHOIR	
*Flute Conique	16	*Quintaton	16	Lieblich Gedeckt	8
*Diapason	8	Geigen Principal	8	Dulciane	8
Principal	8	Rohrgedeckt	8	Principal	4
Bourdon	8	*Spitzflöte	8	*Koppelflöte	4
Gemshorn	8	Salicional	8	*Nazard	2 2/3
*Octave	4	Voix Celeste	8	*Blockflöte	2
*Chimney Flute	4	*Geigen Octave	4	*Tierce	1 3/5
*Octave Quint	2 2/3	Flauto Traverso	2	Clarinet	8
*Superoctave	2	Harmonic Piccolo	2	Tremulant	
*Fourniture IV	1 1/3	*Plein Jeu III	2		
*Cymbal III	1/2	*Bassoon	16		
Trumpet	8	Trompette	8		
		Oboe	8		
		*Clarion	4		
		Tremulant			

PEDAL
*Resultant (added later) 32
*Contre Bass   16
Bourdon   16
Flute Conique (ext.) 16
Quintaton (ext.)   16
*Principal   8
Violoncello (ext.)   8
Stopped Flute (ext.)   8
Flute Conique (ext.)   8
Fifteenth (ext.)   4
*Flute (ext.)   4
*Mixture   III
Trombone   16
*Fagotto (ext.)   16

COUPLERS
Great to Pedal
Great Super to Pedal
Swell to Pedal
Swell Super to Pedal
Choir to Pedal
Choir Super to pedal
Swell to Great
Swell Sub to Great
Swell Super to Great
Swell to Choir
Swell Sub to Choir
Swell Super to Choir
Great to Choir

Choir to Great
Choir Sub to Great
Choir Super to Great
Great Super
Great Unison Off
Swell Sub
Swell Super
Swell Unison Off
Choir Sub
Choir Super
Choir Unison Off

AUGUSTINE UNITED (PRESBYTERIAN) CHURCH, 444 River, Winnipeg.
Karn, 1905, 3/28.
T. Eaton Company, 1951. Renovation.
R. Buck & B. Mantle, Winnipeg, c. 1975. Renovation. Minor renovations, pipework, 1983.

GREAT
Double Diapason   16
Open Diapason   8
Doppel Flute   8
Gamba   8
Principal   4
Harmonic Flute   4
Fifteenth   2
Mixture   III
Trumpet   8

SWELL
Bourdon   16
Diapason   8
Stopped Diapason   8
Viol di Gamba   8
Voix Celeste   8
Aeoline   8
Flauto Traverso   4
Piccolo   2
Cornopean   8
Oboe   8
Tremulant

CHOIR
Geigen Principal   8
Melodia   8
Dulciana   8
Wald Flute   4
Flageolet   2
Clarionette   8
Tremulant

PEDAL
Open Diapason   16
Bourdon   16
Violoncello   8

COUPLERS
Great to Pedal
Swell to Pedal
Swell Super to Pedal
Choir to Pedal
Swell Sub to Great
Swell to Great
Swell Super to Great
Choir Sub to Great
Choir to Great
Choir Super to Great

Swell Sub to Choir
Swell to Choir
Swell Super to Choir
Great Super
Swell Sub
Swell Super
Choir Sub
Choir Super

E. Foidart, Winnipeg; S. Miller, Calgary, 1994. Additions, revisions,
Gabriel Kney console, 2/31.

GREAT		SWELL		PEDAL	
Principal	8	Bourdon	16	Offenbass	16
Harmonic Flöte	8	Gedackt	8	Subbass	16
Gambe	8	Viole da Gamba	8	Offenflöte	8
Octav	4	Celeste	8	Viole	8
Traversflöte	4	Principal	4	Choral Bass	4
Quinte	2 2/3	Waldflöte	4	Mixtur II	2 2/3
Octavin	2	Nasat	2 2/3	Posaune	16
Mixtur III	1 1/3	Hohlflöte	2	Trompete	8
Trompete (prepared)	8	Terz	1 3/5	Rohr Schalmey	4
Dulzian	8	Scharf III	1		
		Trompette	8	COUPLERS	
		Oboe	4	Great to Pedal	
		Tremulant		Swell to Pedal	
				Swell to Great	

BRANDON UNIVERSITY, SCHOOL OF MUSIC, 270-18th St., Brandon.
Gabriel Kney, 1989, 2/9. Mechanical action.

MANUAL I		MANUAL II		PEDAL	
Gedeckt	8	Quintadena	8	Subbass	16
Praestant	4	Offenflöte	4	Gedecktbass	8
Blockflöte	2	Terz	1 3/5		
Quint	1 1/3			COUPLERS	
				I to Pedal	
				II to Pedal	
				II to I	

BROADWAY FIRST BAPTIST CHURCH, 790 Honeyman, Winnipeg.
Casavant, Opus 1231, 1927. From Tivoli Theatre 1958. Revisions,* 2/14 + chimes,
percussion.

GREAT		SWELL		PEDAL	
Diapason	8	Stopped Diapason	8	Bourdon	16
Melodia	8	Salicional	8	Flute	8
Dulciana	8	Voix Celeste	8	Drum	
*Principal	4	*Principal	4		
*Block Flute	2	*Nazard	2 2/3	COUPLERS	
Chimes (from Swell)		*Fifteenth	2	Swell 16	
		Oboe	8	Swell 4	
		Chimes		Swell to Great 16	
		Xylophone		Swell to Great 8	
		Tremulant		Swell to Great 4	
				Great 4	
				Great to Pedal 8	
				Great to Pedal 4	
				Swell to Pedal 8	
				Swell to Pedal 4	

BROADWAY METHODIST CHURCH, Winnipeg. See ST. STEPHEN'S BROADWAY
UNITED CHURCH.

BURROWS BETHEL MENNONITE CHURCH (ST. GILES PRESBYTERIAN),
294 Burrows, Winnipeg.
Canadian Pipe Organ, 1913, 3/30.
Hill, Norman & Beard, 1954. Restoration.

GREAT		SWELL		CHOIR	
Open Diapason	8	Bourdon	16	Geigen Principal	8
Violin Diapason	8	Open Diapason	8	Dulciana	8
Doppel Flute	8	Stopped Diapason	8	Melodia	8
Gemshorn	8	Dolcissimo	8	Harmonic Flute	4
Principal	4	Viol di Gamba	8	Piccolo	2
Harmonic Flute	4	Voix Celeste	8	Clarinet	8
Fifteenth	2	Flauto Traverso	4	Tremulant	
Trumpet	8	Flautino	2		
		Dolce Cornet	III		
		Cornopean	8		
		Oboe	8		
		Vox Humana	8		
		Tremulant			

PEDAL		COUPLERS			
Open Diapason	16	Great to Pedal 8		Choir to Great 8	
Bourdon	16	Choir to Pedal 8		Choir to Great 4	
Lieblich Gedackt	16	Swell to Pedal 8		Great to Great 4	
Bass Flute	8	Swell to Pedal 4		Swell to Choir 8	
		Swell to Pedal 16		Choir to Choir 16	
		Swell to Swell 4		Choir to Choir 4	
		Swell to Great 8			
		Swell to Great 4			

CALVARY TEMPLE - MAIN AUDITORIUM, 400 Hargrave, Winnipeg.
Hybrid: Pipes from Casavant and other makers 1975, 3/33 + chimes. Keates-Geissler console 1991.

GREAT		SWELL		POSITIV	
Principal	8	Principal	8	Geigen Diapason	8
Rohrflöte	8	Gamba	8	Gedeckt	8
Principal	4	Voix Celeste	8	Principal	4
Nachthorn	4	Stopped Diapason	8	Koppelflöte	4
Fifteenth	2	Principal	4	Sesquialtera	II
Mixture V	1 1/3	Waldflöte	4	Cremorne	8
Chimes		Nazard	2 2/3	Tremulant	
		Mixture	III		
		Contra Oboe	16		
		Trumpet	8		
		Clarion	4		
		Tremulant			

PEDAL		COUPLERS		
Diapason	16	Great to Pedal	Positiv Sub to Great
Bourdon	16	Great Super to Pedal	Positiv to Great
Gedeckt	16	Swell to Pedal	Positiv Super to Great
Diapason	8	Swell Super to Pedal	Swell to Positiv 16
Stopped Flute	8	Positiv to Pedal	Swell to Positiv 8
Choral Bass	4	Positive Super to Pedal	Swell to Positiv 4
Trumpet	16	Swell Sub to Great	
Contra Oboe	16	Swell to Great	
Trumpet	8	Swell Super to Great	
Clarion	4		

CALVARY TEMPLE - CHAPEL, 400 Hargrave, Winnipeg.
Kimball, Opus 6583/6627, c. 1910, 2/23 + percussion. Acquired 1940s.
Installed in present chapel 1986. Percussion removed.*

ORCHESTRA		ACCOMPANIMENT		PEDAL	
Concert Flute	8	Horn Diapason	8	Bourdon	16
Tibia Clausa	8	Claribel Flute	8	Flute	8
Violin Cello	8	Viola	8	String Bass	8
Violin	8	Tibia Clausa	8		
Viole (Celeste)	8	Traverse Flute	4	*PERCUSSION	
Solo Flute	4	Gambette	4	Bass Drum	
Orchestral Flute	4	Twelfth	2 2/3	Cymbal	
Nazard	2 2/3	Flautina	2	Tympani	
Piccolo	2	Trumpet	8	Crash Cymbal	
Oboe	8			Snare Drum Tap	
Vox Humana	8	COUPLERS		Snare Drum Roll	
Tremolo		Accompaniment Sub 16		Tambourine	
		Accompaniment Unison Off		Castanet	
		Accompaniment Super 4		Tom-tom	
		Orchestra Sub 16		Chinese Block	
		Orchestra Unison Off		Triangle	
		Orchestra Super 4		Xylophone	
				Bells	
				Carillons	
				Westminster Chimes	

CANADIAN MENNONITE BIBLE COLLEGE, 600 Shaftesbury, Winnipeg.
Karl Wilhelm, 1977, 2/10. Mechanical action.

I		II		PEDAL	
Rohrflöte	8	Gedackt	8	Bourdon	16
Prinzipal	4	Rohrflöte	4	Bourdon	8
Mixtur III	1	Gemshorn	2	Rohrgedackt	4
Kornett	III				

COUPLERS
II to I
I to Pedal
II to Pedal

CENTRAL CONGREGATIONAL CHURCH, Winnipeg.
Warren, c. 1883, 2/?? Specifications unknown. Removed, building demolished.

CENTRAL UNITED CHURCH, 327-8th St., Brandon.
Casavant, Opus 1384, 1930, 2/25 + chimes. From St. John's United, Winnipeg 1988.

GREAT		SWELL		PEDAL	
Bourdon	16	Principal	8	Open Diapason	16
Open Diapason	8	Stopped Diapason	8	Bourdon	16
Melodia	8	Viola di Gamba	8	Bourdon (ext.)	16
Dulciana	8	Voix Celeste	8	Octave (ext.)	8
Principal	4	Aeoline	8	Stopped Flute (ext.)	8
Harmonic Flute	4	Traverse Fulte	4	Fagotto (ext.)	16
Tromba	8	Piccolo	2	Chimes (from Swell)	
Clarinet	8	Dolce Cornet	IV		
Chimes (from Swell)		Contra Fagotto	16	COUPLERS	
Tremulant		Oboe	8	Great to Pedal	
		Vox Humana	8	Great to Pedal Super	
		Chimes		Swell to Pedal	
		Tremulant		Swell to Pedal Super	
				Swell to Great	
				Swell to Great Sub	
				Swell to Great Super	
				Great Sub	
				Great Super	
				Swell Sub	
				Swell Unison Off	
				Swell Super	

CHRIST CHURCH ANGLICAN, Winnipeg.
1. Bolton, Winnipeg, c. 1886. Specifications unknown. Renovation, Casavant 1904.
2. Casavant, Opus 683, 1916, 2/16. Destroyed by fire.

GREAT		SWELL		PEDAL	
Open Diapason	8	Open Diapason (ext.)	8	Bourdon	16
Violin Diapason		Stopped Diapason	8	Gedeckt	16
(ext.)	8	Viola da Gamba	8	Stopped Flute (ext.)	8
Melodia	8	Voix Celeste	8		
Dulciana (ext.)	8	Principal	4	COUPLERS	
Harmonic Flute	8	Fifteenth	2	Great to Pedal	
		Oboe (ext.)	8	Swell to Pedal	
		Cornopean	8	Swell to Great Unison	
		Tremulant		Swell to Great Sub	
				Swell to Great Super	
				Swell Sub	
				Swell Super	
				Great Super	

CHRIST LUTHERAN CHURCH, 815 Inkster, Winnipeg.
George S. Hutchings, Opus 425, 1897, 2/17. Mechanical action.
Stuart Organ Co., Aldenville MA, Opus 30R, 1979. Installed 1980.

GREAT		SWELL		PEDAL	
Open Diapason	8	Stopped Diapason	8	Sub Bass	16
Bourdon	8	Viola	8	Principal	8
Principal	4	Viola Celeste (TC)	8	Choral Bass	4
Mixture (15th & III)	IV	Flute	4	Trombone	16
		Nazard (TC)	2 2/3		
		Fifteenth	2	COUPLERS	
		Tierce (TC)	1 3/5	Great to Pedal	
		Nineteenth	1 1/3	Swell to Pedal	
		Trumpet	8	Swell to Great	
		Tremulant			

CHRISTIAN REFORMED CHURCH, 225 Sutton, Winnipeg.
E. Foidart, Winnipeg, 1977. Pipes: Casavant, Germany; Console: Germany.
2/19 from 6 ranks.*

GREAT		SWELL		PEDAL	
*Principal	8	*Gemshorn	8	*Bourdon	16
*Rohrflöte	8	*Gedeckt	8	Bourdon	8
Octave	8	Gemshorn	4	Principal	8
Flute	4	Chimney Flute	4	Gemshorn	4
Nazard	2 2/3	Fifteenth	2	Block Flöte	2
Blockflöte	2	Tierce	1 3/5		
		Sifflöte	1	COUPLERS	
		*Krummhorn	8	Great to Pedal	
		Tremulant		Swell to Pedal	
				Swell to Great	

CISTERCIAN ABBEY, Holland.
Guilbault-Thérien, 1981, 2/12. Mechanical action.

GRAND ORGUE		POSITIF		PÉDALE	
Principal	8	Bourdon	8	Soubasse	16
Flûte à cheminée	8	Flûte	4		
Principal	4	Principal	2	ACCOUPLEMENTS	
Flûte à bec	2	Quinte	1 1/3	Positif au Grand Orgue	
Mixture	III-IV	Sesquialtera	II	Grand Orgue à la Pédale	
Cromorne	8	Tremblant doux		Positif à la Pédale	

CLARK LEATHERDALE FUNERAL HOME, 232 Kennedy, Winnipeg.
Casavant, Opus 1490, 1934, 2/7.

GREAT		SWELL		PEDAL	
Open Diapason	8	Salicional	8	Bourdon	16
Dulciana	8	Melodia	8		
Wald Flute	4	Oboe	8	COUPLERS	
		Tremulant		Great to Pedal	
				Great to Pedal Super	
				Swell to Pedal	
				Swell to Pedal Super	
				Swell to Great	
				Swell to Great Sub	
				Swell to Great Super	
				Great Sub	
				Great Super	
				Swell Sub	
				Swell Super	

COLLEGE THEATRE, Winnipeg.
Warren, 2/?? Specifications unknown. Removed, building closed.

CRESCENT FORT ROUGE UNITED CHURCH (FORT ROUGE METHODIST),
525 Wardlaw, Winnipeg.
Casavant, Opus 441, 1911. Revisions 1978,* 3/33.

GREAT		SWELL		CHOIR	
Double Open Diapason	16	Bourdon	16	Geigen Principal	8
Open Diapason I	8	Open Diapason	8	Melodia	8
Open Diapason II	8	Stopped Diapason	8	Dulciana	8
Gemshorn	8	*Dolcissimo (removed)	8	Dolce Flute	4
Doppel Flute	8	Viola da Gamba	8	Piccolo	2
Octave	4	Voix Celeste	8	Clarinet	8
Fifteenth	2	Traverse Flute	4	Tremulant	
*Mixture	III	Gemshorn	4		
Trumpet	8	*Nazard	2 2/3		
		Octavino	2		
		Cornet	III		
		Cornopean	8		
		Oboe & Bassoon	8		
		Vox Humana	8		
		Tremulant			

PEDAL		COUPLERS		
Double Open Diapason	16	Great to Pedal	Swell to Choir Sub	
Bourdon	16	Swell to Pedal	Swell to Choir Super	
Gedeckt (ext.)	16	Choir to Pedal	Choir to Great Unison	
Bass Flute(ext.)	8	Swell to Great Unison	Swell Sub	
Stopped Diapason		Swell Sub to Great	Swell Super	
(ext.)	8	Swell Super to Great	Choir Sub	
		Swell to Choir Unison	Choir Super	
			Great at Octave	

CRESTVIEW UNITED CHURCH, 316 Hamilton, Winnipeg.
C. Franklin Legge, Opus 84, 1930, 2/27 from 6 ranks* + chimes. Installed 1982.

GREAT	SWELL	PEDAL
*Open Diapason 8, 4, 2	Stopped Diapason 8, 4, 2	*32 Resultant, 16, 8
*Stopped Diapason (flute)	*Viola da Gamba 8, 4	Open Diapason 8, 4
8, 4, 2 2/3, 2, 1 3/5	*Celeste 8	Stopped Diapason 8, 4
*Oboe 8, 4	Oboe 8, 4	Viola da Gamba 8
Chimes		Oboe 8
		No couplers
		Tremulant

CRYSTAL CITY UNITED CHURCH, Crystal City.
C. Franklin Legge, Opus 35, c. 1920, 2/16 from 5 ranks.* Installed 1927.

GREAT		SWELL		PEDAL	
*Open Diapason	8	Lieblich Gedeckt	16	*Bourdon	16
*Melodia	8	Clarabella	8	Echo Bass	16
*Dulciana	8	Salicional	8	Bass Flute	8
Principal	4	Flute d'Amour	4		
Fifteenth	2	Violina	4	COUPLERS	
		Twelfth	2 2/3	Great to Pedal	
		Piccolo	2	Swell to Pedal	
		*Trumpet	8	Swell Sub to Great	
				Swell to Great	
				Swell Super to Great	

(Original Oboe ranks stolen by an organ tuner in the 1940s;   Swell Sub
Trumpet ranks acquired c. 1988.)   Swell Super

ELIM CHAPEL (ST. STEPHEN'S PRESBYTERIAN), 546 Portage, Winnipeg.
1. Toronto maker unknown, 1903, 2/??. Specifications unknown.
   From Winnipeg College of Music 1903.
2. Casavant, Opus 266, 1906, 3/26; Opus 445 $^1/_2$, 1911, additions,* 3/32.é
3. Casavant, Opus 2137, 1952, additions,** 3/32 + chimes. Destroyed by fire 1974.

GREAT		SWELL		CHOIR	
Open Diapason	8	Bourdon	16	Melodia	8
Doppel Flute	8	Open Diapason	8	*Concert Flute	8
Violin Diapason	8	Stopped Diapason	8	Dulciana	8
Principal	4	Viola da Gamba	8	*Viole d'Orchestre	8
Fifteenth	2	Aeoline	8	Flute	4
Mixture	III	Voix Celeste	8	Clarinet	8
Trumpet	8	Traverse Flute	4	*Orchestral Oboe	8
**Chimes		Gemshorn	8	*Vox Humana	8
		Octavin	2	Tremulant	
		Cornopean	8	**Chimes	
		Oboe	8		
		Tremulant			
		**Chimes			

PEDAL		COUPLERS
Double Open Diapason	16	Great to Pedal
*Bourdon	16	Great Super to Pedal
Gedeckt (ext.)	16	Swell to Pedal
*Violoncello	8	Swell Super to Pedal
Octave (ext.)	8	Choir to Pedal
*Stopped Diapason		Choir Super to Pedal
(ext.)	8	Swell to Great
**Chimes		Swell Sub to Great
		Swell Super to Great
		Swell to Choir
		Swell Sub to Choir
		Swell Super to Choir

4. Casavant, Opus 3404, 1978, 3/20. Renovations, additions 1983-88,* 3/26.

GREAT		SWELL		CHOIR	
Prinzipal	8	Bordun	8	*Holzgedackt	8
Hohlflöte	8	Viola da Gamba	8	*Erzähler	8
Oktave	4	Voix céleste (TC)	8	*Spitzflöte	8
Rohrflöte	4	Prinzipal	4	*Waldflöte	2
Octave	2	Scharf	III	*Quinte	1 1/3
Kornett (TC)	II	Trompete	8	*Krummhorn	8
Mixtur	IV	Tremulant		*Tremulant	

PEDAL		COUPLERS
Prinzipal (ext.)	16	Great to Pedal 8
Subbass	16	Swell to Pedal 8
Oktave	8	Swell to Pedal 4
Bordun (ext.)	8	Choir to Pedal 8
Oktave	4	Swell to Great 16
Mixtur	II	Swell to Great 8
Fagott	16	Choir to Great 8
		Swell to Choir 8

FIRST BAPTIST CHURCH, 102-3rd Ave. SE., Portage la Prairie.
Karn, c. 1900, 2/11. Electric blower 1930s.

GREAT		SWELL		PEDAL	
Open Diapason	8	Stopped Diapason		Bourdon	16
Stopped Diapason	8	Treble	8		
Melodia	8	Stopped Diapason		COUPLERS	
Dulciana	8	Bass	8	Great to Pedal	
Principal	4	Aeoline	8	Swell to Pedal	
		Harmonic Flute	4	Swell to Great	
		Oboe Gamba	8	Swell to Great Super	
		Tremolo			
				Bellows Signal	

FIRST BAPTIST CHURCH, Winnipeg.
H. W. Bolton, Winnipeg, 1883, 2/11. Removed, building demolished.

GREAT		SWELL		PEDAL	
Open Diapason	8	Stopped Diapason Bass	8	Bourdon	16
Stopped Diapason Bass	8	Salicional	8		
Stopped Diapason		Violina	8		
Treble	8	Flute d'Amour	8		
Dulciana	8	Flute Harmonique	4		
Principal	4				

FIRST CHURCH OF CHRIST, SCIENTIST, 511 River, Winnipeg.
Casavant, Opus 313, 1908, 2/17. From Wesley Methodist 1919-20.
Hill, Norman & Beard, 1955. Reconstruction, new console, 2/25 from 20 ranks + chimes.

GREAT		SWELL		PEDAL	
Contra Dulciana	16	Bourdon	16	Open Diapason	16
Open Diapason	8	Open Diapason	8	Bourdon	16
Stopped Diapason	8	Hohl Flute	8	Dulciana (Great)	16
Dulciana (ext.)	8	Viol da Gamba	8	Dulciana (Great)	8
Principal	4	Voix Celeste (TC)	8	Bass Flute (ext.)	8
Flute Ouverte	4	Principal	4	Octave Flute (ext.)	4
Dulcet (ext.)	4	*Quartane II	2 2/3		
Fifteenth	2	Fifteenth	2	COUPLERS	
Trumpet	8	Oboe	8	Great to Pedal 8	
		Cornopean	8	Great to Pedal 4	
		Chimes (g-g")		Swell to Pedal 8	
		Tremulant		Swell to Pedal 4	
				Swell to Swell 16	
		* changed to		Swell Unison Off	
		Sesquialtera	II	Swell to Swell 4	
		1996		Swell to Great 16	
				Swell to Great 8	
				Swell to Great 4	
				Great to Great 16	
				Great Unison Off	
				Great to Great 4	

The organ is installed behind a decorative screen consisting of a palm frond pattern design, a symbolic motif in ancient medicine referring to health and healing, which is repeated elsewhere throughout the church. A newspaper account commented: "The organ is completely obscured from view, increasing the charm and mystery of the musical service."

FIRST ENGLISH EVANGELICAL LUTHERAN, 484 Maryland, Winnipeg.
Canadian Pipe Organ, 1919, 2/7.

GREAT		SWELL		PEDAL	
Open Diapason	8	Salicional	8	Bourdon	16
Dulciana	8	Stopped Diapason	8		
Wald Flute	4	Oboe Gamba	8	COUPLERS	
		Tremulant		Great to Pedal	
				Swell to Pedal	
				Swell to Great	
				Swell to Great Super	
				Swell at Octaves	
				Great at Octaves	
				Bellows Signal	

FIRST FEDERATED CHURCH OF UNITARIANS (now Sri Sathya Sai Baba Centre),
790 Banning, Winnipeg.
Hook & Hastings, Opus 1153, 1883, 2/11. Mechanical action. Installed 1924.

GREAT		SWELL		PEDAL	
Open Diapason	8	Stopped Diapason	8	Sub Bass	16
Stopped Diapason Bass	8	Unison Bass	8		
Melodia	8	Viola	8	COUPLERS	
Dulciana	8	Flute	4	Great to Pedal	
Octave	4	Oboe	8	Swell to Pedal	
		Tremulant		Swell to Great Unison	
				Swell to Great at 8va	
				Bellows Signal	

FIRST LUTHERAN CHURCH, 580 Victor, Winnipeg.
1. Casavant, Opus 267, 1906, 2/22. To St. Boniface Cathedral 1921. Church building sold.
2. Canadian Pipe Organ, 1921, 3/??. New church building.
3. Hill, Norman & Beard, 1959. Reconstruction, console, relocation in rear balcony, 3/26.

GREAT		SWELL		CHOIR	
Open Diapason	8	Open Diapason	8	Dulciana	8
Gemshorn	8	Stopped Diapason	8	Melodia	8
Doppel Flute	8	Vox Angelica	8	Lieblich Flute	4
Principal	4	Voix Celeste	8	Piccolo	2
Fifteenth	2	Octave Geigen	4	Clarinet	8
		Flauto Traverso	4	Tremulant	
		Nasat	2 2/3		
		Super Octave	2		
		Dolce Cornet	III		
		Contra Oboe	16		
		Cornopean	8		
		Tremulant			

PEDAL		COUPLERS			
Open Wood	16	Swell to Pedal		Swell to Great	
Bourdon	16	Swell Octave to Pedal		Swell Octave to Great 4	
Octave	8	Choir to Pedal		Choir Sub Octave to	
Bass Flute	8	Great to Pedal		Great 16	
Choral Bass	4	Swell Sub Octave		Choir Sub Octave	
		Swell Octave		Swell to Choir	

FIRST MENNONITE CHURCH, 922 Notre Dame, Winnipeg.
Canadian Pipe Organ, c. 1915, 2/14. From St. Jude's Anglican.
R. Buck & B. Mantle, Winnipeg, 1991. Reconstruction, installation. 2/37 from 20 ranks
+ chimes.

GREAT		SWELL		PEDAL	
*Dulciana	16, 8, 4	*Viola	8	*Resultant	32
*Diapason	8	*Celeste	8	*Bourdon	16, 8
Principal	4	*Melodia	8	*Open Diapason	8
*Fifteenth	2	*Traverse Flute	4	*Octave	4
*Mixture III	1 1/3	*Quint	2 2/3	Dulciana	16, 8
*Gedeckt	8	*Piccolo	2	Oboe	16, 8, 4
*Harmonic Flute	4	*Tierce	1 3/5	*Posaune	16
Oboe	8	*Oboe	16, 8, 4	Trumpet	8
*Trumpet	8	Trumpet	8	Clarion	4
Clarion	4	Clarion	4	Chimes	
Chimes		Tremulant			
		Chimes			

COUPLERS
Great to Pedal
Swell to Pedal
Swell to Great
Swell Super to Great
Great Super
Swell Sub
Swell Super

FIRST METHODIST CHURCH, Brandon.
Casavant, Opus 190, 1903, 2/15. Removed.

GREAT		SWELL		PEDAL	
Open Diapason	8	Open Diapason (ext.)	8	Bourdon	16
Melodia	8	Stopped Diapason	8	Flute	8
Dulciana (ext.)	8	Viola da Gamba	8		
Octave	4	Voix Celeste	8	COUPLERS	
Fifteenth	2	Harmonic Flute	4	Swell to Great	
Mixture	III	Oboe & Bassoon	8	Great to Pedal	
Trumpet	8	Tremulant		Swell to Pedal	
				Swell Super to Great	
				Great at Octaves	

Bellows Signal

FIRST PRESBYTERIAN CHURCH, 339-12th St., Brandon.
Casavant, Opus 1283, 1928, 2/19 + chimes.

GREAT		SWELL		PEDAL	
Open Diapason	8	Gedeckt	16	Open Diapason	16
Melodia	8	Open Diapason	8	Bourdon	16
Dulciana	8	Stopped Diapason	8	Gedeckt (Great)	16
Principal	4	Viola da Gamba	8	Stopped Flute (ext.)	8
Lieblich Flöte	4	Voix Celeste	8		
Chimes (from Swell)		Aeoline	8	COUPLERS	
		Traverse Flute	4	Great to Pedal	
		Piccolo	2	Great to Pedal Super	
		Closed Horn	8	Swell to Pedal	
		Vox Humana	8	Swell to Pedal Super	
		Tremulant		Swell to Great Unison	
		Chimes (C)	35 bells	Swell to Great Sub	
				Swell to Great Super	
				Swell Sub	
				Swell Super	
				Great Sub	
				Great Super	

FIRST PRESBYTERIAN CHURCH, 61 Picardy, Winnipeg.
1. C. Franklin Legge, 3/25. From Province Theatre 1934. Removed.
2. von Beckerath, 1963, 2/30. Mechanical action.

HAUPTWERK		RÜCKPOSITIV		PEDAL	
Quintadena	16	Gedackt	8	Subbass	16
Principal	8	Quintadena	8	Principal	8
Rohrflöte	8	Principal	4	Rohrgedackt	8
Spitzflöte	8	Rohrflöte	4	Octave	4
Octave	4	Octave	2	Nachthorn	2
Gemshorn	4	Nasat	1 1/3	Mixtur	IV
Nasat	2 2/3	Sifflöte	1	Fagott	16
Octave	2	Sesquialtera	II	Trompete	8
Waldflöte	2	Scharf	III	Schalmei	4
Mixtur	IV-VI	Krummhorn	8		
Trompete	8			COUPLERS	
				Rückpositiv to Hauptwerk	
				Hauptwerk to Pedal	
				Rückpositiv to Pedal	

FIRST UNITED CHURCH, 37-3rd Ave. W., Dauphin.
Casavant, Opus 1675, 1941, 2/25 from 4 ranks.*

GREAT		SWELL		PEDAL	
*Bourdon (TC)	16	Double Dulciana (TC)	16	Bourdon	16
*Open Diapason	8	Viola da Gamba	8	Cello	8
*Viola da Gamba	8	Rohr Flute	8	Stopped Flute	8
Rohr Flute	8	Dulciana	8	Dulcet	4
*Dulciana	8	Violina	4		
Octave	4	Lieblich Flute	4	COUPLERS	
Lieblich Flute	4	Dulcet	4	Great to Pedal	
Dulcet	4	Nazard	2 2/3	Swell to Pedal	
Twelfth	2 2/3	Fifteenth	2	Swell to Great	
Piccolo	2	Tierce	1 3/5		
		Oboe (synthetic)	8		
		Tremulant			

The organ dedication recital was played by Hugh Bancroft, All Saints', Winnipeg, in 1941. The organ was relocated into the new church building in 1962. Mrs. Edythe Winters served as organist in Dauphin for 59 years, first in Grace Methodist Church from 1917, and then in the United church until 1976; she still remained active in 1993 at the age of 93. Her son, Kenneth Winters, also a musician, became organist-choirmaster at St. Philip's Anglican Church, Winnipeg, in 1954 (q.v.).

FORT ROUGE METHODIST CHURCH SUNDAY SCHOOL, Winnipeg.
Casavant, Opus 268, 1906, 2/17. Removed.

GREAT		SWELL		PEDAL	
Open Diapason	8	Open Diapason (ext.)	8	Bourdon	16
Melodia	8	Stopped Diapason	8	Flute	8
Dulciana (ext.)	8	Viola da Gamba	8		
Octave	4	Voix Celeste	8	COUPLERS	
Harmonic Flute	4	Traverse Flute	4	Swell to Great	
Fifteenth	2	Piccolo	2	Great to Pedal	
Mixture	III	Oboe & Bassoon	8	Swell to Pedal	
Trumpet	8	Tremulant		Great at Octaves	
				Swell Sub to Great	

Bellows Signal

FORT ROUGE METHODIST CHURCH, Winnipeg. See CRESCENT FORT ROUGE UNITED CHURCH.

GARDINER FUNERAL HOME, Winnipeg.
Möller, Opus 6150, 1933, 2/20 from 5 ranks.
Blanchard Bros., Winnipeg, 1966. Reconstruction, 2/22 from 6 ranks.* Removed, building closed.

GREAT		SWELL		PEDAL	
*Principal	8	Bourdon	16	Bourdon	16
*Gedeckt	8	Gedeckt	8	Gedeckt	8
*Gemshorn	8	Gemshorn	8	Gemshorn	8
Octave	4	*Voix Celeste	8	Spitzflöte	4
Flute	4	*Spitzflöte	4	Piccolo	2
Nasat	2 2/3	Flute	4		
Piccolo	2	Piccolo	2		
*Oboe	8	Superquint	1 1/3		
		Oboe	8		
		Tremolo			

GARRICK THEATRE, Winnipeg.
Wicks "Giant," Opus 823, 1928, 3/150 from 12 ranks. Removed 1953.

This three-manual, highly-unified instrument consisted of four divisions: Orchestral, Accompaniment, Solo, and Pedal. In addition to the usual ranks of diapason, flute, strings, and reed pipes common to standard pipe organs, it featured several ranks unique to theatre organs: tibia, kinura, and saxophone, dispersed throughout the three manuals at all pitch levels: 16', 8', 4', 2 2/3', 2', 1 3/5'. Tremolo was available on the Orchestral Organ, Solo Organ, and Vox Humana. All pipe ranks were on 7" wind pressure. In addition, the organ featured various percussion devices, some on "second touch": tympani, bass drum, snare drum, snare drum roll, wood drum, tom-tom, cymbal, crash cymbal, triangle, marimba harp, xylophone, chimes, and orchestral bells. Percussion devices were on 9 1/2" wind pressure. The open-top console was finished in ivory and decorated.

GLORIA DEI LUTHERAN CHURCH, 637 Buckingham, Winnipeg.
George Stevens, 1850, 2/16. Mechanical action. Installed 1977.

GREAT		SWELL		PEDAL	
Open Diapason	8	Open Diapason	8	Sub Bass	16
Dulciana	8	Viol de Gamba	8		
Clarabella	8	Stop Diapason Treble	8	COUPLERS	
Stop Diapason Treble	8	Stop Diapason Bass	8	Great and Swell	
Stop Diapason Bass	8	Principal	4	Pedals to Swell Bass	
Principal	4	Oboe	8		
Flute	4	Tremolo		Blowers Signal	
Twelfth	2 2/3				
Fifteenth	2				

GORDON-KING MEMORIAL UNITED (KING MEMORIAL UNITED [PRESBYTERIAN]
CHURCH), 127 Cobourg, Winnipeg.
Casavant, Opus 1272, 1928, 2/25.

GREAT		SWELL		PEDAL	
Open Diapason I	8	Bourdon	16	Open Diapason	16
Open Diapason II	8	Open Diapason	8	Bourdon	16
Doppel Flute	8	Stopped Diapason	8	Gedeckt (Swell)	8
Dulciana	8	Aeoline	8	Octave (ext.)	8
Principal	4	Viola da Gamba	8	Stopped Flute (ext.)	8
Harmonic Flute	4	Voix Celeste	8		
Fifteenth	2	Traverse Flute	4	COUPLERS	
Clarinet	8	Piccolo	2	Great to Pedal	
		Dolce Cornet	III	Great to Pedal Super	
		Cornopean	8	Swell to Pedal	
		Oboe	8	Swell to Pedal Super	
		Clarinet	8	Swell to Great Unison	
		Tremulant		Swell to Great Sub	
				Swell to Great Super	
				Swell Sub	
				Swell Super	
				Great Super	

GRACE METHODIST CHURCH, Portage la Prairie.
Kilgen, c. 1920, 2/13. To Sparling United, Winnipeg 1937.

GRACE UNITED (METHODIST) CHURCH, Winnipeg.
1. Warren, 1885, 2/??. Specifications unknown. To Westminster Presbyterian 1894.
2. R. S. Williams & Son, 1894, 3/34. Removed, parts used in Casavant, Opus 301, 1907.

GREAT		SWELL		CHOIR	
Double Open Diapason	16	Bourdon Treble	16	Geigen Principal	8
Open Diapason	8	Bourdon Bass	16	Dulciana	8
Gamba	8	Open Diapason	8	Melodia	8
Doppel Flute	8	Viol di Gamba	8	Harmonic Flute	4
Wald Flute	4	Concert Flute	8	Harmonic Piccolo	2
Principal	4	Aeoline	8	Clarinette	8
Twelfth	2 2/3	Stopped Diapason	8	Tremulant	
Fifteenth	2	Traverse Flute	4		
Mixture	III	Violina	4		
Trumpet	8	Flautino	2		
		Mixture	II		
		Vox Humana	8		
		Oboe	8		
		Tremulant			

PEDAL		COUPLERS	
Double Open	16	Swell to Great	
Violone	16	Swell to Choir	
Bourdon	16	Choir to Great	
Violoncello	8	Great to Pedal	
Trombone	16	Swell to Pedal	
		Choir to Pedal	
		Bellows Signal	

3. Casavant, Opus 301, 1907, 4/46. Damaged in fire 1917.
4. Casavant, Opus 696, 1917, 4/47 + chimes. Rebuilt after fire, with addition.* Removed 1955.

GREAT		SWELL		CHOIR	
Double Open	16	Bourdon	16	Violin Diapason	8
Open Diapason	8	Open Diapason	8	Melodia	8
Geigen Principal	8	Stopped Diapason	8	Dulciana	8
Doppel Flute	8	Clarabella Flute	8	Harmonic Flute	4
Gemshorn	8	Viola da Gamba	8	Flageolet	2
Wald Flute	8	Voix Celeste	8	Clarinet	8
Principal	4	Dolcissimo	8	Tremulant	
Fifteenth	2	Traverse Flute	4		
Mixture	III	Violina	4	SOLO	
Trumpet	8	Flautino	2	Stentorphone	8
*Chimes		Dolce Cornet	III	Quintadena	8
		Contra Fagotto	16	Rohr Flute	8
		Cornopean	8	Harmonic Flute	4
		Oboe	8	Orchestral Oboe	8
		Vox Humana	8	Cor Anglais	8
		Tremulant		Tuba	8
				Tremulant	

PEDAL		COUPLERS		
Double Open	16	Great to Pedal	Choir to Great
Bourdon	16	Swell to Pedal	Choir Sub Octave to Great
Gedeckt (Swell)	16	Choir to Pedal	Choir at Octaves
Flute (ext.)	8	Solo to Pedal	Solo to Great
Cello	8	Swell to Great	Solo to Swell
Bourdon (ext.)	8	Swell to Choir	Solo to Choir
Trombone	16	Swell at Octaves	Great at Octaves
Trumpet	8	Swell Super Octave to Great	
		Swell Sub Octave to Great	

GREENWOOD UNITED CHURCH, Winnipeg.
Casavant, Opus 1421, 1931, 2/7; Opus 1521: electro-pneumatic action, 1936. Removed 1981. To University of Manitoba, St. John's College Chapel, 1983. Church building demolished.

GREAT		SWELL		PEDAL	
Open Diapason	8	Salicional	8	Bourdon	16
Dulciana	8	Melodia	8		
Lieblich Flute	4	Oboe	8	COUPLERS	
		Tremulant		Great to Pedal	

COUPLERS
Great to Pedal
Great to Pedal Super
Swell to Pedal
Swell to Pedal Super
Swell to Great
Swell to Great Sub
Swell to Great Super
Great Sub
Great Super
Swell Sub
Swell Super

HARROW UNITED CHURCH, 955 Mulvey, Winnipeg.
Casavant, Opus 1224, 1927, 2/7. From St. Andrew's River Heights 1958.

GREAT		SWELL		PEDAL	
Open Diapason	8	Salicional (ext.)	8	Bourdon (ext.)	16
Dulciana	8	Melodia	8		
Wald Flute	8	Oboe	8	COUPLERS	
		Tremulant		Great to Pedal	
				Great to Pedal Super	
				Swell to Pedal	
				Swell to Pedal Super	
				Swell to Great Sub	
				Swell to Great Unison	
				Swell to Great Super	
				Swell Sub	
				Swell Super	
				Great Sub	
				Great Super	

HOLY GHOST ROMAN CATHOLIC CHURCH, Winnipeg.
Casavant, origin unknown, c. 1916, 2/20. Removed 1993.

GREAT		SWELL		PEDAL	
Open Diapason	16	Bourdon	16	Bourdon Discant (Sw.)	16
Open Diapason	8	Open Diapason	8	Bourdon	16
Melodia	8	Stopped Diapason	8	Violoncello	8
Floete d'Amour	4	Viola di Gamba	8		
Principal	4	Voix Celeste	8	COUPLERS	
Fifteenth	2	Harmonic Flute	4	Great to Pedal	
Mixture	III	Violina	4	Swell to Pedal	
Trumpet	8	Flautino	2	Great Super	
		Oboe	8	Swell to Great	
		Tremolo		Swell to Great Sub	
				Swell to Great Super	

HOLY TRINITY ANGLICAN CHURCH, 256 Smith, Winnipeg.
1. S. R. Warren & Son, 1878, 2/24. Specifications unkown. Enlarged 1884. Additions 1892, 3/39. Removed.
2. Canadian Pipe Organ, 1912, 4/50.
3. Casavant, Opus 2014, 1950. Console, electrification, additions,* 4/53.

GREAT		SWELL		CHOIR	
Open Diapason	16	Bourdon	16	Geigen Principal	8
Open Diapason No. 1	8	Open Diapason	8	Melodia	8
Open Diapason No. 2	8	Clarabella	8	Dulciana	8
Violin Diapason	8	Stopped Flute	8	Unda Maris	II
Doppel Flöte	8	Viola da Gamba	8	Harmonic Flute	4
Gemshorn	8	Voix Celeste	8	Nazard	2 2/3
Wald Flute	4	Dolcissimo	8	Piccolo	2
Principal	4	Traverse Flute	4	Clarinet	8
Twelfth	2/3	Violina	4	Tremulant	
Fifteenth	2	Flautino	2		
Mixture	III	Dolce Cornet	V	SOLO	
Trumpet	8	Contra Fagotto	16	*Stentorphone	8
		Cornopean	8	*Gross Flute	8
		Oboe	8	Grosse Gambe	8
		Vox Humana	8	Viole d'Orchestre	8
		Tremulant		Orchestral Flute	4
				Piccolo	2
				Orchestral Oboe	8
				Tuba	8
				Tremulant	

PEDAL		COUPLERS		
*Resultant	32	Great to Pedal	Solo to Great Unison	
Double Open	16	Great to Pedal Super	Solo to Great Sub	
Open Diapason	16	Swell to Pedal	Solo to Great Super	
Bourdon	16	Swell to Pedal Super	Solo to Swell Unison	
Gedeckt	16	Choir to Pedal	Solo to Swell Sub	
Octave	8	Choir to Pedal Super	Solo to Swell Super	
Bourdon	8	Solo to Pedal	Solo to Choir Unison	
Cello	8	Solo to Pedal Super	Solo to Choir Sub	
Trombone	16	Swell to Great Unison	Solo to Choir Super	
*Tromba	8	Swell to Great Sub	Great Super	
		Swell to Great Super	Swell Sub	
		Swell to Choir Unison	Swell Unison Off	
		Swell to Choir Sub	Swell Super	
		Swell to Choir Super	Choir Sub	
		Choir to Great Unison	Choir Unison Off	
		Choir to Great Sub	Choir Super	
		Choir to Great Super	Solo Sub	
			Solo Super	

4. Hill, Norman & Beard, 1962, 4/59. Rebuilt, Positiv added. Mechanical work 1969, 1993.

GREAT	
Double Open Diapason	16
Open Diapason I	8
Open Diapason II	8
Principal	8
Stopped Diapason	8
Octave	4
Spitz Principal	4
Wald Flute	4
Twelfth	2 2/3
Fifteenth	2
Quartane	II
Mixture	III
Trumpet	8

SWELL	
Quintaten	16
Geigen Diapason	8
Clarabella	8
Viola da Gamba	8
Erzähler	8
Erzähler Celeste (TC)	8
Octave	4
Traverse Flute	4
Octave Quint	2 2/3
Fifteenth	2
Mixture	IV
Double Trumpet	16
Trompette	8
Oboe	8
Clarion	4
Tremulant	

POSITIV	
Chimney Flute	8
Octave	4
Koppelflöte	4
Nasat	2 2/3
Blockflöte	2
Tierce	1 3/5
Larigot	1 1/3
Sifflöte	1
Orchestral Trumpet	16
Orchestral Trumpet	8
Orchestral Trumpet	4
Tremulant	

SOLO	
Viole de Gambe	8
Gedeckt	8
Dulciana	8
Unda Maris	8
Traverse Flute	4
Nazard	2 2/3
Flautina	2
Clarinet	8
Orchestral Oboe	8
Tremulant	

PEDAL	
Resultant Bass	32
Open Diapason (Wood)	16
Open Diapason (Metal)	16
Bourdon	16
Quintaten	16
Bourdon	8
Principal	8
Spitz Flute	4
Quartane	II
Trombone	16
Trumpet	8

COUPLERS
Great to Pedal
Swell to Pedal
Positiv to Pedal
Solo to Pedal
Great Super to Pedal
Swell Super to Pedal
Positiv Super to Pedal
Solo Super to Pedal
Swell Sub to Great
Swell to Great
Swell Super to Great
Positiv Sub to Great
Positiv to Great
Positiv Super to Great
Solo Sub to Great
Solo to Great
Solo Super to Great
Solo Sub to Swell
Solo to Swell
Solo Super to Swell
Swell Sub to Positiv
Swell to Positiv
Swell Super to Positiv
Solo Sub to Positiv
Solo to Positiv
Solo Super to Positiv
Great Octave
Swell Octave
Swell Sub Octave
Solo Octave
Solo Sub Otave

HOME STREET MENNONITE CHURCH (HOME STREET UNITED), 318 Home, Winnipeg.
Woodstock Pipe Organ Builders, c. 1920, 2/15 + chimes. (Removed since installation*)

GREAT		SWELL		PEDAL	
Open Diapason	8	Open Diapason	8	Major Bass	16
Melodia	8	Stopped Diapason	8	Bourdon	16
Dulciana	8	Viol d' Gamba	8	Stopped Flute	8
Principal	4	*Voix Celeste	8	Chimes (from Swell)	
*Flute Harmonic	4	Flauto Traverso	4		
Chimes (from Swell)		Piccolo	2	COUPLERS	
		Oboe	8	Great Sub	
		Tremolo		Great Super	
		Chimes		Great to Pedal	
				Great to Pedal Super	
				Swell to Pedal	
				Swell to Pedal Super	

IMMACULATE CONCEPTION ROMAN CATHOLIC CHURCH, Winnipeg.
Eusèbe Brodeur, 1896, 2/19. Destroyed by fire c. 1975.

GREAT		SWELL		PEDAL	
Montre	8	Principal	8	Bourdon	16
Bourdon	8	Clarabelle	8	Violoncello	16
Salicional	8	Gamba	8		
Dulciana	8	Voix céleste	8	COUPLERS	
Flûte harmonique	4	Violina	4	Swell to Great	
Prestant	4	Flutina	4	Swell to Pedal	
Nazard	2 2/3	Hautbois	8	Great to Pedal	
Doublette	2	Tremolo			
Mixture	III			Pumper Signal	
Trompette	8				

KNOX PRESBYTERIAN CHURCH, Portage la Prairie. See TRINITY UNITED.
1. Karn-Warren, 1904, 2/20. Specifications unknown. Destroyed in tornado 1922.
2. Casavant, Opus 966, 1923, 2/29.

KNOX PRESBYTERIAN CHURCH, Souris.
Casavant, Opus 727, 1917, 2/12. To St. Paul's United, Souris 1946.

KNOX UNITED (PRESBYTERIAN) CHURCH, 400 Edmonton, Winnipeg.
1. First organ, maker unknown (from USA), 1882.
2. Warren, c. 1885, 2/??. Specifications unknown. To Knox Presbyterian Church, Regina, 1906.
3. Casavant, Opus 259, 1906, 3/32. Moved to new building 1917.
   Opus 1947, 1949: console and additions,* 3/34.

GREAT		SWELL		CHOIR	
Double Open Diapason	16	Lieblich Bourdon	16	Gamba	8
Open Diapason (Large)	8	Open Diapason	8	Melodia	8
Open Diapason (Small)	8	Stopped Diapason	8	Dulciana	8
Rohrflöte	8	Dolce	8	Suabe Flute	4
Principal	4	Echo Gamba	8	Piccolo	2
Harmonic Flute	4	Voix Celeste	8	*Tierce	3/5
Fifteenth	2	Principal	4	Clarionet	8
Mixture	III	Fifteenth	2	*Tremulant	
Trumpet	8	Dolce Cornet	III		
		Horn	8		
		Oboe and Bassoon	8		
		Vox Humana	8		
		Tremulant			

PEDAL		COUPLERS
Open Diapason	16	Swell to Great
Bourdon	16	Swell to Choir
Lieblich Bourdon		Choir to Great
(Swell)	16	Swell Sub Octave to Great
*Stopped Flute (ext.)	8	Great at Octaves
Bass Flute (ext.)	8	Swell to Pedal
Trombone	16	Great to Pedal
		Choir to Pedal

4. Casavant, Opus 2992, 1968, 3/40 + percussion. New specifications, pipes. Additions* to 1997, 3/44 + percussion.

GREAT		SWELL		POSITIV	
Quintaden	16	Salizional	8	Gedeckt	8
Prinzipal	8	Vox coeleste	8	Prinzipal	4
Rohrflöte	8	Gedecktflöte	8	Koppelflöte	4
Octav	4	Weidenpfeife	4	Gemshorn	2
Spitzflöte	4	*Dolce	8	Quintflöte	1 1/3
Quinte	2 2/3	Nachthorn	4	Sifflöte	1
Oktav	2	Nasat	2 2/3	Sesquialtera II	2/3
Blockflöte	2	Waldflöte	2	Scharf IV	1
Mixtur IV	1 1/3	Terz	1 3/5	Krummhorn	8
Trompette	8	Scharf IV	1/3	Tremulant	
		Fagott	16		
		Oboe	8		
		Tremulant			

PEDAL		COUPLERS			
*Contra Prinzipal	32	Great to Pedal		Positiv to Great	
(Resultant)		*Great Super to Pedal		*Positiv Super to Great	
Prinzipal	16	Swell to Pedal		*Positiv Sub to Great	
Subbass	16	*Swell Super to Pedal			
Oktav	8	Positiv to Pedal		PERCUSSION	
Gedecktpommer	8	*Posiiv Super to Pedal		Zimbelstern (gift of	
Choral Bass	4	*Great Super to Great		Dr. Dan Wilmot)	
Rohrpfeife	4	Swell to Great		*Schulmerich Carillon	
Nachthorn	2	*Swell Super to Great		Americana, sanctuary and	
Mixture IV	2	*Swell Sub to Great		tower, 1995 (Maunders	
*Contra Posaune	32	Swell to Positiv		McNeill Foundation)	
(Resultant)		*Swell Super to Positiv			
Posaune	16				
*Trompette	8				
Schalmei	4				

KNOX UNITED CHURCH - CHAPEL. 400 Edmonton, Winnipeg.
Casavant, c. 1970, 2/16 from 5 ranks.*

GREAT	SWELL	PEDAL	
*Diapason 8, 4	*Salicional 16, 8, 4	*Open	16
*Flute 16, 8, 4, 2	Flute 8, 4, 2	Flute	8
*Dulciana 8, 4			

The early history of this organ is unknown, but it was not originally installed in Manitoba. For several years it was in a Winnipeg residence until it was purchased by a member of the choir of Westminster Church in the late 1970s. Following its acceptance by Knox Church, it was stored for a time by a local organ technician before being installed in the chapel.

LA MAISON VICARIALE, St. Boniface.
Casavant, Opus 490, 1912, 2/11. Removed.

GRAND ORGUE		RÉCIT		PÉDALE	
Montre	8	Principal (ext.)	8	Bourdon	16
Mélodie	8	Bourdon	8		
Dulciane (ext.)	8	Aeoline	8	ACCOUPLEMENTS	
Prestant	4	Voix céleste	8	Grand Orgue à la Pédale	
		Flûte harmonique	4	Récit à la Pédale	
		Hautbois	8	Récit au Grand Orgue	
		Trémolo		unisson	
				Récit au Grand Orgue	
				grave	
				Récit au Grand Orgue aigu	
				Octave aiguë Grand Orgue	

LYCEUM THEATRE, Winnipeg.Smith, 3/?? Unit organ. Specifications unknown. Removed, building closed.

MESSIAH LUTHERAN CHURCH, 400 Rouge, Winnipeg.
Karl Wilhelm, 1974, 1/7. Mechanical action.

MANUAL		PEDAL	
Gedackt	8	Bourdon	16
Principal	4		
Rohrflöte	4	COUPLER	
Spitz	2	Manual to Pedal	
Quinte	2 2/3		
Octave	1		

Although the church building was erected in 1967, an organ was not in place until five years later. The organ committee decided on a pipe organ over an electronic instrument, and visited several local churches to inspect their pipe organ installations. A proposal for a small two-manual organ was received from Gabriel Kney, but the decision was made in favour this one-manual organ, at a cost of $11,000.

MORDUE FUNERAL CHAPEL, Winnipeg.
Wicks "Sonatina," Opus 2071, 1940, 2/20 from 4 ranks. To University of Winnipeg Chapel 1982.

NEEPAWA UNITED (METHODIST) CHURCH, Neepawa.
1. Warren. Specifications unknown. From a church in St. Catherines, Ontario. Installed 1921.
    Blanchard Bros., Winnipeg. Electric blower 1943. Removed.
2. T. Eaton Co. / William F. Legge, 1947, 2/21. Removed.

GREAT		SWELL		PEDAL	
Flute Conique	16	Principal	8	Open Diapason	16
Diapason	8	Principal	4	Violone	16
Flute	8	Flute	8	Stopped Flute	16
Gamba	8	Flute	4	Principal	8
Octave	4	Viola	8	Flute	8
Flute	4	Viol Celeste	8		
Twelfth	2 2/3	Oboe	8	COUPLERS	
Fifteenth	2	Tremulant		Swell to Great 16-8-4	
Trumpet	8			Great to Pedal 8-4	
				Swell to Pedal 8-4	
				Manuals 16-8-4	

Arthur Leach, the pumper of the Warren tracker organ in the early years, was paid .25¢ an hour. The interior of the organ contained some World War II graffiti, such as drawings of bullets shooting through the helmets of enemy soldiers. Due to the lack of ongoing technical assistance and the costs of a visiting tuner from Winnipeg—the instrument was never properly voiced for the building—the Eaton/Legge organ was replaced by an electronic organ in 1968, over the objections of the local organist, followed by an Allen organ in 1989.

OUR SAVIOUR'S LUTHERAN CHURCH, 600 Minto, Winnipeg.
William F. Legge, 1954, 2/35 from 7 ranks* + chimes.

GREAT		SWELL		PEDAL	
Bourdon	16	Gedackt (TC)	16	Bourdon	16
Contra Gamba (TC)	16	Stopped Diapason	8	Open Diapason	8
*Open Diapason	8	Viol d'Gamba	8	Stopped Flute	8
*Stopped Diapason	8	*Voix Celeste (TC)	8	Cello	8
*Gamba	8	Dolce	8	Dolce	8
*Dolce	8	Flute d'Amour	4	Quint	5 1/3
*Principal	4	Violina	4	Octave	4
Flute	4	Octave Celeste	4	Flute	4
Violina	4	Piccolo	2	Fagotto	16
Dulcet	4	Oboe	8	Oboe	8
Nazard	2 2/3	Chimes (25 notes)			
Super Octave	2	Tremulant			
*Fagotto	16				
Oboe	8				
Oboe	4				

The decision in favour of the Legge organ was made over Casavant, whose estimate was considered too high. William Legge came to Winnipeg and consulted with the architect regarding the installation. However, a later opinion was that more attention should have been paid to acoustical considerations. In 1967 Blanchard Bros., Winnipeg, reported to the church on the condition of the organ. In their opinion, the organ chamber was one of the most poorly designed that they had ever seen: the tonal opening was higher than the speaking level of the pipes, the inner surfaces were covered with a paper composite board that absorbed sound, the shutters were facing in the wrong direction and did not open sufficiently, and an interior heater was against safety standards. The chest design was not well suited to local climatic conditions. Pipe speech was poor, due to faulty original voicing, regulation was unequal, and the pedal division lacked an independent voice. These deficiences, along with tonal gaps, made the organ difficult to play. Replacement of the pipes of British manufacture was considered too expensive. (Letter from Blanchard Bros. to W. A. Broddy, Our Saviour's Lutheran Church, 1 March 1967.)

PARISH CHURCH, ROMAN CATHOLIC, 233 Pembina, Ste. Agathe.
Casavant, Opus 2122, 1952, 2/7.

GRAND ORGUE		RÉCIT		PÉDALE	
Montre	8	Salicional	8	Bourdon	16
Dulciane	8	Bourdon	8		
Flûte bouchée	8	Hautbois	8	ACCOUPLEMENTS	
		Trémolo		Grand Orgue à la Pédale	
				Grand Orgue aigu à la Pédale	
				Récit à la Pédale	
				Récit aigu à la Pédale	
				Récit au Grand Orgue	
				Récit grave au Grand Orgue	
				Récit aigu au Grand Orgue	
				Grand Orgue aigu	
				Récit grave	
				Récit aigu	

PARISH CHURCH, ROMAN CATHOLIC, Hwy. 12, S. of Hwy. 1E., Ste. Anne des Chênes.
1. First organ, 1904. Specifications unknown. Removed.
2. Casavant, Opus 983, 1923, 2/12.

GRAND ORGUE		RÉCIT		PÉDALE	
Montre	8	Principal (ext.)	8	Bourdon	16
Mélodie	8	Bourdon	8	Flûte	8
Dulciane (ext.)	8	Viole de Gambe	8		
Prestant	4	Voix céleste	8	ACCOUPLEMENTS	
		Flûte harmonique	4	Grand Orgue à la Pédale	
		Cor	8	Récit à la Pédale	
		Trémolo		Récit au Grand Orgue unisson	
				Récit au Grand Orgue aigu	
				Récit au Grand Orgue grave	
				Octave grave Récit	
				Octave aiguë Récit	
				Octave aiguë Grand Orgue	

The first organ in the church was installed in 1904, a gift from a parish in Québec. The organist in 1993, Alice Langill, served in that position for 50 years.

PARISH CHURCH, ROMAN CATHOLIC, St. Norbert.
1   Casavant, Opus 102, 1899, 2/12. Mechanical action. Destroyed by fire 1929.

GRAND ORGUE		RÉCIT EXPRESSIF		PÉDALE	
Montre	8	Mélodie	8	Bourdon	16
Flûte harmonique	8	Salicional	8		
Dulciana	8	Voix céleste	8	REGISTERS	
Prestant	4	Flûte harmonique	4	MÉCANIQUE	
Doublette	2	Hautbois	8	Récit au Grand Orgue	
Kéraulophone	8			Récit à Pédale	
				Grand Orgue à Pédale	
				Octave grave Récit au	
				Grand Orgue	
				Trémolo	
				Souffleur	

2. Edward Lye, Opus 12, 1906, 2/12. Mechanical action. Removed from Sacré-Coeur 1992.
J. Musselwhite, Winnipeg, 1997. Reconstruction, installation.

GREAT		SWELL		PEDAL	
Open Diapason	8	Stop'd Diapason Bass	8	Bourdon	16
Stopped Diapason	8	(unenclosed)		Open Diapason	8
Melodia	8	Viola	8		
Dulciana	4	Viola di Gamba	8	COUPLERS	
Principal	4	Traverse Flute	4	Great to Pedal	
		Piccolo	2	Swell to Pedal	
		Tremolo		Swell to Great	
				Bellows Signal	

PARISH CHURCH, ROMAN CATHOLIC, St. Pierre-Jolys.
Casavant, Opus 670, 1916, 2/9. Removed.

GRAND ORGUE		RÉCIT		PÉDALE	
Montre	8	Bourdon	8	Bourdon	16
Mélodie	8	Viole de gambe	8		
Dulciana (ext.)	8	Voix céleste	8	ACCOUPLEMENTS	
		Flûte harmonique	4	Grand Orgue à la Pédale	
		Hautbois	8	Récit à la Pédale	
		Tremolo		Récit au Grand Orgue	
				unisson	
				Récit au Grand Orgue grave	
				Récit au Grand Orgue aigu	
				Octave Grave Récit	
				Octave aiguë Récit	
				Octave aiguë Grand Orgue	

After 70 years of service, the organ was in poor condition and was demolished when a new
church building was erected in 1983. Some wood from the organ case was used in a decorative fashion in the interior of the new building. The pipe organ was succeeded by an
electronic instrument.

PRESBYTERIAN CHURCH, Birtle.
Bolton & Baldwin, Winnipeg, 1887, 1/5. Removed.

MANUAL		PEDAL	
Open Diapason	8	Bourdon	16
Stopped Diapason	8		
Dulciana	8		
Principal	4		
Tremulant			

PROVINCE THEATRE, Winnipeg.
C. Franklin Legge, 1917, 3 manuals, 2,000 pipes. Specifications unknown.
To First Presbyterian 1934.

ROBERTSON MEMORIAL UNITED CHURCH, 648 Burrows, Winnipeg.
Casavant, Opus 1889, 1947, 2/25 from 5 ranks.*

GREAT		SWELL		PEDAL	
Lieblich Gedeckt (TC)	16	Contra Dulciana (TC)	16	*Bourdon	16
*Open Diapason	8	Rohr Flöte	8	Octave	8
*Rohr Flute	8	Salicional	8	Cello	8
*Salicional	8	Dulciana	8	Stopped Flute	8
*Dulciana	8	Salicet	4	Dulcet	4
Octave	4	Lieblich Flöte	4		
Lieblich Flöte	4	Dulcet	4	COUPLERS	
Dulcet	4	Nazard	2 2/3	Great to Pedal	
Nazard	2 2/3	Piccolo	2	Swell to Pedal	
Fifteenth	2	Tierce	1 3/5	Swell to Great	
		Tremulant			

ROMAN CATHOLIC CATHEDRAL, The Pas.
Casavant, Opus 1538, 1939, 2/22 from 3 ranks.* Removed c. 1970.

GRAND ORGUE		RÉCIT		PÉDALE	
*Bourdon	16	Principal	8	Bourdon	16
*Principal	8	Bourdon	8	Bourdon	8
Bourdon	8	Quintaton	8	Principal	4
*Dulciane	8	Dulciane	8	Flûte	4
Violina	5	Violina	4	Dulcet	4
Flûte d'amour	4	Flûte d'amour	4		
Dulcet	4	Dulcet	4		
Nazard	2 2/3	Hautbois (syn.)	8		
Doublette	2	Trémolo			

SACRÉ-COEUR ROMAN CATHOLIC CHURCH, Winnipeg.
Edward Lye, Opus 12, 1906, 2/12. Mechanical action. From Trinity Lutheran 1968. Removed
1992.
To Parish Church, St. Norbert, 1997.

ST. AIDAN'S ANGLICAN CHURCH, 274 Campbell, Winnipeg.
1.   Casavant, Opus 1777, 1945, 2/27 from 7 ranks.* Removed.

GREAT		SWELL		PEDAL	
Lieblich Gedeckt (TC)	16	Contra Dulciana (TC)	16	*Bourdon	16
*Open Diapason	8	Rohr Flöte	8	Octave	8
*Rohr Flöte	8	Viola da Gamba	8	Cello	8
*Viola da Gamba	8	*Voix Celeste	8	Stopped Flute	8
*Dulciana	8	Dulciana	8	*Bassoon	16
Octave	4	Violina	4		
Lieblich Flöte	4	Lieblich Flöte	4		
Dulcet	4	Dulcet	4		
Nazard	2 2/3	Nazard	2 2/3		
Fifteenth	2	Piccolo	2		
		Tierce	1 3/5		
		Oboe	8		
		Tremulant			

2.   Casavant, Opus 2682, 1962, 2/25.

GREAT		SWELL		PEDAL	
Nachthorngedeckt	16	Rohrflöte	8	Violone	16
Principal	8	Salicional	8	Nachthorngedeckt	
Spitzflöte	8	Voix Celeste (GG)	8	(Great)	16
Octave	4	Geigen Principal	4	Spitzprincipal	8
Koppelflöte	4	Nazard	2 2/3	Nachthorngedeckt	
Superoctave	2	Blockflöte	2	(Great)	8
Fourniture IV	1 1/3	Plein Jeu III	1	Choralbass	4
Trompette	8	Fagott	16	Mixture II	2 2/3
		Trompette	8	Lieblich Posaune	16
		Hautbois	4		
		Tremulant			

COUPLERS

Great to Pedal 8	Swell to Pedal 8-4
Great Unison Off	Swell to Great 16-8-4
Great 4	Swell 16
	Swell Unison Off
	Swell 4

ST. ALBAN'S ANGLICAN CHURCH, 486 Rathgar, Winnipeg.
Warren, 1891, 2/16. From All Saints' Anglican Church 1917.
F. Radcliffe, Winnipeg, c. 1953. Reconstruction, additions, 2/24.

GREAT		SWELL		PEDAL	
Open Diapason	8	Bourdon (TC)	16	Bourdon	16
Concert Flute	8	Diapason	8	Diapason	8
Viol d' Gamba	8	Stopped Diapason	8	Bass Flute	8
Dulciana	8	Viol d' Gamba	8	Cello	8
Octave	4	Stopped Flute	4	Tuba (Great)	8
Flute	4	Gambette	4		
Dulcet	4	Nazard	2 2/3	COUPLERS	
Tuba	8	Piccolo	2	Swell to Great	
Clarion	4	Oboe Syn.	8	Great to Pedal	
		Tuba (Great)	8	Swell to Pedal	
		Tremulant			

ST. ANDREW'S PRESBYTERIAN CHURCH, Winnipeg.
Casavant, Opus 197, 1904, 3/28. Destroyed by fire 1968.

GREAT		SWELL		CHOIR	
Double Open Diapason	16	Bourdon	16	Geigen Principal	8
Open Diapason	8	Horn Diapason	8	Melodia	8
Doppel Flute	8	Viola di Gamba	8	Dulciana	8
Gamba	8	Stopped Diapason	8	Wald Flute	4
Principal	4	Aeoline	8	Flageolet	2
Harmonic Flute	4	Voix Celeste	8	Clarionet	8
Fifteenth	2	Traverse Flute	4	Tremulant	
Mixture	III	Piccolo	2		
Trumpet	8	Cornopean	8		
		Oboe & Bassoon	8		
		Tremulant			

PEDAL		COUPLERS	
Open Diapason	16	Great to Pedal	
Bourdon	16	Swell to Pedal	
Violoncello	8	Choir to Pedal	
		Choir Sub Octave to Great	
		Swell to Great	
		Swell to Choir	
		Great at Octaves	

Bellows Signal

ST. ANDREW'S RIVER HEIGHTS UNITED CHURCH, 255 Oak, Winnipeg.
1. Casavant, Opus 1224, 1927, 2/7. Moved to new building c. 1950. To Harrow United 1958.

GREAT		SWELL		PEDAL	
Open Diapason	8	Salicional (ext.)	8	Bourdon (ext.)	16
Dulciana	8	Melodia	8		
Wald Flute	8	Oboe	8	COUPLERS	
		Tremulant		Great to Pedal	
				Great to Pedal Super	
				Swell to Pedal	
				Swell to Pedal Super	
				Swell to Great Sub	
				Swell to Great Unison	
				Swell to Great Super	
				Swell Sub	
				Swell Super	
				Great Sub	
				Great Super	

2. Casavant, Opus 2463, 1958, 3/39. Pipes relocated 1981.

GREAT		SWELL		CHOIR	
Quintaton	16	Geigen Principal	8	Cor de Nuit	8
Diapason	8	Rohrflöte	8	Erzähler	8
Gedeckt	8	Salicional	8	Erzähler Celeste (GG)	8
Gemshorn	8	Voix Celeste (GG)	8	Prestant	4
Octave	4	Geigen Principal	4	Koppelflöte	4
Octave Quint	2 2/3	Flauto Traverso	4	Rohrnazard	2 2/3
Super Octave	2	Plein Jeu	III	Blockflöte	2
Mixture	IV	Contre-Hautbois (ext.)	16	Tierce	1 3/5
		Trompette	8	Clarinet	8
		Hautbois Unit	8	Tremulant	
		Clairon	4		
		Tremulant			

PEDAL		COUPLERS			
Contrabasse	16	Great Super		Choir Sub	
Bourdon	16	Great Unison Off		Choir Unison Off	
Quintaton (Great)	16	Great to Pedal		Choir Super	
Cor de Nuit (ext.)	16	Great Super to Pedal		Choir Unison to Great	
Spitzprincipal	8	Swell Sub		Choir Sub to Great	
Gedeckt (ext.)	8	Swell Unison Off		Choir Super to Great	
Cor de Nuit (ext.)	8	Swell Super			
Choralbass	4	Swell Unison to Great			
Cymbal	II	Swell Sub to Great			
Posaune	16	Swell Super to Great			
Fagotto (ext.)	16	Swell Unison to Choir			
		Swell Sub to Choir			
		Swell Super to Choir			

ST. AUGUSTIN ROMAN CATHOLIC CHURCH, 327-4th St., Brandon.
Casavant, Opus 479, 1912, 2/20.

GREAT		SWELL		PEDAL	
Diapason	8	Bourdon	16	Double Open	16
Melodia	8	Diapason	8	Bourdon	16
Dulciana	8	Stopped Diapason	8	Gedeckt (ext.)	16
Principal	4	Viola da Gamba	8	Bourdon (ext.)	8
Fifteenth	2	Aeoline	8		
Trumpet	8	Voix Celeste	8	COUPLERS	
		Flauto Traverso	8	Great to Pedal	
		Piccolo	2	Swell to Pedal	
		Cornopean	8	Swell to Great Sub	
		Oboe	8	Swell to Great Unison	
		Tremulant		Swell to Great Super	
				Swell Sub	
				Swell Super	
				Great Super	

ST. BONIFACE ROMAN CATHOLIC CATHEDRAL, St. Boniface.
1. Louis Mitchell, 1875. Specifications unknown (2/12). Removed, divided, relocated 1909.
2. Casavant, Opus 267, 1906, 2/22. From First Lutheran 1921.
3. Casavant, Opus 2282, 1955. Console, additions, revisions, 3/47. Destroyed by fire 1968.

GRAND ORGUE		RÉCIT		POSITIF	
Bourdon	16	Principal	8	Principal violon	8
Montre	8	Bourdon	8	Cor de nuit	8
Principal étroit	8	Viole de gambe	8	Erzähler	8
Mélodie	8	Voix céleste	8	Erzähler céleste (GG)	8
Gemshorn	8	Principal	4	Violon	4
Prestant	4	Flûte harmonique	4	Flûte bouchée	4
Flûte harmonique	4	Piccolo	2	Nazard	2 2/3
Quinte	2 2/3	Cornet	III	Flautino	2
Doublette	2	Basson	16	Tierce	1 3/5
Acuta	II	Trompette	8	Clarinette	8
Trompette	8	Hautbois	8	Trémolo	
		Voix humaine	8		
		Clairon	4		
		Trémolo			

PÉDALE		ACCOUPLEMENTS
Flûte	16	Grand Orgue 8-4 à la
Violon	16	Pédale
Bourdon	16	Récit 8-4 à la Pédale
Bourdon doux (Great)	16	Positif 8-4 à la Pédale
Quinte	2 2/3	Récit 16-8-4 au Grand
Flûte	8	Orgue Récit 16-8-4 au
Violoncello (ext.)	8	Positif
Bourdon (ext.)	8	Positif 16-8-4 au Grand
Basse chorale (ext.)	8	Orgue
Bombarde	16	Grand Orgue 8-4 au Positif
Basson ((ext.)	16	Grand Orgue 4
Trompette (ext.)	8	Récit 16-8-4, Unisson off
Clairon	4	Positif 16-8-4, Unisson off

ST. EDWARDS'S ROMAN CATHOLIC CHURCH, 818 Arlingon, Winnipeg.
Canadian Pipe Organ, c. 1915, 2/23.

GREAT		SWELL		PEDAL	
Open Diapason	8	Bourdon	16	Double Open Diapason	16
Melodia	8	Open Diapason	8	Bourdon	16
Dulciana	8	Stopped Diapason	8	Gedackt	16
Octave	4	Aeoline	8	Bass Flute	8
Harmonic Flute	4	Viola da Gamba	8		
Fifteenth	2	Voix Celeste	8	COUPLERS	
Trumpet	8	Traverse Flute	4	Great to Pedal	
		Piccolo	2	Swell to Pedal	
		Dolce Cornet	III	Swell to Great	
		Cornopean	8	Swell to Great Sub	
		Oboe	8	Swell to Great Super	
		Vox Humana	8	Swell at Octave Sub	
		Tremulant		Swell at Octave Super	
				Great at Octave Super	

ST. GEORGE'S ANGLICAN CHURCH, Winnipeg.
Warren, 1894, 1/??. Specifications unknown. Removed.

ST. GEORGE'S CRESCENTWOOD ANGLICAN CHURCH, 168 Wilton, Winnipeg.
1.   Casavant, Opus 1167, 1926, 2/7. Rebuilt, Swell additions c. 1945. Removed.

GREAT		SWELL		PEDAL	
Open Diapason	8	Salicional (ext.)	8	Bourdon (ext.)	16
Dulciana	8	Melodia	8		
Wald Flute	4	Oboe (TC)	8	COUPLERS	
		Tremulant		Great to Pedal	
				Swell to Pedal	
				Swell to Great Unison	
				Swell to Great Sub	
				Swell to Great Super	
				Swell Sub	
				Swell Super	
				Great Super	

2. Hill, Norman & Beard, 1954, 3/36.

GREAT		SWELL		CHOIR	
Contra Geigen	16	Viola da Gamba	8	Hohl Flute	8
Open Diapason	8	Lieblich Gedeckt	8	Echo Salicional	8
Geigen Principal	8	Voix Celeste	8	Unda Maris	8
Chimney Flute	8	Geigen Principal	4	Fugara	4
Octave	4	Quint Mixture	III	Flute	4
Octave Geigen	4	Contra Oboe	16	Flageolet	2
Gemshorn	4	Trompette	8	Trompette (Swell)	8
Nasat	2 2/3	Clarion	4		
Block Flute	2	Tremulant			
Tierce	1 3/5				
Sifflöte	1				

PEDAL		COUPLERS		
Resultant Sub Bass	32	Swell to Pedal		Choir to Great
Geigen Bass	16	Swell Octave to Pedal 4		Great Octave
Sub Bass	16	Choir to Pedal		Choir Sub Octave
Bourdon	16	Great to Pedal		Choir Octave
Principal	8	Swell Sub Octave		Swell to Choir
Bass Flute	8	Swell Octave		
Octave Flute	4	Swell Unison Off		
Oboe Bass	16	Swell to Great		
Trompette (Swell)	8	Swell Octave to Great		
Trompette Clarion	4			

ST. GILES PRESBYTERIAN CHURCH, Winnipeg. See BURROWS BETHEL
MENNONITE CHURCH.

ST. IGNATIUS ROMAN CATHOLIC CHURCH, 255 Stafford, Winnipeg.
Casavant, Opus 1324, 1929, 3/29 + harp.

GREAT		SWELL		CHOIR	
Open Diapason	8	Bourdon	16	Geigen Principal	8
Doppel Flute	8	Open Diapason	8	Melodia	8
Gemshorn	8	Stopped Diapason	8	Dulciana	8
Harmonic Flute	4	Viola di Gamba	8	Wald Flute	4
Octave	4	Voix Celeste	8	Piccolo	2
Trumpet	8	Flauto Traverso	4	Clarinet	8
		Flautino	2	Tremulant	
		Dolce Cornet	III		
		Cornopean	8		
		Oboe	8		
		Vox Humana	8		
		Tremulant			
		Harp			

PEDAL		COUPLERS	
Open Diapason	16	Great to Pedal	Choir to Great
Bourdon	16	Swell to Pedal	Choir to Great Sub
Gedeckt (Swell)	16	Choir to Pedal	Choir to Great Super
Octave (ext.)	8	Swell to Pedal Super	Great Sub
Stopped Flute (ext.)	8	Swell to Great	Great Super
Trombone	16	Swell to Great Sub	Swell Sub
		Swell to Great Super	Swell Super
		Swell to Choir	Choir Sub
		Swell to Choir Sub	Choir Super
		Swell to Choir Sub	

ST. JAMES ANGLICAN CHURCH, 195 Collegiate, Winnipeg.
Woodstock Pipe Organ Builders, c. 1925, 2/14.

GREAT		SWELL		PEDAL	
Open Diapason	8	Open Diapason	8	Bourdon	16
Claribel Flute	8	Viol d' Gamba	8	Lieblich Gedeckt	16
Dulciana	8	Stopped Diapason	8	Flute	8
Flute Harmonique	4	Flauto Traverso	4		
Principal	4	Piccolo	2	COUPLERS	
		Oboe	8	Great to Pedal	
		Tremolo		Great to Pedal Super	
				Swell to Pedal	
				Swell to Pedal Super	
				Swell Sub	
				Swell Super	
				Swell to Great Sub	
				Swell to Great Unison	
				Swell to Great Super	
				Great Super	

ST. JAMES LUTHERAN CHURCH, 871 Cavalier, Winnipeg.
Gerhard Brunzema, 1982, 1/10. Mechanical action. Divided manual, bass and treble.

MANUAL			PEDAL	
Gedackt		8	Subbass	16
Hohlflöte	(B/T)	8		
Rohrflöte	(B/T)	8	COUPLER	
Prestant		4	Manual to Pedal	
Octave		2		
Flöte	(T)	2		
Sesquialtera	(T)	II		
Mixtur		III		

ST. JOHN'S ANGLICAN CATHEDRAL, 135 Anderson, Winnipeg.
1. Compensating Pipe Organ, 1902, hybrid reeds/pipes, 2/14. Replaced smaller model.
   Removed.

GREAT		SWELL		PEDAL	
Bourdon	16	Clarionet	16	Bourdon	16
Open Diapason	8	Stopped Diapason	8	Violone	16
Melodia	8	Harp Aeolian	8		
Aeoline	8	Salicional	8	COUPLERS	
Principal	4	Violin Diapason	4	Great to Pedal	
		Flute d'Amour	4	Swell to Pedal	
		Piccolo	2	Swell to Great	
				Octaves to Great	
				Tremulant	
				Blowers Signal	

2. Casavant, Opus 1198, 1927, 2/19. Additions: 1951, 1953, choir 1955; revisions 1980; 3/39.

GREAT

Open Diapason	8
Principal	8
Rohrflöte	8
Octave	4
Spitzflöte	4
Super Octave	2
Mixture	IV
Trumpet	8

SWELL

Bourdon	16
Open Diapason	8
Stopped Diapason	8
Viola da Gamba	8
Voix Celeste	8
Principal	4
Flauto Traverso	4
Flautino	2
Mixture	III
Fagotto	16
Trompette	8
Oboe	8
Clarion	4
Tremulant	

CHOIR

Erzahler	8
Cor de Nuit	8
Koppelflöte	4
Nazard	2 2/3
Piccolo	2
Tierce	1 3/5
Cromorne	8
State Trumpet (unencl.)	8
Tremulant	

PEDAL

Resultant	32
Open Diapason	16
Bourdon	16
Gedeckt (Swell)	16
Octave (ext.)	8
Stopped Flute (ext.)	8
Octave	4
Fagotto (Swell)	16
Trombone	16
Tromba	8

COUPLERS

Great to Pedal 8
Swell to Pedal 8
Choir to Pedal 8
Swell to Pedal 4
Swell to Great 8
Swell to Great 16
Swell to Great 4
Swell to Choir 8
Swell to Choir 16
Swell to Choir 4
Choir to Great 8
Choir to Great 16
Choir to Great 4

ST. JOHN'S UNITED CHURCH, Winnipeg.
Casavant, Opus 1384, 1930, 2/25 + chimes. To Central United, Brandon 1988.

ST. JUDE'S ANGLICAN CHURCH, Winnipeg.
Canadian Pipe Organ, c. 1915, 2/14. To First Mennonite 1991.

ST. LUKE'S ANGLICAN CHURCH, 130 Nassau, N., Winnipeg.
1. Casavant, Opus 424, 1910, 3/30. Echo organ 1912,* 3/36.

GREAT
Double Open Diapason 16
First Open Diapason   8
Second Open Diapason   8
Doppel Flöte   8
Dolce   4
Octave   4
Fifteenth   2
Trumpet   8

SWELL
Bourdon   16
Horn Principal   8
Stopped Diapason   8
Aeoline   8
Viola da Gamba   8
Voix Celeste   8
Flauto Traverso   4
Piccolo   2
Dolce Cornet   III
Cornopean   8
Oboe   8
Vox Humana   8
Tremulant

CHOIR
Melodia   8
Dulciana   8
Dolce Flute   4
Flageolet   2
Clarinet   8
Tremulant

*ECHO (played from Choir)
Concert Flute   4
Gedeckt   8
Dulciana   8
Vox Angelica   8
Piccolo   2
Orchestral Oboe   8

PEDAL
Double Open Diapason 16
Bourdon   16
Gedeckt (Swell)   16
Flute (ext.)   8
Bourdon (ext.)   8

COUPLERS
Choir to Pedal
Great to Pedal
Swell to Pedal
Swell to Great
Swell Sub Octave to Great
Swell Super Octave to
   Great
Swell at Octaves
Swell to Choir
Choir to Great
Choir Sub Octave to Great
Great at Octaves
*Echo to Swell
*Echo to Great
*Echo to Great Sub
*Echo Sub Octave
*Echo Super Octave
*Echo to Pedal

2. Hill, Norman & Beard, 1953. Reconstruction, additions, 4/61.
   R. Buck & B. Mantle, Winnipeg, 1979. Revisions, 4/59.

GREAT		SWELL		CHOIR	
Quintaten	16	Principal	8	Gedeckt Pommer	8
Open Diapason I	8	Viola da Gamba	8	Diapason Cantabile	8
Open Diapason II	8	Gamba Celeste	8	Chimney Flute	4
Doppelflöte	8	Hohlflöte	8	Nazard	2 2/3
Octave	4	Geigen Octave	4	Blockflöte	2
Twelfth	2 2/3	Waldflöte	4	Larigot	1 1/3
Fifteenth	2	Super Octave	2	Cymbale	III
Quint Mixture	IV	Mixture	III	Harmonic Trumpet	8
		Orchestral Oboe	8	Octave Trumpet	4
WEST GREAT		Tremulant		Clarinet	8
Viola	16			Tremulant	
Open Diapason	8	WEST SWELL			
Principal	4	Viole de Gamba	8	SOLO	
Quinte	2 2/3	Flute Ouverte	8	Carillon Harp	8
Super Octave	2	Unda Maris	8	Marimba Harp	8
		Principal	4	Harmonic Trumpet	8
		Mixture	III	Octave Trumpet	4
		Double Trumpet	16		
		Trumpet	8		
		Cornopean	8		
		Clarion	4		
		Tremulant			

PEDAL		COUPLERS			
Resultant Bass	32				
Open Wood Bass	16	PEDAL		SWELL	
Quintaten	16	Swell & Pedal Pistons		West Swell On	
Sub Bass	16	Coupled		Swell Sub Octave	
Bass Flute	8	Great & Pedal Pistons		Swell Unison Off	
Spitzflöte	8	Coupled		Swell Octave	
Choral Bass	4	Solo to Pedal			
Quartane	II	Swell to Pedal		CHOIR	
Trombone	16	Swell Octave to Pedal		Solo to Choir	
Trumpet	8	Great to Pedal		Swell to Choir	
		Choir to Pedal		Great to Choir	
WEST PEDAL					
Bourdon	16	GREAT		SOLO	
Contra Viola	16	West Great On		West Swell to Solo	
Gedeckt	8	Swell Sub Octave to Great		West Swell Octave to Solo	
Octave	8	Swell to Great		West Great to Solo	
		Swell Octave to Great		West Great Octave to Solo	
		Choir to Great			
		Great Super			

ST. MARGARET'S ANGLICAN CHURCH, Winnipeg.
Canadian Pipe Organ, c. 1915, 2/7. To St. Paul's Anglican, Dauphin 1974.

ST. MARY'S ACADEMY, 550 Wellington Crescent, Winnipeg.
Casavant, Opus 352, 1909, 2/10.

GREAT		SWELL		PEDAL	
Open Diapason	8	Violin Diapason	8	Bourdon	16
Melodia	8	Stopped Diapason	8		
Dulciana	8	Aeoline	8	COUPLERS	
Principal	4	Harmonic Flute	4	Swell to Pedal	
		Oboe	8	Great to Pedal	
		Tremuulant		Swell to Great	
				Swell Sub to Great	
				Swell Super to Great	
				Great at Octaves	
				Bellows Signal	

ST. MARY'S ANGLICAN CHURCH, 36-2nd St. SW., Portage la Prairie.
Karn-Warren, c. 1900, 2/??.
Hill, Norman & Beard, 1953. Reconstruction, new console, 2/10.

GREAT		SWELL		PEDAL	
Open Diapason	8	Wald Flute	8	Bourdon	16
Stopped Diapason	8	Salicional	8	Bass Flute	8
Principal	4	Salicional	4	Oboe Bass	16
		Contra Oboe	16		
		Tremulant			
		COUPLERS			
		Great to Pedal		Swell Octaves	
		Swell to Pedal		Swell Sub Octaves	
		Swell Octaves to Pedal 4		Swell Unison Off	
		Great Octaves		Swell to Great	
				Swell Octaves to Great	

ST. MARY'S ROMAN CATHOLIC CATHEDRAL, 353 St. Mary, Winnipeg.
1. Louis Mitchell, 1883, 2/18. Removed.

GREAT		SWELL		PEDAL	
Open Diapason	8	Horn Diapason	8	Bourdon	16
Open Flute	8	Bass	8	Violoncello	16
Dulciana	8	Melodia	8		
Flute Harmonique	4	Viol de Gamba	8	COUPLERS	
Principal	4	Violon	4	Swell to Great	
Fifteenth	2	Wald Flute	4	Great to Pedal	
Mixture	II	Oboe	8	Swell to Pedal	
Cymbal	III	Tremolo		Octave-Kopel	
Trumpet	8				
Ventil				Bellows Signal	

2. Casavant, Opus 751, 1918, 2/18; Opus 2416, 1957: console, renovations, additions,* 2/26.

GREAT		SWELL		PEDAL	
Bourdon	16	Open Diapason	8	Double Open Diapason	16
Open Diapason	8	Stopped Diapason	8	Bourdon	16
*Flute Ouverte		Viola da Gamba	8	*Gedeckt (Sw. ext.)	16
/Melodia	8	Voix Celeste	8	Stopped Flute (ext.)	8
Dulciana	8	*Aeoline	8	*Spitzprincipal	8
Principal	4	Harmonic Flute	4	*Flute	4
Fifteenth	2	Violina	4		
Mixture	III	*Nazard	2 2/3	COUPLERS	
Trumpet	8	*Piccolo	2	Great to Pedal	
		*Tierce	1 3/5	*Great Super to Pedal	
		*Trumpet	8	Swell to Pedal	
		Oboe	8	*Swell Super to Pedal	
		Tremulant		Swell to Great	
				Swell Sub to Great	
				Swell Super to Great	
				*Great Sub	
				*Great Unison Off	
				Great Super	
				Swell Sub	
				*Swell Unison Off	
				Swell Super	

ST. MATTHEW'S ANGLICAN CATHEDRAL, 403-13th St., Brandon.
1. Karn, c. 1906. Specifications unknown. Removed.
2. Casavant, Opus 2514, 1959, 3/39.

GREAT		SWELL		CHOIR	
Quintaton	16	Rohrflöte	8	Cor de Nuit	8
Principal	8	Spitzviola	8	Erzähler	8
Spitzflöte	8	Voix Celeste (GG)	8	Unda Maris	8
Octave	4	Geigen Octave	4	Dolceprincipal	4
Chimney Flute	4	Harmonic Flute	4	Koppelflöte	4
Octave Quinte	2 2/3	Fifteenth	2	Nazard	2 2/3
Superoctave	2	Cymbel III	1	Blockflöte	2
Fourniture	IV	Bassoon-Hautbois	16	Tierce	1 3/5
		Trompette	8	Cromorne	8
		Hautbois	8	Tremulant	
		Clarion	4		
		Tremulant			

PEDAL		COUPLERS			
Contrebasse	16	Great to Pedal		Choir to Great	
Gemshorn	16	Great Super to Pedal		Choir Sub to Great	
Quintaton (Great)	16	Swell to Pedal		Choir Super to Great	
Octave (ext.)	8	Swell Super to Pedal		Great Super	
Gedeckt	8	Choir to Pedal		Great Unison Off	
Gemshorn (ext.)	8	Choir Super to Pedal		Swell Sub	
Flute (ext.)	4	Swell to Great		Swell Unison Off	
Mixture III	4	Swell Sub to Great		Swell Super	
Posaune	16	Swell Super to Great		Choir Sub	
Bassoon (ext.)	16	Swell to Choir		Choir Unison Off	
Hautbois (ext.)	8	Swell Sub to Choir		Choir Super	
		Swell Super to Choir			

ST. MATTHEW'S ANGLICAN CHURCH, 641 St. Matthews, Winnipeg.
1. Casavant, Opus 1394, 1930, 3/40. Destroyed by fire 1944.
2. Casavant, Opus 1901, 1948, 3/40. Same specifications as Opus 1394.

GREAT		SWELL		CHOIR	
Open Diapason (ext.)	16	Gedeckt	16	Geigen Principal	8
Open Diapason I	8	Principal	8	Melodia	8
Open Diapason II	8	Stopped Diapason	8	Dulciana	8
Hohl Flöte	8	Aeoline	8	Flute d'Amour	4
Gemshorn	8	Gamba	8	Nazard	2 2/3
Harmonic Flute	4	Voix Celeste (GG)	8	Flageolet	2
Principal	4	Flute Traverso	8	Clarinet	8
Twelfth	2 2/3	Piccolo	2	Tuba	8
Fifteenth	2	Dolce Cornet	III	Tremulant	
Tuba (from Choir)	8	Contra Fagotto	16		
		Cornopean	8		
		Oboe	8		
		Vox Humana	8		
		Clarion	4		
		Tremulant			

PEDAL		COUPLERS	
Resultant	32	Great to Pedal	Choir to Great
Open Diapason	16	Great to Pedal Super	Choir to Great Sub
Bourdon	16	Swell to Pedal	Choir to Great Super
Gedeckt (Swell)	16	Swell to Pedal Super	Great Super
Octave (ext.)	8	Choir to Pedal	Swell Sub
Stopped Flute	8	Choir to Pedal Super	Swell Super
Trombone	16	Swell to Great	Choir Sub
Contra Fagotto		Swell to Great Sub	Choir Super
(Swell)	16	Swell to Great Super	
Tromba (ext.)	8	Swell to Choir	
		Swell to Choir Sub	
		Swell to Choir Super	

ST. PAUL'S ANGLICAN CHURCH, 404-1st St. SW., Dauphin.
Canadian Pipe Organ, c. 1915, 2/7. From St. Margaret's Anglican, Winnipeg 1974.

GREAT		SWELL		PEDAL	
Open Diapason	8	Stopped Diapason	8	Bourdon	16
Principal	4	Salicional	8		
Wald Flute	4	Oboe Gamba	8	COUPLERS	
		Tremulant		Swell to Great	
				Swell at Octaves	
				Swell to Great Super	
				Swell to Great Sub	
				Swell to Pedal	
				Great to Pedal	
				Great at Octaves	

ST. PAUL'S UNITED CHURCH, Brandon.
Casavant, Opus 2260, 1955, 3/38. Destroyed by fire.

GREAT		SWELL		CHOIR	
Quintaton	16	Geigen Diapason	8	Melodia	8
Open Diapason	8	Rohrflöte	8	Dulciana	8
Principal	8	Viola da Gamba	8	Lieblich Flute	4
Hohl Flute	8	Voix Celeste (GG)	8	Nazard	2 2/3
Gemshorn	8	Aeoline	8	Piccolo	2
Flute d'Amour	4	Flauto Traverso	4	Tierce	1 3/5
Fifteenth	2	Flautino	2	Cor Anglais	8
Mixture	III	Cornet	III	Tuba	8
Tuba (from Choir)	8	Contra Fagotto	16	Tremulant	
		Trumpet	8		
		Oboe	8		
		Clarion	4		
		Tremulant			

PEDAL		COUPLERS			
Resultant (12 Quints)	32	Great to Pedal		Swell Unison to Great	
Contrabass	16	Great Super to Pedal		Choir Super to Choir	
Bourdon	16	Swell to Pedal		Choir Sub to Great	
Gedeckt (Great)	16	Swell Super to Pedal		Choir Super to Great	
Principal	8	Choir to Pedal		Great Sub	
Bass Flute (ext.)	8	Choir Super to Pedal		Great Super	
Choralbass (ext.)	4	Swell Unison to Great		Swell Sub	
Trombone	16	Swell Sub to Great		Swell Unison Off	
Fagotto (ext.)	16	Swell Super to Great		Swell Super	
		Swell Unison to Choir		Choir Sub	
		Swell Sub to Choir		Choir Unison Off	
				Choir Super	

ST. PAUL'S UNITED (METHODIST) CHURCH, 47-5th Ave. W., Souris.
Casavant, Opus 727, 1917, 2/12. From Knox Presbyterian Church, Souris 1946.

GREAT		SWELL		PEDAL	
Open Diapason	8	Open Diapason	8	Bourdon	16
Melodia	8	Stopped Diapason	8		
Dulciana (ext.)	8	Viola da Gamba	8		
Principal	8	Aeoline	8		
		Voix Celeste	8		
		Harmonic Flute	4		
		Oboe	8		
		Tremulant			

ST. PETER'S ANGLICAN, Winnipeg.
Karn, 1910, 2/14. To St. Thomas Anglican 1932.

ST. PHILIP'S ANGLICAN CHURCH, 240 Taché, Winnipeg.
Casavant, Opus 1273, 1928, 2/7.

GREAT		SWELL		PEDAL	
Open Diapason	8	Salicional (ext.)	8	Bourdon (ext.)	16
Dulciana	8	Melodia	8		
Wald Flute	4	Oboe	8	COUPLERS	
		Tremulant		Great to Pedal	
				Great to Pedal Super	
				Swell to Pedal	
				Swell to Pedal Super	
				Swell to Great Unison	
				Swell to Great Sub	
				Swell to Great Super	
				Great Sub	
				Great Super	
				Swell Sub	
				Swell Super	

Kenneth Winters, prominent music broadcaster on CBC radio, became organist-choirmaster at St. Philip's Anglican Church in 1954. While in Winnipeg, he engaged in teaching, vocal coaching, singing, and writing music and arts reviews for the *Winnipeg Free Press*, before moving to Toronto. He was one of the editors of the first English edition of the *Encyclopedia of Music in Canada*, published in 1981; second edition 1992. His mother, Mrs. Edythe Winters, served as organist at First United Church, Dauphin, for 48 years (q.v.).

ST. STEPHEN'S BROADWAY UNITED (BROADWAY METHODIST) CHURCH, 396 Broadway, Winnipeg.
1. Casavant, Opus 276, 1907, 3/36; Opus 2136, 1952: console, renovations, additions, * 3/39. Destroyed by fire 1968.

GREAT		SWELL		CHOIR	
Double Open Diapason	16	Lieblich Gedeckt	16	Geigen Principal	8
Open Diapason	8	Horn Diapason	8	Melodia	8
Violin Diapason	8	Stopped Diapason	8	Dulciana	8
Doppel Flute	8	Viola da Gamba	8	Dolce Flute	4
Gemshorn	8	Voix Celeste	8	*Nazard	2 2/3
Principal	4	Dolcissimo	8	Piccolo	2
Harmonic Flute	4	Traverse Flute	4	*Tierce	1 3/5
Twelfth	2 2/3	Gemshorn	4	Clarinet	8
Fifteenth	2	Flautino	2	Tremulant	
Mixture	III	Mixture	III		
Trumpet	8	Cornopean	8		
		Oboe & Bassoon	8		
		Vox Humana	8		
		Tremulant			

PEDAL		COUPLERS			
Double Open	16	Swell to Great		Swell at Octaves	
Bourdon	16	Swell to Great Sub		Great at Octaves	
Gedeckt (Swell)	16	Swell to Great Super		Swell to Pedal	
Bass Flute (ext.)	8	Swell to Choir		Great to Pedal	
Stopped Diapason (ext.)	8	Choir to Great		Choir to Pedal	
Trombone	16	Choir to Great Sub			
*Tromba (ext.)	8				

2. Casavant, Opus 3090, 1971, 3/31.

GREAT		SWELL		POSITIV	
Quintaden	16	Salizional	8	Gedackt	8
Prinzipal	8	Vox coelestis (GG)	8	Prinzipal	4
Rohrflöte	8	Gedacktflöte	8	Koppelflöte	4
Oktav	4	Gemshorn	4	Oktav	2
Spitzflöte	4	Waldflöte	2	Quintflöte	4
Flachflöte	2	Scharf .	III	Sesquialtera (TC)	II
Mixtur	IV	Fagott	16	Zimbel	III
Trompete	8	Oboe	8	Krummhorn	8
		Tremulant		Tremulant	

PEDAL		COUPLERS
Prinzipal	16	Great to Pedal
Subbass	16	Swell to Pedal
Oktav	8	Positiv to Pedal
Gedacktpommer	8	Swell to Great
Choralbass	4	Positiv to Great
Mixtur	IV	Swell to Positiv
Posaune	16	

ST. STEPHEN'S PRESBYTERIAN, Winnipeg. See ELIM CHAPEL

ST. THOMAS ANGLICAN CHURCH, 1567 William W., Winnipeg.
Karn, 1910, 2/14. From St. Peter's Anglican Church 1932.
F. Radcliffe, Winnipeg, c. 1950. Reconstruction.
R. Buck & B. Mantle, Winnipeg, and volunteers, 1987-89. Renovated.

GREAT		SWELL		PEDAL	
Open Diapason	8	Open Diapason	8	Bourdon	16
Melodia	8	Stopped Diapason	8	Bass Flute	8
Dulciana	8	Aeoline	8		
Principal	4	Viol di Gamba	8	COUPLERS	
Fifteenth	2	Voix Celeste	8	Great to Pedal	
		Flauto Traverso	4	Swell to Pedal	
		Oboe Gamba	8	Swell to Great Sub	
		Tremulant		Swell to Great Unison	
				Swell to Great Super	
				Great at Octaves	
				Swell at Octaves	

SPARLING UNITED CHURCH, 1609 Elgin, Winnipeg.
Kilgen, c. 1920, 2/13. From Grace Methodist Church, Portage la Prairie 1937.

GREAT		SWELL		PEDAL	
Open Diapason	8	Violin Diapason	8	Bourdon	16
Dulciana	8	Stopped Diapason	8	Bass Flute	8
Chimney Flute	8	Salicional	8		
(Melodia to 1967)		Aeoline	8	COUPLERS	
Octave	4	Flute Harmonic	4	Great to Pedal 8	
Flute d'Amour	4	Oboe Gamba	8	Swell to Pedal 8	
		Tremolo		Swell to Great 8	
				Swell to Great 4	
				Swell to Great 16	
				Great to Great 4	

TIVOLI THEATRE, Winnipeg.
Casavant, Opus 1231, 1927, 2/12 + chimes, percussion. To Broadway First Baptist Church 1958. Theatre closed.

GREAT		SWELL		PEDAL	
Open Diapason	8	Violin Diapason	8	Bourdon	16
Melodia	8	Stopped Diapason	8	Flute	8
Dulciana	8	Salicional	8	Drum	
Castanets (1-37)		Voix Celeste	8		
Chimes (Swell)		Flauto Traverso	4	COUPLERS	
Xylophone (Swell)		Oboe	8	Great to Pedal	
		Vox Humana	8	Great to Pedal Super	
		Chimes (Deagan, C)		Swell to Pedal	
			20 notes	Swell to Pedal Super	
		Xylophone	37 bars	Swell to Great Unison	
				Swell to Great Sub	
				Swell to Great Super	
				Swell Sub	
				Swell Super	
				Great Super	

TRINITY BAPTIST CHURCH (NASSAU STREET BAPTIST), 549 Gertrude, Winnipeg.
Karn, 1911, 3/23.
Hill, Norman & Beard, 1954. Reconstruction, 3/26.

GREAT		SWELL		CHOIR	
Open Diapason	8	Geigen Diapason	8	Doppel Flute	8
Stopped Diapason	4	Hohl Flute	8	Dulciana	8
Principal	4	Viola da Gamba	8	Viole d'Orchestre	8
Twelfth	2 2/3	Viole Celeste	8	Harmonic Flute	4
Quartane	II	Principal	4	Clarinet	8
		Lieblich Gedeckt	4	Tremulant	
		Quint Mixture	III		
		Contra Oboe	16		
		Cornopean	8		
		Tremulant			

PEDAL		COUPLERS			
Resultant Bass	32	Swell to Pedal		Choir to Great 8	
Bourdon	16	Swell Octave to Pedal		Choir Sub Octave	
Principal	8	Choir to Pedal		Choir Octave	
Bass Flute	8	Great to Pedal		Choir Unison Off	
Octave	4	Swell Sub Octave		Swell to Choir	
Octave Flute	4	Swell Octaves			
Contra Oboe	16	Swell Unison Off			
		Swell to Great 8			
		Swell to Great 4			

TRINITY LUTHERAN CHURCH, Winnipeg.
Edward Lye, Opus 12, 1906, 2/10. Mechanical action. To Sacré-Coeur 1968.

When the Trinity Lutheran congregation occupied a new church building in 1968, they
wanted no reminders of their earlier building, erected in 1905. Among the relics of the past
they wished to discard was the organ, although the architect of the new building advised that
space could be be made for the organ pipes on the wall of the new edifice. Blanchard Bros.,
local organ technicians, proposed to rebuild and electrify the organ at a cost of $14,000, and
Casavant Frères submitted an estimate for a new organ of appropriate size at a cost of
approximately $65,000. The organ issue was a matter of considerable controversy among
members of the congregation. Some members thought the Lye organ cabinet "old fashioned"
and were more concerned with the interior appearance of the building than with sound
quality, while others preferred an electronic organ for other reasons. Trinity Church representatives approached Sacré-Coeur and made arrangements for the relocation of the organ at
an agreed-upon price of $2,000. The instrument was succeeded by a used Hammond electric
organ at a cost of $12,500.

TRINITY UNITED (KNOX PRESBYTERIAN) CHURCH, 15 Tupper S., Portage la Prairie.
1. Karn, 1904, 2/20. Specifications unknown. Demolished in tornado 1922.
2. Casavant, Opus 966, 1923, 2/20. Reconstruction 1977. Electric action 1987.

GREAT		SWELL		PEDAL	
Open Diapason	8	Bourdon	16	Open Diapason	16
Melodia	8	Open Diapason	8	Bourdon	16
Dulciana	8	Stopped Diapason	8	Gedeckt (Swell)	16
Principal	4	Aeoline	8	Stopped Flute (ext.)	8
Harmonic Flute	4	Viola di Gamba	8		
Trumpet	8	Voix Celeste	8	COUPLERS	
		Traverse Flute	4	Great to Pedal	
		Piccolo	2	Swell to Pedal	
		Cornopean	8	Swell to Great Unison	
		Oboe	8	Swell to Great Sub	
		Tremulant		Swell to Great Super	
				Swell Sub	
				Swell Super	
				Great Super	

UNITARIAN CHURCH, Winnipeg. See FIRST FEDERATED CHURCH OF UNITARIANS.

UNIVERSITY OF MANITOBA, ST. JOHN'S COLLEGE CHAPEL, Fort Garry Campus, Winnipeg.
Casavant, Opus 1521, 1936. Removed from Greenwood United Church 1981.
E. Foidart, Winnipeg, 1983. Installation, additions, 2/10.

GREAT		SWELL		PEDAL	
Principal	8	Melodia	8	Bourdon	16
Gedackt	8	Viola	8	Flute	8
Gemshorn	4	Voix Celeste (TC)	8		
		Harmonic Flute	4	COUPLERS	
		Oboe	8	Great to Pedal	
		Tremulant		Great Super to Pedal	
				Swell to Pedal	
				Swell Super to Pedal	
				Swell to Great	
				Swell Super to Great	

UNIVERSITY OF MANITOBA, SCHOOL OF MUSIC, Fort Garry Campus, Winnipeg.
Casavant, Opus 2919, 1967, 2/21

GREAT		POSITIV		PEDAL	
Prinzipal	8	Gedackt	8	Subbass	16
Rohrflöte	8	Spitzflöte	4	Prinzipal	8
Oktave	4	Prinzipal	2	Gedacktpommer	8
Koppelflöte	4	Quintflöte	1 1/3	Choralbass	4
Nasat	2 2/3	Sesquialtera III	2 2/3	Rauschpfeife II	2 2/3
Blockflöte	2	Zimbel III	1/3	Fagott	16
Mixtur IV	1	Krummhorn	8		
Trompete	8	Tremulant		COUPLERS	

COUPLERS
Positiv to Great
Positiv to Pedal
Great to Pedal

For a discussion of the specifications of this organ, see Lawrence Ritchey, *An Examination of
Tonal Design in the Casavant Organ of the Eva Clare Hall, The School of Music, The University of
Manitoba,* n.d., Music Library, The University of Manitoba.

UNIVERSITY OF MANITOBA, SCHOOL OF MUSIC STUDIO, Fort Garry Campus,
Winnipeg.
von Beckerath, 1968, 2/3. Mechanical action.

I Gedackt	8	I/Pedal
II Flute Dolce	8	II/Pedal
Pedal: Stopped Flute	8	

UNIVERSITY OF WINNIPEG CHAPEL, 515 Portage, Winnipeg.
Wicks "Sonatina," Opus 2071, 1940, 2/20 from 4 ranks.*
From Mordue Funeral Chapel. Installed 1982.

GREAT			SWELL		PEDAL	
Bourdon		16	Bourdon	16	*Sub Bass (12 reeds)	16
Flute		8	Quintadena	8	Gedeckt	8
*Salicional	(TC)	8	*Stopped Flute	8	Flute	4
*Dulciana	(TC)	8	Viola	8	Violina	4
Flute d'Amour		4	Dulciana	8		
Violina		4	Flute	4		
Piccolo		2	Dulciana	4		
			Nazard	2 2/3		
			Oboe	8		

VICTORIA HALL, Winnipeg.
Maker unknown, 1884, 2/11. Removed. Building demolished.

FIRST MANUAL		SECOND MANUAL		PEDAL	
Viol di gamba	8	Sordino	8	Contra Bass	16
Horn	8	Prin'pl Violin	8		
Concert Flute	8	Ripieno No. 1	8	COUPLERS	
Clarionet	8	Ripieno No. 2	8	Manual Couplers	
Harmonic Flute	4			Pedal Coupler No. 1	
Piccolo	2			Pedal Coupler No. 2	

WESLEY METHODIST CHURCH, Winnipeg.
Casavant, Opus 313, 1908, 2/17. To First Church of Christ, Scientist 1919-20.

GREAT		SWELL		PEDAL	
Open Diapason	8	Bourdon	16	Open Diapason	16
Melodia	8	Open Diapason	8	Bourdon	16
Dulciana	8	Stopped Diapason	8		
Octave	4	Viola di Gamba	8	COUPLERS	
Fifteenth	2	Voix Celeste	8	Great to Pedal	
Trumpet	8	Harmonic Flute	4	Swell to Pedal	
		Piccolo	8	Swell to Great	
		Dolce Cornet	II	Swell Sub Octave to Great	
		Oboe & Bassoon	6	Swell Super Octave to	
		Tremulant		Great	
				Swell at Octaves	
				Great at Octaves	

WESTMINSTER UNITED(PRESBYTERIAN) CHURCH, 745 Westminster, Winnipeg.
1. Warren, 1885. Specifications unknown. From Grace Methodist Church 1894. Removed.
2. Karn, 1899, 2/24. Specifications unknown. Removed.
3. Casavant, Opus 481, 1912, 4/49; Opus 2078, 1951: console and additions, 4/52.
    Tonal revisions 1985, 1986, 4/54 + bells.

GREAT		SWELL		CHOIR	
Double Open Diapason	16	Bourdon	16	Melodia	8
Open Diapason I	8	Geigen Principal	8	Dulciana	8
Open Diapason II	8	Stopped Diapason	8	Unda Maris (TC)	8
Clarabella Flute	8	Viola da Gamba	8	Gemshorn	4
Principal	4	Voix Celeste (TC)	8	Traverse Flute	4
Harmonic Flute	4	Waldflute	4	Flageolet	2
Twelfth	2 2/3	Octave	4	Quint Flute	1 1/3
Fifteenth	2	Nazard	2 2/3	Clarinet	8
Blockflute	2	Principal	2	Tremulant	
Mixture	IV	Tierce	1 3/5		
Trumpet	8	Mixture	IV	Bells - Schulmerich	25
		Contra Fagotto	16	Cymbelstern	9
		Oboe	8		
		Cornopean	8	SOLO	
		Clarion	4	Stentorphone	8
		Tremulant		Grosse Flute	8
				Cello	8
				Violina	4
				Orchestral Flute	4
				Harmonic Piccolo	2
				Orchestral Oboe	8
				Cor Anglais	8
				Tuba	8
				Tremulant	

PEDAL		COUPLERS		
Resultant	32	Great to Pedal		Swell to Choir Sub
Open Diapason	16	Great to Pedal Super		Swell to Choir
Violone	16	Swell to Pedal		Swell to Choir Super
Gedeckt (Swell)	16	Swell to Pedal Super		Solo to Choir Sub
Flute	8	Choir to Pedal		Solo to Choir
Cello	8	Choir to Pedal Super		Solo to Choir Super
Principal	8	Solo to Pedal		Great Sub
Choral Bass	4	Solo to Pedal Super		Great Unison Off
Contra Trombone	32	Swell to Great Sub		Great Super
Trombone	16	Swell to Great		Swell Sub
Tromba	8	Swell to Great Super		Swell Unison Off
		Choir to Great Sub		Swell Super
		Choir to Great		Choir Sub
		Choir to Great Super		Choir Super
		Solo to Great Sub		Solo Super
		Solo to Great		Solo Sub
		Solo to Great Super		

YOUNG UNITED (METHODIST) CHURCH, 222 Furby, Winnipeg.
1. Casavant, Opus 277, 1907, 2/16. Console, additions* 1973, 2/18 + chimes. Destroyed by fire 1987.

GREAT		SWELL		PEDAL	
Open Diapason	8	Open Diapason	8	Bourdon	16
Melodia	8	Stopped Diapason	8	Lieblich Gedeckt (ext.)	16
Dulciana	8	Viola da Gamba	8	Stopped Flute (ext.)	8
Octave	4	Voix Celeste	8		
Fifteenth	2	*Aeoline	8	COUPLERS	
Mixture	III	Flute Traverso	4	Great to Pedal 8	
Trumpet	8	Piccolo	2	*Great to Pedal 4	
*Chimes		Oboe	8	Swell to Pedal 8	
		*Chimes		*Swell to Pedal 4	
		Tremulant		Swell to Great 16	
				Swell to Great 8	
				*Swell to Great 4	
				Great to Great 16	
				Great Unison Off	
				Great to Great 4 (deleted)	
				Swell to Swell 16	
				Swell Unison Off	
				Swell to Swell 4	

Bellows Signal (deleted)

2. Létourneau, Opus 32, 1993, 2/29. Mechanical action.

GREAT		SWELL		PEDAL	
Quintaton	16	Holzgedackt	8	Subbass	16
Principal	8	Salicional	8	Principal	8
Metalgedackt	8	Voix céleste (TC)	8	Gedackt	8
Octave	4	Principal	4	Octave	4
Rohrflöte	4	Koppelflöte	4	Mixture IV	2 2/3
Nazard	2 2/3	Octave	2	Posaune (ext.)	16
Blockflöte	2	Sifflöte	1	Trumpet (Schnitger)	8
Tierce	1 3/5	Zimbel III	2/3	Clarion (Schnitger)	4
Mixture IV	1 1/3	Bassoon	16		
Trumpet (Dom Bédos)	8	Trumpet		COUPLERS	
		(Cavaillé-Coll)	8	Swell to Great	
		Schalmei		Swell to Pedal	
		(German tapered)	4	Great to Pedal	
		Tremulant			

ZION METHODIST CHURCH, Winnipeg.
1. First organ, earlier building: maker unknown, 1882, 1/??
2. Casavant, Opus 235, 1905, 3/37. Removed, building demolished.

GREAT		SWELL		CHOIR	
Double Open	16	Lieblich Gedeckt	16	Geigen Principal	8
Open Diapason	8	Horn Principal	8	Melodia	8
Violin Diapason	8	Stopped Diapason	8	Dulciana	8
Doppel Flöte	8	Viola da Gamba	8	Dolce Flute	4
Gemshorn	8	Voix Celeste	8	Flageolet	2
Principal	4	Dolcissimo	8	Clarinet	8
Harmonic Flute	4	Flauto Traverso	4	Tremulant	
Twelfth	2 2/3	Gemshorn	4		
Fifteenth	2	Piccolo	2		
Mixture	III	Dolce Cornet	III		
Trumpet	8	Cornopean	8		
		Oboe	8		
		Vox Humana	8		
		Tremulant			

PEDAL		COUPLERS		
Double Open	16	Swell to Great		Swell at Octaves
Bourdon	16	Swell Sub Octave to Great		Great at Octaves
Gedeckt (Swell)	16	Swell Super Octave to		Choir at Octaves
Bass Flute (ext.)	8	Great		Swell to Pedal
Bourdon (ext.)	8	Swell to Choir		Great to Pedal
Violoncello	8	Choir to Great		Choir to Pedal
Trombone	8	Choir Sub Octave to Great		

Glossary

This glossary is intended to assist the reader in gaining a general understanding of those technical terms that are not explained in the text on their first appearance. Some terms have slightly different meanings, while others are interchangeable; these are noted wherever appropriate. An asterisk before a term indicates a reference elsewhere in the glossary.

bellows. The structures made of wedge-shaped wooden frames and ribbed, flexible leather that are raised and lowered in sequence by their weighted tops (actuated by hand levers in early organs and now by electric *blowers) to compress the air that causes the organ pipes to speak. The bellows mechanism is also designed to maintain a steady wind supply. Large organs require several bellows operated in relay, and some of them incorporate tiered reservoirs for supplying different wind pressures for different stops.

blower. In modern organs, an electrically driven rotary or centrifugal fan that compresses air into wind for the pipes. Some early organs were powered by water pressure. The term also referred to the person who pumped a heavy handle to inflate the *bellows.

casework. The cabinet that encloses the organ pipes and protects them from dust and confines mechanical noise. In most 19th-century organs, the visible facade at the front of the case (sometimes consisting of "dummy" or nonfunctioning pipes) obscured the internal mechanism, but many

late 20th-century organs have revived the traditional system of placing the pipes for each *division in separate, shallow, wooden enclo-
sures, open at the front, that visually announce the capabilities of the
instrument. The architecturally pleasing design also allows for a more
direct projection of sound.

Choir Organ. The *division of the organ, including the *wind chest, action,
and pipework, that includes soft stops for accompaniment purposes,
or *orchestral stops for solo use. The Choir division is controlled by
the lowest keyboard on organs having three or more manuals.

chorus. In organ registration, a basic ensemble or grouping of stops, often in families, e.g., "flue" chorus (*diapason *ranks), or "reed" chorus. The classical
tonal chorus is built up from a manual stop of fundamental pitch, to which
is added other unison- and fifth-sounding stops of the same tonal family.

combination pedals, pistons. Devices for operating *stops in predetermined
groups. Combination pedals are placed above the pedal board and are
operated by the organist's foot; earlier actions of this kind were mechanical in nature. Combination pistons, small press-buttons located
between the manuals and operated by the player's thumb or finger,
employ *pneumatic or *electric actions.

compass. The range of notes or pitches: now standardized at 61 notes CC-C in
the manuals and 32 notes CCC-F in the pedals.

crescendo pedal. A foot-operated pedal, set above the console pedal board,
that brings on *stops and intermanual couplers gradually in a
predetermined and fixed order, increasing the sound from the softest
to comprehensive full organ.

diapason. The characteristic *foundation stop unique to the organ, the first
essential of tonal design, and the main *stop on the *Great manual. It
possesses a fullness throughout the *compass and at all *ranks of such
pipes at different pitches, and a clarity required for contrapuntal music. Diapason tone is often called *principal tone. The open, cylindrical, metal facade pipes of traditional organs are diapasons.

divided stop, keyboard. The separation of a *stop into treble and bass halves,
usually at middle C on the keyboard, that allows a solo to be played
with one *registration and a soft accompaniment with another. The
system is sometimes found on small one-manual organs or harmoniums.

division. A group of *ranks of pipes with its own keyboard/pedal board and separate mechanical devices, together with the corresponding *wind chests. The divisions of a four-manual organ are: *Great, *Swell, *Choir, *Solo, and *Pedal. This arrangement augments the usefulness and flexibility of the organ by allowing the player to utilize the unique tonal characteristics of the various divisions in contrasting ways or in combination. Some larger organs have an ancillary "floating" division of highly specialized *ranks without its own manual that can be coupled to any manual.

draw stop. The knob or handle that controls the *ranks of pipes or couplers. Stop knobs are arranged according to *divisions on jambs or panels on both sides of the manuals on the organ console. In earlier organs their action was mechanical; some modern organs (chiefly theatre organs and many electronic instruments) employ electrically operated stop keys (tilting or rocking tablets) above the upper manual for the same purpose.

electric action. The use of electricity to control devices on the organ is as old as the electromagnet, invented in 1826. Systems of electrical action, which appeared around the turn of the century, made it possible to place the organ console at a distance from the *divisions and to locate the organ pipes and mechanism anywhere in the church. The term is sometimes used as a synonym for *electro-pneumatic action.

electro-pneumatic action. Pressing a manual key operates an electrical contact switch that completes a low-voltage circuit to activate an electromagnet controlling a pneumatically operated relay at the distant *wind chest, which results in the opening of the corresponding pipe valve, causing the pipe to speak. Releasing the key opens the electrical circuit, de-energizes the magnet, and reverses the pneumatic events in the wind chest, thus closing the pipe valve. A similar electrical and air-powered system operates the *stops. This system superseded *tubular-pneumatic action in the 1930s.

flue pipe. The method of sound production is the same as in wind instruments like the recorder. In a flue pipe the sound is made by a current of air striking its mouth or opening (the "flue"). Wind passes from the foothole of the pipe to the mouth, where it is then directed alternately to either side of the upper lip, causing the column of air in the pipe to vibrate and produce the sound. A stopped flue pipe, closed at the top, produces a sound an octave lower than an open pipe of the same length. Flue pipes made of metal (such as the *diapasons) or wood (flutes) are the most numerous in the organ, and produce differ-ent timbres depending on their design; the other major type is the *reed pipe, in which the sound is produced by a beating reed. Flue pipes are sometimes referred to as labial pipes. Compare *reed pipe.

foot.   The conical portion at the bottom of the organ pipe that conveys the wind to the *flue.

foundation stop. A stop of 8' pitch for which it takes an open pipe eight feet in length to produce the lowest note of the manuals at normal pitch. The foundation family of stops usually consists of open metal pipes that sound a strong fundamental tone.

free reeds. A type of *reed pipe in which the metal tongue swings freely in its vibrating motion instead of beating against a shallot or orifice; it can be blown louder or softer without altering the pitch. In pipe organs they had resonators of various kinds that imparted different tonal quali-ties. Pipeless free reeds are used in harmoniums.

Great Organ. The main *division of the organ, including the *wind chest, action, and pipework, that contains a majority of *stops of pure organ tone. The nucleus of a Great Organ in the English style is the open *diapason *chorus. The Great division is controlled by the keyboard intermediate between the lower *Choir manual and the upper *Swell manual on three-manual organs.

imitative stop. A *rank of pipes that attempts to simulate *orchestral tones, although they have an individuality of their own due to their inabil-ity to reproduce all the tonal nuances of wind, string, and brass instru-ments of the orchestra.

manual. A keyboard (other than the pedal board) played with the fingers of both hands. Small organs have one or two manuals, larger instruments may have as many as seven. One manual may control several *divi-sions.

mechanical action. An ingenious mechanism for connecting the movements of the manual keys to the air release valves within the *wind chest under the pipes. This system was employed in the earliest organs and was developed and refined over the years until it was superseded by systems of *tubular-pneumatic and *electro-pneumatic action, but the system has been reintroduced into some contemporary organs.

A sensitive player can control the pipe speech through the way in which the keys are depressed. Sometimes called *tracker action.

mixture. A compound *stop of two or more *ranks of the highest-pitched *diapason- or *principal-*scaled *choruses, designed to break back in pitch with the ascending scale on the keys. The number of ranks is indicated in Roman numerals on the stop knobs controlling the manual or pedal *divisions. Mixtures produce the penetrating sound characteristic of most organs of most periods.

orchestral stop. An *imitative stop whose tone colour attempts to approximate that of instruments of the band or orchestra. Orchestral stops proliferated in organs around the turn of the century, but a reaction to the concept took place in the 1930s with a return to classically oriented tonal principles.

Pedal Organ. The *division of the organ, including its *wind chest, action, and pipework, that provides a bass to manual tones and *choruses. The large keys on the pedal board are operated by the player's feet. In general, pedal stops are an octave lower in pitch than manual stops of the same timbre, although well-designed instruments contain stops at a variety of pitches, including *mixtures.

pneumatic action. The use of air pressure or pneumatic power to reduce the excessive weight required to depress the keys of coupled manuals of large organs with conventional mechanical action. Sometimes the term is used interchangeably with *tubular-pneumatic action.

principal. One or more of the basic *ranks that produce the characteristic foundation tone of the organ from *flue pipes of medium *scale. The term has various detailed meanings in different cultures: in British and American organs it usually denotes an open *diapason of 4' (octave) length and pitch.

rank. A row or assembly of pipes making up a single *stop.

reed pipe. The method of sound production is the same as in wind instruments like the clarinet. In a reed pipe the sound is made when a thin brass blade (the "tongue" or "reed") in the boot of the pipe is set into vibration by the entering wind, which in turn excites the air column in the body of the pipe, or resonator, whose shape affects the timbre. Its pitch, and therefore its tuning, is determined by the rate of vibration of the reed. Reed pipes are sometimes referred to as lingual pipes. Compare *flue pipe.

regal. The first known portable keyboard instrument that produced its sound from a set of beating reeds provided with small resonators, in use from the mid-15th century to the end of the 17th century. Now the term refers to a family of *stops constructed in the same way, incorporated into larger organs.

registration. The selection and combination of *stops (registers) by the player, appropriate for the performance of a piece of music.

roller board. In mechanical-action organs, the frame supporting the rollers (cylindrical wooden rods) that transfer the mechanical key action from one vertical plane to another.

scale. A technical term denoting the comparative size of organ pipes: the relationship of the diameter of a pipe to its speaking length. A narrow-scaled pipe produces a bright sound rich in harmonics, while a wide-scaled pipe emphasises the fundamental pitch with fewer overtones. *Diapasons, the basic tone quality of the organ, are average-scaled.

Solo Organ. The division of the organ, including its *wind chest, action, and pipework, that contains tone colours, some powerful in nature. The Solo division is controlled by the top manual on four-manual organs.

speaking stop. A *stop whose pipes are used only for one *register and do not sound at lower or higher pitches.

specification. The formal description of the resources of an organ: *stop list, *divisions, mechanical adjuncts, *wind pressure, pipe materials, etc. The "disposition" is the manner in which stops are distributed among the manual and pedal divisions.

sticker. In *mechanical-action instruments, a long piece of wood that conveys motion from the key by pushing open a pallet or valve below the pipe. Compare *tracker.

stop. A row or *rank of pipes (or several ranks in a compound *stop such as a *mixture), one for each key, under the single control of a stop knob or *draw stop operated by the player. The exception is in the *unit organ, in which a stop may "borrow" pipes from another stop or division. Traditionally, stops have been classified as *flue stops (foundation, flute, string) and *reed stops. The term "stop" originated in the use of the stop knob to shut off, or stop unwanted tones. See also *divided stop.

Swell Organ. The keyboard *division of the organ, including the *wind chest, action, and pipework, in which the pipes are enclosed in a large wooden box with a louvred front that allows for expressive effects of crescendo and diminuendo by opening and closing the shutters; their operation is controlled by a swell pedal on the console. The Swell division is controlled by the manual immediately above the *Great manual on all organs.

tracker. In *mechanical-action instruments, a thin strip of wood that conveys motion from the key by pulling open a pallet or valve below the pipe. Compare *sticker.

tracker action. A purely mechanical action between the keys and pipe valves, controlled by the fingers of the player. See *mechanical action.

tremulant, tremolo. A mechanical device that imparts an undulating or pulsing effect to the wind supply by causing regular fluctuations in pressure, usually from two to seven times per second; similar to a vibrato.

tubular-pneumatic action. Pressing a manual key transmits a pneumatic signal from a small *wind chest ("touch box") above the key through small-bore lead tubing to another air-operated mechanism ("pouch") at the main *wind chest that opens the pallet or valve beneath the pipe, causing the pipe to speak. A similar air-powered system operates the *stops. This system was superseded by *electro-pneumatic action in the 1930s.

tuning. The act of adjusting the fundamental sound frequency of a pipe to agree with some predetermined pitch. This is particularly important in the organ whose pipes, made of different materials, go out of tune with wide fluctuations in temperature and humidity. Tuning techniques require the adjustment of metal flue collars, reed springs, and wooden stoppers, along with other alterations, to raise or lower the pitch. *Voicing, which alters the tonal characteristics, is a separate operation.

unit organ. An *electric-action instrument in which one or more of its *ranks can be made to sound at several different pitches by a system of wiring linking the keys and *stop switches. This economical system, which obtains the greatest number of stops from the smallest possible number of ranks, is sometimes used in small organs—and even in large theatre organs—to create the illusion of variety, but the practice has been condemned as artistically inferior. Organs that do not employ this system are called "straight" organs.

upperwork. In addition to the *stops of fundamental pitch, well-designed organs contain a number of *ranks that sound the pitches of several higher partial tones simultaneously, such as *mixtures. Their use in *registration contributes to the possible permutations of tone colour available to the player.

voicing. The regulation of each organ pipe for proper speech, loudness, and tone quality. On *flue pipes this is done by altering the mouth of the pipe; on *reed pipes it is done by altering the curvature of the reed or adjusting its mounting. In both types, the hole at the *foot of the pipe may have to be adjusted to admit more wind. Voicing is first done at the factory and again on location at the time of installation. *Tuning, which alters the pitch, is a separate operation.

wind chest. A rectangular wooden box, containing compressed wind supplied by the *bellows, upon which the pipes are arranged in an orderly manner. The pipe valves and stop-action mechanisms are part of the wind chest. Each *division of the organ has its own wind chest.

wind pressure. The compressed air, provided by the *bellows, required to cause the organ pipes to speak. Wind pressure is measured in millimetres or inches of water displaced in a gauge or manometer, and varies according to the size of the organ and its *divisions: from 25 mm (1.0 inch) to 100 mm (3.9 inches)in organs in smaller buildings, and up to 400 mm (15.7 inches) or higher for extremely loud divisions in large organs.

Bibliography

Manitoba: The Formative Years

Bingham, Neil. *A Study of the Church Buildings in Manitoba of the Congregational, Methodist, Presbyterian and United Churches of Canada*. Manitoba. Historic Resources Branch, 1987.

"Les Cathédrales de Saint-Boniface." *La Liberté*, 12 July 1972.

Chester, Russell E. "Music in Winnipeg, 1900-1907." *The Canada Music Book*, Canadian Music Council, Spring-Summer 1974.

Crossman, Kelly. *A Study of Anglican Church Buildings in Manitoba*. Manitoba. Historic Resources Branch, 1989.

Encyclopedia of Music in Canada, 1992 ed. S.v. "Anglican church music," "Hymns and hymn tunes," "Protestant church music," "Roman Catholic church music in Quebec," "Winnipeg."

"Fifty Years of Music in Winnipeg." *Musical Canada*, August 1920.

Hill, Robert B. *Manitoba: History of its Early Settlement, Development and Resources*. Toronto: William Briggs, 1890.

Kelly, Wayne. "Keyboards for Canadians." *The Beaver*, December 1991-January 1992.

Kitto, Franklin H. *Manitoba, Canada: Its Resources and Development*. Ottawa: Department of the Interior, 1931.

Knox United, Winnipeg, 100 Years 1868-1968. Knox Church publication, 1968.

Mitchell, Elaine A. "A Red River Gossip." *The Beaver*, Spring 1961.

Pierre Falcon. Manitoba. Historic Resources Branch, 1984.

Pritchett, John P. *The Red River Valley, 1811-1849: A Regional Study*. New Haven: Yale University Press, 1942.

The Red River Settlement. Manitoba. Historic Resources Branch, 1991.

Schofield, Frank H. *The Story of Manitoba*, vol. 1. Winnipeg: S. J. Clarke, 1913.

Wheeler, Charles H. "Music in Manitoba." In *The Year Book of Canadian Art 1913*, compiled by the Arts and Letters Club of Toronto, 85-89. London and Toronto: J. M. Dent & Sons.

Reed Organs

Begg, Alexander, and Walter R. Nursey. *Ten Years in Winnipeg: A Narration of the Principal Events in the History of the City of Winnipeg from the Year A.D., 1870 to the Year A.D., 1879 Inclusive.* Winnipeg: Times Printing and Publishing, 1879.

Classey, T. F. "19ᵗʰ Century Canadian Organs." *The York Pioneer*, 1966.

Duga, Jules J. "A Short History of the Reed Organ." *The Diapason*, July 1968.

Encyclopedia of Music in Canada, 1992 ed. S.v. "Protestant church music," "Reed organs," names of builders.

Hatch, Wilma. Oak Lake, Manitoba. Letter to the author, July 1992.

Healy, W. J. *Women of Red River*. Winnipeg: Russell, Lang & Co., 1923.

The New Grove Dictionary of Music and Musicians, 1980 ed. S.v. "Harmonium."

The New Grove Dictionary of Musical Instruments, 1984 ed. S.v. "Reed organ."

"Les Orgues de Saint-Boniface." *La Liberté*, 12 July 1972.

Ochse, Orpha. *The History of the Organ in the United States*. Bloomington: Indiana University Press, 1975.

Whitlaw, Ruth. Deloraine, Manitoba. Letter to the author, 10 November 1992.

Manitoba Pipe Organs and Their Builders

Andersen, Poul-Gerhard. *Organ Building and Design*, trans. Joanne Curnett. London: George Allen and Unwin, 1969.

Bouchard, Antoine. "The Organ in Canada: the First 300 years." *Musicanada*, April 1978.

Bridle, Augustus. "Beginning With the Pipe Organ." *The Canadian Courier*, 12 October 1912.

"Casavant Brothers Complete Century as Organ Builders." *The Diapason*, February 1937.

Encyclopedia of Music in Canada, 1992 ed. S.v. names of Canadian organ builders.

"In memoriam Gerhard Brunzema. "*The Diapason*, August 1992.

New Harvard Dictionary of Music, 1986 ed. S.v. "Organ."

New Oxford Companion to Music, 1988 ed. S.v. "Organ."

Norman, Herbert, and H. John Norman. *The Organ Today*. Newton Abbot, Devon, England: David and Charles, 1980.

Ochse, Orpha. *The History of the Organ in the United States*. Bloomington: Indiana University Press, 1988.

Owen, Barbara. *The Organ in New England*. Raleigh: The Sunbury Press, 1979.

Perin, Monica Wilch. "The Wicks Organ Company." *The American Organist*, February 1989.

Phelps, Lawrence I. "A Short History of the Organ Revival." *Church Music* 67, no. 1 (1967): 13-30.

Sumner, William Leslie. *The Organ: Its Evolution, Principles of Construction and Use.* 4ᵗʰ ed. New York: St. Martin's Press, 1973.

Williams, Peter. *A New History of the Organ From the Greeks to the Present Day.* London: Faber and Faber, 1980.

Williams, Peter. *The Organ in Western Culture, 750-1250.* Cambridge: Cambridge University Press, 1993.

The Golden Age of the Organ: 1875-1919

Boston, Noel, and Lyndesay G. Langwill. *Church and Chamber Barrel-Organs.* Edinburgh: Langwill, 1967.

Encyclopedia of Music in Canada, 1992 ed. S.v. names of Canadian organists.

The Middle Years: 1920-1939

Encyclopedia of Music in Canada, 1992 ed. S.v. names of Canadian organists.

A Period of Recession: 1940-1949

Encyclopedia of Music in Canada, 1992 ed. S.v. names of Canadian organists.

A Time for Renewal: 1950-1959

Encyclopedia of Music in Canada, 1992 ed. S.v. names of Canadian organists.

Recent Times: 1960-1997

Yearbook 1996-97, The Royal Canadian College of Organists.

The Future of the Organ

Andersen, Poul-Gerhard. *Organ Building and Design,* trans. Joanne Curnett. London: George Allen and Unwin, 1969.

Armstrong, Susan. "Creating Awareness of the Pipe Organ With Children." *The American Organist,* June 1996.

Coleberd, R. E. "Pipe Organ Building at the Crossroads." *The Diapason,* June 1994.

Phelps, Lawrence. *More About the Third Kind of Organ.* Macungie, PA: Allen Organ Company, 1986.

Racer, Bill E. "Reaching Children With the Organ." *The American Organist,* September 1993.

Redman, Roy. "Pipes or Loudspeakers?" *The American Organist,* July 1988; letters in reply, November 1988.

Index

Note: Organists whose country or city of origin is not identified are Winnipeg players.